Tools of Engagement

The Instructor's Manual for *Tools of Engagement* by Tom Bunzel includes helpful how-to information for creating meaningful presentations.

The Instructor's Manual is available free online. If you would like to download a copy, please visit:

www.wiley.com/college/bunzel.

Tools of Engagement

PRESENTING AND TRAINING
IN A WORLD OF SOCIAL MEDIA

Tom Bunzel

A Wiley Imprint
www.pfeiffer.com

Copyright © 2010 by John Wiley & Sons, Inc. All Rights Reserved.

Published by Pfeiffer
An Imprint of Wiley
989 Market Street, San Francisco, CA 94103-1741
www.pfeiffer.com

No part of this publication may be reproduced, stored in a retrieval system, or transmitted in any form or by any means, electronic, mechanical, photocopying, recording, scanning, or otherwise, except as permitted under Section 107 or 108 of the 1976 United States Copyright Act, without either the prior written permission of the Publisher, or authorization through payment of the appropriate per-copy fee to the Copyright Clearance Center, Inc., 222 Rosewood Drive, Danvers, MA 01923, 978-750-8400, fax 978-646-8600, or on the web at www.copyright.com. Requests to the Publisher for permission should be addressed to the Permissions Department, John Wiley & Sons, Inc., 111 River Street, Hoboken, NJ 07030, 201-748-6011, fax 201-748-6008, or online at http://www.wiley.com/go/permissions.

Limit of Liability/Disclaimer of Warranty: While the publisher and author have used their best efforts in preparing this book, they make no representations or warranties with respect to the accuracy or completeness of the contents of this book and specifically disclaim any implied warranties of merchantability or fitness for a particular purpose. No warranty may be created or extended by sales representatives or written sales materials. The advice and strategies contained herein may not be suitable for your situation. You should consult with a professional where appropriate. Neither the publisher nor author shall be liable for any loss of profit or any other commercial damages, including but not limited to special, incidental, consequential, or other damages.

Readers should be aware that Internet websites offered as citations and/or sources for further information may have changed or disappeared between the time this was written and when it is read.

For additional copies/bulk purchases of this book in the U.S. please contact 800-274-4434.

Pfeiffer books and products are available through most bookstores. To contact Pfeiffer directly call our Customer Care Department within the U.S. at 800-274-4434, outside the U.S. at 317-572-3985, fax 317-572-4002, or visit www.pfeiffer.com.

Pfeiffer also publishes its books in a variety of electronic formats. Some content that appears in print may not be available in electronic books.

Library of Congress Cataloging-in-Publication Data

Bunzel, Tom.
  Tools of engagement : presenting and training in a world of social media / Tom Bunzel.
    p. cm.
  Includes bibliographical references and index.
  ISBN 978-0-470-57394-5 (pbk.);   ISBN 978-0-470-64427-0 (ebk);   ISBN 978-0-470-64428-7 (ebk);
  ISBN 978-0-470-64429-4 (ebk)
  1. Multimedia systems in business presentations.   2. Social media.   3. Training.
  4. Business communication.   5. Communication in organizations.   I. Title.
  HF5718.22.B86   2010
  658.4'52—dc22
                                                                                2010019084

Acquiring Editor: Matthew Davis
Director of Development: Kathleen Dolan Davies
Production Editor: Mary Garrett
Editorial Assistant: Marisa Kelley

Marketing Manager: Tolu Babalola
Developmental Editor: Susan Rachmeler
Editor: Pam Suwinsky
Manufacturing Supervisor: Becky Morgan

Printed in the United States of America
Printing   10 9 8 7 6 5 4 3 2 1

*This book is dedicated to the loving memory of my parents,
Rudolf and Eva Bunzel, and to Alan Shapero.*

About Pfeiffer

Pfeiffer serves the professional development and hands-on resource needs of training and human resource practitioners and gives them products to do their jobs better. We deliver proven ideas and solutions from experts in HR development and HR management, and we offer effective and customizable tools to improve workplace performance. From novice to seasoned professional, Pfeiffer is the source you can trust to make yourself and your organization more successful.

Essential Knowledge Pfeiffer produces insightful, practical, and comprehensive materials on topics that matter the most to training and HR professionals. Our Essential Knowledge resources translate the expertise of seasoned professionals into practical, how-to guidance on critical workplace issues and problems. These resources are supported by case studies, worksheets, and job aids and are frequently supplemented with CD-ROMs, websites, and other means of making the content easier to read, understand, and use.

Essential Tools Pfeiffer's Essential Tools resources save time and expense by offering proven, ready-to-use materials—including exercises, activities, games, instruments, and assessments—for use during a training or team-learning event. These resources are frequently offered in looseleaf or CD-ROM format to facilitate copying and customization of the material.

Pfeiffer also recognizes the remarkable power of new technologies in expanding the reach and effectiveness of training. While e-hype has often created whizbang solutions in search of a problem, we are dedicated to bringing convenience and enhancements to proven training solutions. All our e-tools comply with rigorous functionality standards. The most appropriate technology wrapped around essential content yields the perfect solution for today's on-the-go trainers and human resource professionals.

Essential resources for training and HR professionals

CONTENTS

List of Figures and Tables		ix
Acknowledgments		xxi
1	Introduction	1
2	How the Presentation World Has Changed	11
3	Engaging with Social Media	33
4	The New Tools of Engagement	61
5	Major Social Networks: Twitter and Ning	109
6	Crafting a Visual Message	137
7	Meeting in Real Time: Using the Power of Now	179
8	What Lies Ahead in Global Communication	223
Glossary		243
About the Author		245
Index		247

LIST OF FIGURES AND TABLES

FIGURES

Figure 2.1	The Conversation Prism from social media and public relations professionals' blogs shows the wide array of communications channels, addressing personal and professional interests, to capture the attention of a potential audience.	17
Figure 3.1	Google Alerts is a good starting point for staying informed about references to key terms or names in various parts of the Internet—particularly those relating to your profile.	55
Figure 3.2	For immediate updates. Google Alerts can create an RSS feed that can be read in Google Reader.	56
Figure 3.3	After selecting View in Google Reader, a new subscription is added in the Google Reader application from which you can monitor the feed online.	56
Figure 3.4	If you've already set up RSS feeds in Outlook, you can subscribe to an individual Google Alert or all feeds in Google Reader to monitor results in RSS Feeds in your Outlook folders.	56
Figure 4.1	The Comments feature of blogs is critical for creating a dialogue with readers.	62
Figure 4.2	You can customize the appearance of your blog on Google using a Layout grid.	62
Figure 4.3	You can add features and functions to your blog with gadgets or add-on programs.	63

Figure 4.4	The Posting tab of the blogging tool will have general text formatting tools, as well as tabs to paste or type text, and a separate tab for HTML. Note also the Labels field at the bottom where search tags (also known as meta-data or metatags) can be placed.	63
Figure 4.5	The source code for any Web page in HTML places the elements of the page in their proper locations for the browser to display. The highlighted portion of code here references an image on a Web page.	64
Figure 4.6	LinkedIn is a business (social) network that integrates with desktop applications like Microsoft Outlook to locate and organize contacts with specific attributes.	69
Figure 4.7	LinkedIn has a Web tool that lets you locate people in your existing contact database who are already part of its network.	69
Figure 4.8	The Advanced Search feature of LinkedIn lets you locate individuals with unique combinations of skill sets or very esoteric attributes through the combination of keywords and other parameters.	70
Figure 4.9	Asking specific questions of your LinkedIn contacts or the community as a whole can generate discussion and connections that yield dividends in your ability to communicate with them, their companies or organizations, or others of like interest.	71
Figure 4.10	You can categorize your query to a specific industry or level of profession to focus the results.	71
Figure 4.11	As you establish a network that reflects your interests and expertise, browsing through questions and answers in your main Answers area of LinkedIn can provide new connections, research, and inspiration.	72
Figure 4.12	The Delicious toolbar in your Web browser lets you add any Web location to your own account and share the tags with others.	73
Figure 4.13	In your Delicious account, you can locate others with the same keywords as tags, add them to your network, or join one of their networks.	74

Figure 4.14	Other Delicious users who share their bookmarks can be located through their tags, added to a network in Delicious, and sometimes contacted through their profile information.	75
Figure 4.15	Facebook provides an open platform for social and professional interaction that lets third-party developers create branded applications and members connect in groups and subnetworks.	78
Figure 4.16	Snag-It's Capture program lets the user set up a series of profiles that can be used to save screens directly to a file or first annotate them in an Editor.	83
Figure 4.17	Snag-It lets the user set the file output options for name, file type, and location.	84
Figure 4.18	By right-clicking on a profile, a hotkey for automatic capture can be set up.	84
Figure 4.19	By using Snag-It's Automatic Capture, Emily could quickly and efficiently compile a folder of screenshots.	85
Figure 4.20	Snag-It's Editor gives the user the ability to annotate and change images before they are saved or after reopening them later on.	85
Figure 4.21	PhotoBucket's batch upload feature lets the user add tags and descriptions to multiple images (to facilitate search) before they are saved and uploaded.	86
Figure 4.22	Opening an image page lets you access the Link and Embed options in PhotoBucket to copy and paste the URL or embed code into a blog or other Web page.	86
Figure 4.23	With an image hosted on PhotoBucket you can use the TwitGoo application to send it directly to Twitter.	87
Figure 4.24	The Twitter post or "tweet" can let the user click the link to view a picture on PhotoBucket.	87
Figure 4.25	An audio hosting site like Podbean.com can let you post MP3 audio files with descriptions and keywords as podcasts, which can be aggregated in an MP3 player (iTunes) and subscribed to as RSS feeds.	96
Figure 4.26	An RSS feed can be managed from Microsoft Outlook or used to bring the content directly into an MP3 player. Use	97

	a link from the standard RSS symbol icon or use a Subscribe link to get the feed URL.	
Figure 4.27	Users can subscribe to an RSS feed from Internet Explorer by clicking the RSS symbol, going to the feed page, and clicking Subscribe to this feed, giving them a subscribe dialogue box that lets them rename the feed and add it to their favorites (where Outlook or iTunes can access the subscription).	97
Figure 4.28	A document repository like Scribd can host supporting reference material for linking and embedding and sustain an active community around your content.	98
Figure 4.29	Picnik has the most common features of an image editor but lives entirely online, and it's free.	99
Figure 4.30	Picnik lets you save the image file locally or send it directly to Twitter, Flickr, and other Web sites.	100
Figure 4.31	With the image on Flickr, it can be shared in an e-mail by using its URL on the Flickr site or sent to a blog.	100
Figure 4.32	In the Get the Button screen, you can choose a style of button, which services you wish to distribute content to, and whether you want code for any Web page or for one of three major blogging tools: WordPress, TypePad, and Blogger.	102
Figure 4.33	In the Get the Code window, select the code and copy it to your clipboard.	102
Figure 4.34	The ShareThis widget on a Web site or blog lets the visitor share your content, by e-mail, on popular sites and other blogs.	103
Figure 4.35	This ShareBox lets the account holder track the sharing history of the widget she has created. (In this instance I shared my own blog to Delicious.com.)	103
Figure 4.36	Widgetbox is an online tool for creating, distributing, and tracking widget applications.	105
Figure 4.37	Widgetbox has a visual interface for creating a widget in a set size and generating code.	106
Figure 5.1	Each Twitter post has options to reply to the post or mark it as a favorite.	112
Figure 5.2	Clicking Direct Message in the right column gives you a chance to send a direct post to anyone following you, using a drop-down list or @ prefix.	113

Figure 5.3	The Profile page shows how others see you and also shows your most recent posts.	113
Figure 5.4	You can create your own background image for your Profile page on Twitter in any good image editor by saving it in a Web image format. A good procedure is to create a new image in the resolution you want and paste in your elements, saving it as a JPG file.	114
Figure 5.5	Making your image wide and short lets it tile throughout the page and provides space in the middle for the Twitter content to scroll down.	115
Figure 5.6	Seesmic Desktop lays out your Twitter or Facebook updates in a series of columns from which you can quickly respond, or follow or unfollow other users.	116
Figure 5.7	Naming a userlist and then adding appropriate people lets you pay attention to their specific concerns and respond quickly and effectively.	116
Figure 5.8	Whrrl creates a quick and easy slide show of uploaded pictures and text.	118
Figure 5.9	The user simply drags and drops the uploaded pictures and creates text slides to construct a story.	119
Figure 5.10	The final version is online with a Web link to post on Twitter, Facebook, or in any Web page or e-mail, along with a comment thread that can build viral interest.	119
Figure 5.11	The configuration chosen in the layout is reflected in the Main Page that you see on your Ning social network.	130
Figure 5.12	In the Manage window of your Ning network, you can open option windows for Network Information, Features, Appearance, and Tab Manager.	131
Figure 5.13	Your new social network's Main Page can be configured with all of the features of popular social networks like Facebook, but it is entirely branded to you, with your own Web address, keywords, banner, and network information.	132
Figure 6.1	Videos hosted on YouTube feature snippets of code that let the user embed the videos in any Web page.	142
Figure 6.2	Copying and pasting the embed code from YouTube into the HTML tab of a blogging tool will make it appear in the Web page.	143

Figure 6.3	The user can play the referenced video from directly within the Web page in the dimensions that the embed code generates in a Web browser.	143
Figure 6.4	To create a branded template for a presentation, first establish the color values of the logo or collateral material.	146
Figure 6.5	Modifying a presentation's Slide Master creates a consistent look that can represent the identity of an entity or organization.	147
Figure 6.6	Colors chosen individually can be applied in a custom theme (in PowerPoint's Design tab) to create a consistent look throughout a slide show.	147
Figure 6.7	Using Arrange All from the View tab in PowerPoint allows you to move slides between one presentation and another.	148
Figure 6.8	You can download an Add-In for PowerPoint that lets you save and print your notes (or handouts or slides) in PDF format.	150
Figure 6.9	Adding a Fade In Entrance Animation to AutoShapes can highlight parts of an image to let the presenter call attention to detail.	150
Figures 6.10 and 6.11	Converting a set of bullets to SmartArt can make a significant difference in how your information is presented and absorbed.	151
Figure 6.12	Converting a slide show to HTML format makes it available in a Web browser, but the presenter is not there to tell a story.	156
Figure 6.13	Windows Media Recorder lets you set your options through a recording wizard; to capture PowerPoint and narration, use Screen Capture and enable your microphone to record simultaneously.	158
Figure 6.14	Camtasia Studio can be set up and started from within the Add-In tab directly inside PowerPoint.	159
Figure 6.15	The versatile Editing program in Camtasia Studio lets you revise the final video before saving it as a new file in the production stage.	159
Figure 6.16	Camtasia Studio's Production Wizard lets you choose encoding options for your final output that balance quality with the size of the final file.	160
Figure 6.17	The Video Upload lets you enter a full description and searchable tags. You can revise this information or add more search tags in YouTube by clicking on Edit.	163

Figure 6.18	Audacity is a free full-featured audio editor that can convert, import, and export MP3 files for podcasts or to be synchronized as slidecasts on SlideShare.com.	164
Figure 6.19	Slidecasts on SlideShare.com are PowerPoint slides with audio narration and have many of the same properties as videos on YouTube, but they are hosted in a community dedicated to presentations.	164
Figure 6.20	An MP3 file of the audio narration to a presentation (exported from Camtasia and converted in Audacity) can be linked to the slides in SlideShare to create a slidecast.	164
Figure 6.21	You can use the Synchronization Workspace in SlideShare to create a slidecast.	165
Figure 6.22	If you deselect Link narration in your PowerPoint slides, you can embed the audio to create a narrated presentation for AuthorSTREAM.	165
Figure 6.23	Like YouTube and SlideShare, AuthorSTREAM has a form on the upload screen to include a searchable description and keyword tags.	166
Figure 6.24	When uploaded to AuthorSTREAM, a presentation can be played with accompanying narration on the Web site or linked to or embedded just like a YouTube video. It can also be converted to video and sent to YouTube (for a small fee).	166
Figure 6.25	Using an evocative symbol or metaphor can help communicate key concepts emotionally far more effectively than text or charts.	167
Figure 6.26	Gargiulo's story-based communication skills model can be used as an assessment tool or for coaching and facilitation.	170
Figure 6.27	Gargiulo's diagrammatic snapshot of today's learning options.	172
Figures 6.28–6.30	Creative storytelling and PowerPoint animation can add impact to a visual metaphor.	175
Figure 7.1	Many Web conferencing programs let you meet instantly by inviting other participants by phone or e-mail.	185
Figure 7.2	Participants can join the meeting by entering information into their Web browser or clicking a link provided through e-mail or discussed by telephone.	185

Figure 7.3	The presenter in a Web conference or webinar can share her desktop view or display any open program to the audience.	186
Figure 7.4	The presenter can show a clear screen to the audience (instead of a cluttered desktop) and then click a program from the Task Bar to show it on a shared desktop.	186
Figure 7.5	During a Web conference or webinar, opening the PowerPoint program will show the Editor to the audience. You can click the Full Screen view or press F5 to show your presentation.	187
Figure 7.6	While online, the presenter can open a window to monitor the pace and see what the audience is seeing, handle Q&A, or present polling questions.	188
Figure 7.7	To get feedback from the audience during a conference or webinar, you can ask a polling question and show the results during the presentation.	191
Figure 7.8	The main program for the Web conference provider will let you begin or schedule a conference or webinar (GoToMeeting Corporate shown here).	191
Figure 7.9	The Schedule window provides a form to describe the event, pick a date and time, and set up audio services (instead of limiting the audio to computer speakers and microphones).	192
Figure 7.10	When setting up your own webinar, using your own branding in the invitation and waiting room, with a background and logo, adds consistency and professionalism.	192
Figure 7.11	The Registration page can be set up to collect specific information in a form to add to a database for follow-up and research. You can mail a copy back to yourself for a preview or to copy and paste into other e-mail invitations.	193
Figure 7.12	Webinar invites can be received and responded to with direct links to the Registration page from any e-mail program.	193
Figure 7.13	The Registration Web page for attendees has fields in a form with a Register now (submit form) button. These are the fields chosen when the webinar is set up (as was shown in Figure 7.11).	194

Figure 7.14	As the webinar begins, the presenter can see the attendee names as they enter, greet them, and make sure that the conference is being recorded for archived video.	195
Figure 7.15	Before the webinar, the Tools submenu should be checked to make sure that all services are available and that Recording is enabled if the conference is to be archived as a video file.	195
Figure 7.16	The webinar coordinator should check the Preferences window to make sure that audio is enabled and that the proper video output and folder locations are selected.	196
Figure 7.17	To avoid heartache or heartburn, make sure that someone is responsible to begin recording just prior to the speaker introduction.	196
Figure 7.18	If the service provider for the webinar has archived the video online, users should fill out a form to view the archived the file so that you can collect more information.	197
Figure 7.19	To show the speaker on screen, you can move the preview panel for a webcam program into the viewable desktop area of the Web conference or webinar.	200
Figures 7.20 and 7.21	Outlook's Contact database lets you add color-coded categories to sort through large numbers of individuals and companies.	202
Figure 7.22	Copy2Contact is a utility that lets the user select a block of data and press a hotkey to place the information directly into the appropriate fields of the Contact database or Calendar.	202
Figure 7.23	When you set up a scheduled DimDim conference, you can enter an Agenda that will be included in your e-mail invitations to others.	204
Figure 7.24	A DimDim meeting has the standard Web conference features, including a video window for webcam views of speakers and a shared Whiteboard.	204
Figure 7.25	You can invite additional participants from within a DimDim meeting so that you can start the meeting, set it up, and then have others join the event.	205

Figure 7.26	By copying AutoShapes or Text Boxes to the Office Clipboard and then pasting them into Word, you can create a whiteboard-like brainstorming diagram that you can save in Word format.	205
Figure 7.27	You can add an Event tab under your Profile in Facebook or click it directly if it's already been enabled.	206
Figure 7.28	The Create Event window in Facebook is a great place to detail the particulars of a webinar or conference and then invite others within your Friends or any Groups or Networks to which you have access on Facebook.	207
Figure 7.29	The Customize window lets you decide who can attend or be invited to the event and set it up for Facebook search.	207
Figure 7.30	After saving your event, you have the option of publishing it to your Wall and to your Facebook Friends' home pages.	208
Figure 7.31	The Event page lets you see who is registered and post a direct link to the registration page for a conference or webinar in the Links panel.	208
Figure 7.32	OpenOffice's Impress presentation program has many of the standard slide show features of PowerPoint and lives online, letting the user present directly through the browser and access other resources from within the program.	209
Figure 7.33	Zoho's Show online presentation tool also mimics PowerPoint, with many similar capabilities, and now works with SharePoint.	209
Figure 7.34	SlideRocket's sharing capability extends its reach; users can send links in Twitter posts or embed presentations in other Web pages, such as blogs.	210
Figure 7.35	SlideRocket's ability to import and export PowerPoint expands its versatility.	211
Figure 7.36	For an online application, SlideRocket provides a full array of tools to create and present slide shows with graphics, video, and animation entirely through a Web browser.	211
Figure 7.37	When you paste information from the Internet into a OneNote page, the URL from the original source is also included, making OneNote an excellent research tool.	212

Figure 7.38	When you send a PowerPoint file to OneNote through the print feature, its slides become searchable and you can begin to add reference information in OneNote.	213
Figure 7.39	A Live Sharing Session in OneNote lets all participants collaborate on a shared page in a section of OneNote (while speaking on the phone or conference line). Shown here is the IP address information screen from a previous task pane in the process to begin the Live Sharing Session.	214
Figure 7.40	Microsoft Publisher has the ability to merge newsletter content with an e-mail list.	216
Figure 7.41	Microsoft Publisher's E-mail Merge File Wizard task pane takes you through the process of connecting with a database or contact list in Outlook.	217
Figure 7.42	E-mail Merge in Microsoft Publisher lets you place fields or containers for data into the document and preview how it will look when merged.	218
Figure 7.43	When you click Merge to E-mail in Microsoft Publisher, you can confirm the address field and add a subject line.	218
Figure 7.44	After generating an E-mail Merge in Microsoft Publisher, you can check the final results in your e-mail Outbox folder before sending.	219
Figure 8.1	Enhancing the connection between the organization and its customers and thereby strengthening a brand or identity are the key perceived values of social technologies.	224
Figure 8.2	Presenter Pro is a portable application for iPhone that provides tips, techniques, and planning features that can be accessed anywhere and any time.	226
Figure 8.3	A twine is similar to a group on a social network, but soon content begins to accumulate through the connections to kindred twines.	228
Figure 8.4	A twine evolves as other members contribute content that is related in meaning to your concept and content you have uploaded or linked to and the comments of members.	229
Figure 8.5	The Explore area of Twine provides an overview of the most popular topics and members; drilling down locates more specific entries with member comments and interactivity.	230

Figure 8.6	Google Wave promises a new real-time communications platform for instant communication and collaboration among participants.	231
Figure 8.7	IBM's Quantum Mirage uses the wave nature of electrons instead of wire to move information on a molecular scale.	235

TABLES

Table 4.1	Capital Payroll Services Social Media Strategy Plan	90
Table 6.1	Gargiulo's Three Dimensions and Nine Skills of Communication	171

ACKNOWLEDGMENTS

I am indebted to many people who supported me through difficult times during the planning and writing of this book. Specifically I deeply thank and express gratitude to Terrence Gargiulo, Debra Swihart, Freeman Michaels, and Dr. Orli Peter, without whom this project would never have happened, and also Matthew Davis and Lindsay Morton from John Wiley & Sons, along with my excellent editor, Susan Rachmeler, copy editor Pam Suwinsky, and senior production editor Mary Garrett.

Tools of Engagement

Introduction

chapter
ONE

Times are rapidly changing in the presentation field in the early twenty-first century. Travel constraints, budget concerns, and the advent of new technology have mandated that many individuals who might have in the past addressed their audiences directly and personally need to do so electronically, across large distances.

In addition, the instantaneous nature of the Internet has made it possible for individuals and businesses to connect with each other in new and amazing ways, forging online communities and networks that comingle personal and professional issues.

The software and technology that enables this process is continually changing and is quite complex. While Fortune 500 corporations may still avail themselves of proprietary broadband networks that support sophisticated and expensive videoconferencing, more and more organizations are using reasonably priced software over the Internet to reach out to customers, clients, colleagues, students, constituencies, and other audiences.

But how to make sense of this varied and vast assortment of tools and feature sets?

In this book we discuss the technological, logistical, and thematic requirements of reaching out to a world that sees a presentation or a communication in an entirely new way: as a video, an e-mail, a slide show, a real-time broadcast, a Twitter update or "tweet," or even something not yet conceived. We provide an overview of the latest trends and programs, demonstrate proven and popular software, and take the reader through many possible scenarios of presenting, communicating, and learning in the new social media universe.

Web 2.0—a term used to designate the collection of information-sharing and collaboration tools available on the World Wide Web—breaks the oligarchy of the expert and the power grip of corporations and institutions on the individual's access to information and ability to influence opinion and behavior. As blogging, Facebook, Twitter, and other evolving applications find their user bases, end users are building communities of trust with one another to get their information needs filled and are no longer relying on old business models through which they seek support from or trust corporations or other institutions.

At the same time, savvy corporations are leveraging these communities as active participants in their businesses so that they can learn from these user communities and let users' experience enhance and build their brands.

So how are the fields of communication, training, and learning affected by the next generation of end users and the social tools that are proliferating?

With individuals' short attention spans (witness the 140-character limit of an update or tweet on Twitter) and the ubiquity of mobile devices and video, communication between institutions and individuals will not be anything like the old single-event PowerPoint presentations in an auditorium or boardroom. And with the growth of Web conferencing and webinars, location is of secondary importance; anyone can meet anywhere, any time. In addition, a meeting will not be a single disconnected event but will result from a series of prior relationship-building events held within the social media space.

Tools of Engagement is not a book devoted directly to social media—there are many of those already in print; some are referenced in the coming pages. Instead, we investigate how the new social tools and programs interface, influence, and inform the presentation and training landscape that currently exists and to address a key issue: how to convey an important message in the most effective way in the current environment.

HOW THIS BOOK IS ORGANIZED

The chapters that follow cover the following landscape:

In Chapter Two, we take the reader through an overview of how presentation has changed and has been influenced by the new social media landscape in the early twenty-first century.

Then, in Chapter Three, we concentrate on the nature of social media as a game changer as it shifts the focus of training, learning, and marketing from selling to building relationships of trust and establishing an effective identity in this new world.

We discuss in Chapter Four how to implement some of the more popular social media tools and strategies with an overview of representative programs and Web sites; in Chapter Five we focus on two of the major social networks (Twitter for everyone, Ning for targeted networks), all with an emphasis on training and communication.

In Chapter Six, we begin to integrate the new trends with more familiar communication tools and go into some detail in how to leverage existing skills in graphics and PowerPoint (and its new online cousins) to deliver a visual message.

The very nature of meetings as part of an ongoing conversation with an audience is a theme throughout the book, so in Chapter Seven we address various scenarios for conveying information at a specific venue—particularly when the venue is virtual—or in a Web page. We cover the steps necessary to get an online meeting scheduled, plan its contents, rehearse and prepare, deliver meaningful content over the Web, and follow up with a strategic plan to take full advantage of all aspects of the event going forward as the presenter or trainer continues the conversation.

In Chapter Eight we speculate about what is likely to come next and about the meaning of the incredible changes that are taking place in how we present, communicate, and learn.

Throughout the book, case studies and scenarios are used to demonstrate the various ways to communicate across many platforms effectively and for a variety purposes. We also present specific examples of representative programs and tools and how they can be implemented. None of these examples are meant to be endorsements; the landscape changes so rapidly we discuss current programs that perform specific tasks and concentrate on their intent and focus.

To demonstrate the most important features and benefits of these tools, screen shots are provided as illustrations throughout the book.

For your reference while reading, a Glossary has been included at the end of this book.

In keeping with the theme of engaging in an ongoing dialogue, the material in the book will be supplemented after publication by a Web site that includes an introduction to the new features in PowerPoint 2010 presented as a visual guide with screenshots and tips and techniques; contributions to an active blog; and the delivery of webinars and updates in the coming year.

WHO WILL BENEFIT FROM THIS BOOK?

I was amazed when I returned to Tech TV's *Call for Help* for a second appearance that the target audience for learning about PowerPoint had expanded well beyond busy executives. In addition to being used in the boardroom and the auditorium, PowerPoint had become a staple for communication in universities, middle and elementary schools, philosophical and denominational institutions, as well as in the consumer world among families (creating videos or photo histories), and literally anyone with an interest in digital media.

On the Internet today, the influence of PowerPoint is everywhere: photo-hosting programs feature slide shows, consumer slide show programs inhabit the "cloud" (a constellation of programs that interact and reference each others' content on Web servers), and video has become a staple of blogs and social networks.

The popularity of PowerPoint has expanded dramatically by the need to use its capabilities online and reach a much wider audience in a Web conference, blog, Facebook page, YouTube video, or a format as yet unknown. However, while PowerPoint can be vital as the visual focus of a Web conference or online seminar ("webinar"), and its slides and narration can be used to create a YouTube video, the new world of social media has all but left PowerPoint behind as the presentation program of choice.

Instead, younger business users in particular favor the immediacy and ubiquity of social networking tools like Facebook and LinkedIn, and for presentations new online tools like SlideRocket, with its ability to "mash up" content from sources like YouTube and Google Docs, are opening a brave new world of online communication. Many of these new tools communicate directly not just with users but with each other. YouTube video, for example, is linked directly to blogs and e-mail, allowing its users to find audiences that an ordinary PowerPoint file could never reach.

Everyone has a visual story to tell, regardless of the technology of choice.

Trade shows like InfoComm and the Consumer Electronics Show in Las Vegas have replaced the COMDEX convention because the point is not about the technology anymore. It's about how to use the myriad of platforms and tools and integrate them to sell, persuade, inspire, teach, or perform any of a wide range of presentation tasks.

Our primary audiences for the information covered in the coming pages are managers in traditional corporations who need to create and sustain a high-performing team or organization; executives who seek to create a participative and innovative corporate culture; sales and marketing organizations that thrive on customer feedback and loyalty; and customer service and public relations organizations that seek to improve customer relationships.

Other audiences include:

- Human resource (HR) managers and training professionals who want to expand the reach and impact of their material using today's Internet tools and reaching current Web users
- Executives and managers who need to reach colleagues and prospects without travel
- Small business users and professionals (including doctors, dentists, attorneys) who need the competitive advantage of educating and training others electronically
- Technical professionals with detailed financial or strategic messages who need to convey information to large and small groups without leaving their desks

As our economy transforms, the audience for this book broadens. Our secondary audience includes the growing number of small-business entrepreneurs and independent business owners as well as consultants and small businesses who need to reach wider audiences to educate their clientele as they market themselves.

Also included:

- Educators and students who want to use digital media to more effectively communicate beyond the classroom
- Organizations that want to combine video, imagery, and audio to inspire their members over the Internet
- Individuals with important messages to deliver online to expand their influence and businesses, like consulting and training

The audience for this book is growing vastly as potential communicators, educators, and indeed presenters (which includes almost everyone in business, education, law, or other institutions or organizations) realize that a combination of tools and skills can enable them to reach larger audiences across oceans, time zones, and other geographic and physical barriers.

IMPACT ON TRAINING AND DEVELOPMENT

Perhaps the biggest impact of social media is on education, in the broadest sense of the word. With the complexity of modern life, from the woman who reads blogs to learn about the best formula for her baby (and affects the company that makes and distributes the product) to the financial planner who must absorb and then convey complex ideas (and build trust among his clients), the integration of social tools with issues of learning and communication has become critical for nearly everyone.

And of course, the landscape for organizational education, training, and development of institutional learning programs is also changing dramatically. In corporate human resources departments, there is an increasing focus on the need for alignment with a company's strategic visions. Increasingly, HR departments are expected to provide more than just administrative or training services—they need to support all phases of the company's goals and to maximize efficiency and profit. Traditional HR training sessions generally require time away from work; an online event can have high impact in one hour without employees leaving their desks. By fostering stronger connections among top executives, middle management, and staff, strategic HR online initiatives can add significant value by effectively communicating and facilitating the organization's strategic plans.

Integrating social media into the unstructured activities that comprise the organization's learning initiatives can also yield tremendous and unexpected benefits. In the customer service area, social networks like Best Buy's Blue Shirt Nation have galvanized a workforce and created energetic alignment with the company's goals by engaging the sales staff and listening carefully to their input and concerns.

As more and more people adopt social technologies and become connected, these platforms become critical in the initiatives of any individual or group to reach customers and employees with information, training, or any important message.

Consequently, in a blended scenario of traditional and unstructured approaches to training, the inclusion of research, connections, partnerships, and other resources gleaned through social technologies will become a key in successful implementation. For example, coaching and skill building will not occur in a vacuum; levels of trust and engagement will be required for maximum efficacy. The holistic nature of these varied practices will create a need to understand and implement the most effective tools for maximum impact on the widest audience.

Instructor-led traditional training has also been affected by the new Web technologies. With the changing nature of today's workforce and student population, the issue of a "backchannel"—the trend toward communication and criticism among audiences during an event—is just one of many new factors in how training and presentation professionals are perceived and evaluated. With instant and potentially unmonitored feedback, for example, even the common civility and attentiveness with which presenters are received by an audience has become a matter of concern for organizations, educators, and presentation professionals.

Whether information or training is delivered traditionally by an instructor or facilitator, directly within a designed course, through a Web-based program, or through a live online learning event, preparation with and integration of social technologies will greatly affect the relevance, retention, and overall success or failure of any presentation initiative.

Understanding and mastering the new concepts and social tools, as well as online delivery scenarios, will become paramount for anyone in the business of training development and education.

SOCIAL MEDIA'S IMPACT ON THE BOTTOM LINE

While we present a number of case studies and examples in the coming pages, the jury is still out in many areas on how to best use social media in a communications strategy. The key word here is *strategy*. As we will see, blogging for no reason is not a recipe for success in marketing, training, or any other endeavor. Just as an effective presentation in the sales arena ends with a call to action, social tools must have a clearly defined purpose in their implementation to realize a return on investment—and that is why the coming chapters use real-world examples as well as creative scenarios to demonstrate their effective integration with more traditional communication tools.

Examples of companies that are effectively using social tools to expand markets include Bill Marriott's popular blog for the hotel chain, a sales boost reported by Southwest Airlines from its social media efforts, $3 million garnered by Dell Outlet from its initiative on Twitter, and the 90,000 customers the Wiggly Wigglers blog has gained among photo enthusiasts.

Social media blurs the lines between marketing and training in many ways for large organizations and particularly for small businesses and entrepreneurs who need to deliver a message that doesn't directly sell but that needs to result in more than just good will.

Another interesting aspect of this trend toward a convergence between marketing and training or education is that these movements toward relationship and engagement, along with the tools that support them, have resulted in social change as well as a transformation in how organizations and individuals communicate and learn. Key factors like trust, credibility, and attention are no longer taken for granted but must be earned by those seeking to communicate and influence.

TOOLS MATTER IN A SOCIALLY CONNECTED WORLD

In the pages that follow, we will see how a current movement in social media is breathing the life of humanity back into technology and corporations and other organizations by fostering greater connection and community among users of the Internet.

In their seminal book, *Trust Agents: Using the Web to Build Influence, Improve Reputation, and Earn Trust*,[1] Chris Brogan and Julien Smith (2009) avoid getting caught up in the "hows" of social media and only tangentially mention some key tools. In *Tools of Engagement*, we take things a bit further and empower the reader with a broad overview of how social media informs and supports effective communication: the key element of commerce, education, worship, family, and much more.

In the emerging marketplace of commerce and ideas, a meeting will never again be an isolated event but will result from a matrix of prior interactions in the social media space.

In the sales environment, the call to action will not be a single "close," but instead the result of a facilitated set of communications (perhaps still including slides but probably many images and video in lieu of bullets, based on numerous prior relationships and communications), and the signed contract will not happen so much by manipulation but rather through a tacit understanding and acceptance of a win-win scenario.

In the persuasion, training, and educational areas in which static presentations have been used at large venues, universities, and other institutions, or in motivational settings, the same type of evolution is taking place. In the near future, few speakers of any substance who have not already connected and listened to their audience prior to an event via Twitter or Facebook will be taken seriously. Authority in the world of social media is not automatic; it is a precious commodity.

The key to communications success is to blend the various social media technologies into a coherent strategy, using each for its unique ability to build story and community rather than as a piece of software (like simply learning how to use one program such as PowerPoint and relying on that to carry the show).

In this effort, we do not cover many programs or platforms in great depth; many of the tools covered in the coming pages could—and some do—have entire books as well as online tutorials devoted to them. Instead we illuminate trends and relationships as the exchange of information and learning among humans is changing from one of *broadcast*, where those with power and purported knowledge distribute it as they see fit, to building *relationships of trust and community*, where everyone is empowered to participate and influence and one's reputation and credibility are earned on the basis of tangible contributions and human interaction.

Some of the tools, like Microsoft PowerPoint, covered in this smorgasbord of communication and learning are familiar, but they contribute to the overall strategy of exchange of information in new and dynamic ways. Others are just emerging—like the applications that inhabit the cloud and share information among themselves in new and exciting ways.

What follows is a study of how these new technologies are evolving in the emerging Internet world, with tips and insights and some speculation. It just may be that the tools and the concepts of this cresting wave, groundswell, or movement are deeply influencing and affecting the evolution of mankind's most important technology of all: ourselves.

QUESTIONS TO PONDER

1. How do you feel when someone uses a PDA (personal digital assistant) or cell phone in your presence, breaking away directly or indirectly from their attention on you? Can you see the benefits of an "always connected" audience for your message, or is it a threat in your mind?

2. Is training and development your main focus, or do you see it as a secondary aspect of your communication needs? How has the explosion of information

in the world today affected how you communicate? Which aspects of your message involve education in some way?

3. What tools are you currently using, or would you like to learn, to reach out and communicate more effectively with others in your field?

Note
1. Chris Brogan and Julien Smith, *Trust Agents: Using the Web to Build Influence, Improve Reputation, and Earn Trust.* Hoboken, NJ: Wiley, 2009.

How the Presentation World Has Changed

chapter
TWO

A long time ago there was a young man who worked in resorts for a continuing education program for physicians. Every week a new expert in the field of infectious diseases would arrive at the location to speak to the attending doctors about how various antibiotics could be used most effectively. Before each session, the young man would receive a carousel of 35 mm slides from the expert and place it on a slide projector, test a slide, make sure it was in focus, and let the speaker control the process with a remote control device attached to a long cable. With each new slide there was an audible click, which presumably woke up the audience, who were generally snoozing in the darkened room.

Among the other duties the young man had was circulating an attendance sheet that the doctors would sign to get their tax deduction verification; once signed, many of the doctors would scoot out the back to play golf.

For decades, presentations hardly changed—they remained the province of an authority figure who pumped out information.

As computers became popular and then laptops emerged, projectors became more powerful and connected to software programs like PowerPoint, which allowed the presenter to change his slides up until the moment of truth. Some of the slides became animated, with lots of bells and whistles, and it became possible to insert pictures and video into a presentation, but the room was still often dark, and the attendees still disappeared out the back when given the chance.

With the advent of computer software to replace the slide projector, several things became apparent:

- Changing the mode of transmission or hardware was not going to improve communications.
- Using multimedia and animation might make a few people pay attention longer, but in many cases the technologies might not significantly increase retention of information.
- Unless the subject matter or the speaker was particularly compelling, the software and hardware made no difference.
- And finally, unless the entire concept of an authority figure pumping out information changed (to involve the audience meaningfully), the results of a single event, meeting, or conference would vary widely.

This chapter helps us understand the significance and breadth of the current phase in the evolution of the presentation. If we use the term in its broadest sense, *presentation* encompasses all aspects of communication between and among individuals and organizations. Traditional presenters realized that engaging the audience was a key element of success; the Internet has taken this engagement to another level entirely.

As we follow the evolution of the nature of a presentation, we come to realize that it is inevitably part of an *ongoing conversation* within a matrix of communications that is always in flux: the world of social media. The presence of everything written, said, and shown everywhere online, or in the "cloud," constitutes a fundamental shift in how we communicate, from the most powerful network journalist to the individual training professional or executive delivering a seminar.

LIFE IS A SERIES OF PRESENTATIONS

Somewhere along the line, people began to realize that the speaker and the content were critical to the success of a presentation, and that unless the audience cared about the material, the retention of information and any follow-up action would be unsatisfactory. And, since the stakes for many presentations were quite high—millions of dollars in revenue, productivity, or knowledge in the workplace, retention of employees, or the loyalty of members of any organization with a united purpose—small businesses started investing in figuring out what it took to capture the attention of an audience.

Experts in the field like Tony Jeary, who wrote *Life Is a Series of Presentations*,[1] concentrated on how to craft a message in a way that the audience gets it by appealing to their emotions as well as logic. Authors like Dan and Chip Heath published books like *Made to Stick*,[2] which expanded on the theories of how ideas can be communicated effectively, exposing the "curse of knowledge" in which speakers assume that their audience knows or assumes certain facts, and helped media experts come up with stories that made hard-to-grasp concepts "sticky" and even become part of the public consciousness. Speaker coaches worked with presenters on body language and energy, often videotaping them, to make sure that their delivery and rapport with the audience enabled them to impart the message effectively. Strategic experts like Jim Endicott of Distinction Services, who began his career with Genigraphics, the company that output those 35 mm slides, realized the unique ability of presentation software to communicate and consulted with corporations on making sure the visuals and content of the slide show communicated the value proposition of the presenter in the most effective way.

But while PowerPoint (the dominant presentation software program from Microsoft) found its way into every presentation nook and cranny, from businesses to religious institutions to universities to high schools and even elementary schools, at the beginning of the twenty-first century the game began to change. The attacks in New York City and Washington, D.C., on September 11, 2001, put the first stress on the economy and made travel for the business of presenting more difficult. In addition, the ubiquity of broadband Internet and the proliferation of new and exciting software and more powerful networks made it possible to present remotely or distribute presentations using electronic media.

At first, this simply increased the ability of presenters to reach larger audiences more effectively, but the basic concept remained the same: package your message and use an expert in the field who is proficient and polished in her delivery to distribute the information. But as the audience for these types of presentations became peppered with young people who had grown up with digital media, a shift began to occur. Professors who used PowerPoint in the classroom noticed that their students had laptops, cell phones, and PDAs (personal digital assistants), and students would be communicating as a lecture was being delivered. A sales professional delivering a conventional presentation was in a conference room where the attendees were thumb-typing on BlackBerries and similar devices. Even a chief executive officer delivering an important speech may have noticed that among his flock were those text messaging as he spoke.

Not only was there serious competition for the attention of the audience, which posed a threat to retention of the material presented (along with the ego of the presenter), this new technology could cut both ways. It could undercut the message, or it could *significantly increase potential audience involvement in the entire process of communication.* The results could be dramatically positive or extremely adverse.

So the question now becomes, Does the conventional presenter see this trend as a threat to her position at the front of the room, or can she harness the energy of the audience not as merely passive recipients of information but as active participants in the process of learning, communication, and, dare we suggest, awareness?

WHAT IS THE WORLD OF SOCIAL MEDIA?

A few years after the young man at the beginning of this chapter left the tourist industry, he got interested in computers and became an instructor for a large training organization for which he taught classes on software. During one of these classes, a question came up to which the young man did not know the answer. Instead of becoming flustered or trying to fake the response, he threw it back to the audience, where someone else knew the specific answer, and that began a discussion that resolved and shed more light on the issue.

However, upon the instructor's return home, he found that his evaluation for the course had been marred by the comment of one of the attendees who said that he was inadequately versed in the subject matter because he had to get an answer to a question from another person in the room (and suggested that he should have known the information himself). This resulted in the instructor getting fewer assignments, and eventually he moved on to other ventures and activities, including writing this book. The point is, if the students in that class had the mindset of the people using the Internet today, I might still be teaching that course.

Why? Because among the new generation of information consumers and Internet users, the entire concept of one expert knowing everything and distributing the font of her wisdom to uninformed people starved for a single point of view is *over*.

From a purely technological point of view, let's take a look at YouTube, the preeminent online video hosting service. Not only does YouTube make a mockery of ownership of content, it encourages the sharing of information by making the code for linking and embedding freely available front and center. This allows anyone with a blog, Web page, or e-mail to easily distribute or display this content. Not only that, but YouTube has created a community around the hosted video so that those who view it can comment upon it and rate it—others can more easily locate, digest, and consume the information they want. In this way, *the entire Internet has become one ongoing conversation*, going in all directions simultaneously.

To be sure, there is still a revered place in this universe for the person with important knowledge to impart, whether in front of the room, on a Web conference, through a blog, or a myriad of media both presently available and coming down the road. But woe to the expert or authority who assumes that her mantle of expertise is sufficient to ensure the attention of her audience.

In their book, *Groundswell: Winning in a World Transformed by Social Technologies*,[3] Charlene Li and Josh Bernoff detail the impact this trend in information exchange is having on corporations; for example, there is now an ongoing conversation with freely proffered opinions about a company's product or service on various sites on the Internet.

Imagine you are a presenter for such a company on a standard sales call in a board or conference room, and people are not paying attention because they are on their BlackBerries finding online material that challenges the premise behind your beautiful PowerPoint slides. If you were a savvy participant in this new social media, your research would have included this information, and you would be prepared. If, however, you were a traditional presenter who came with a first slide talking about your company with a spinning logo and went into a standard sales pitch, the results would not be pretty. You would be tuned out by the BlackBerry-wielding audience, and as you touted the features of your product or service, you would be peppered by interruptions and questions about how it might benefit the potential customer, and what about the flaws that were being noted about your product or service online?

And this trend goes far beyond sales. A college professor or high school teacher will know his students are discussing her subject matter and participating in a way that stimulates learning and discourse; if the opposite is true, she will be confronted with the reality that the material is either not relevant or is being poorly presented.

This phenomenon of electronic commentary and chatter during and even in opposition to a presentation is known as the "backchannel" and is the subject of new books by presentation experts Olivia Mitchell and Cliff Atkinson.

In her free eBook *How to Present with Twitter (and Other Backchannels)*,[4] Olivia Mitchell suggests three steps for taking advantage of the backchannel rather than seeing it as a threat:

1. Survive the experience. Prepare adequately.
2. Respond to the audience's needs. Master the phenomenon.
3. Engage with the backchannel. Use it for your own purposes.

In many ways this trend represents a microcosm of social media's impact on communications: the speaker as oligarch with unchallenged authority is an institution of the past. With mobile phones and PDAs, Twitter is the main medium of the backchannel at this time. (We cover Twitter in some detail in Chapter Five.)

For his part, Atkinson recommends displaying the @ identifier with a presenter's Twitter account prominently in any presentation; for example, on the title page of my presentation I would place "@tombunzel" to let the audience know that they can contact me with Twitter. Atkinson also suggests creating a hashtag (#; covered in Chapter Five) for the presentation to filter Twitter messages about the topic and engage participants in the process. You can search for existing hashtags and learn more about them at www.wthashtag.com; and once you have a hashtag in use, you can archive the tweets using the hashtag at www.twapperkeeper.com. (We cover Twitter in more detail in Chapter Five and Twitter tools that work with PowerPoint in Chapter Six—also see #blogchat reference later in this chapter.)

Atkinson counsels presenters to have a colleague monitor the Twitter stream or backchannel during a presentation and even take Twitter breaks to allow participants to tell the world what is going on. Finally, you can use Twitter and other social media tools to send out your slides; other scenarios for using slides in and with social media are mentioned throughout this book.

Suffice it to say, there will be many fewer if any passive audiences.

A human resource coordinator or information technology manager will be under intense pressure to ride this wave or wipe out under its influence. If your organization decides to adopt a new software system internally, and a staff will need to be reoriented and instructed, you can be sure that the employees will be active online finding out the pros and cons of the new procedures as you implement your own processes.

Whether your organization deems it advisable to give employees a voice and a hand in the choice of such a new product probably depends on the organization's size and culture, but whatever strategy you put into place for implementation, you would be well advised to take into account the chatter and feedback that is sure to accompany the move, either on an internal network that you can monitor, or on the greater Internet, outside the scope of your influence.

To help you get a sense of the wide range of social media, Figure 2.1 represents the exploding landscape of social media in its many applications and permutations.

Some organizations see these new technologies as threats, disrupting their security, diminishing their brand, causing loss of control. As we delve more deeply, however, you may shift to seeing them as opportunities for developing new relationships and gaining a competitive advantage. We examine in following chapters how these social technologies can be powerful enablers when effectively mastered and supplemented with the new presentation and communications technologies.

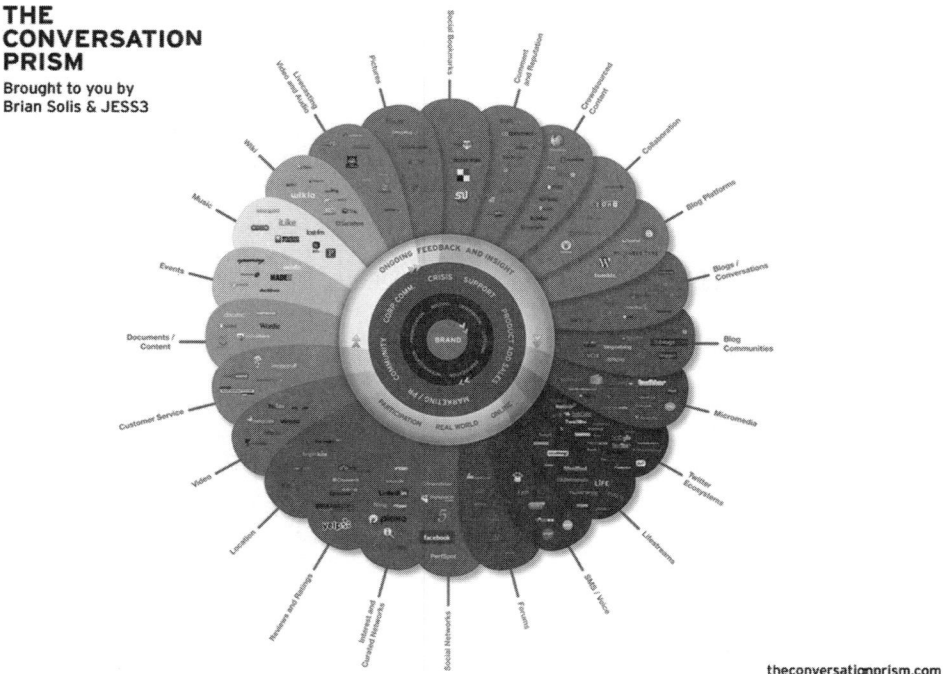

Figure 2.1 The Conversation Prism from social media and public relations professionals' blogs shows the wide array of communications channels, addressing personal and professional interests, to capture the attention of a potential audience.[5]

A PARTIAL OVERVIEW OF SOCIAL MEDIA CATEGORIES AND EXAMPLES

Auction sites (eBay, uBid)

Automated business/professional services (Generate, LexisNexis ExecRelate, and Collexis)

Automated discovery sites (Spoke, Rapleaf, ZoomInfo, Spock, and Wink)

Blogs (and RSS feed)

Business networks (LinkedIn, Plaxo)

Classified (CraigsList)

Consumer sites (Epinions)

Entertainment sites for media

Interactive gaming sites

Microblogging, real time (Twitter)

Music sites (BitTorrent, iTunes, Rhapsody)

News sites (Digg.com)

Niche or special interest networks (Ning, corporate, industry)

Online malls (vintage fashion, MakeMinePink, Buy It Sell It), Amazon (product ratings and reviews)

Social communities and groups (Facebook)

Social bookmarking (delicious)

Sports site (ESPN, CNN/Sports Illustrated, NBA, NASCAR)

Twines, semantic webs

Universal social networks (Facebook, MySpace, Twitter)

User-generated content sites, viral video (YouTube, Flickr, PhotoBucket, Helium)

Virtual worlds (Second Life)

Wikis, participant posted and edited web sites

Tweens (Real Girls Media, BettyConfidential)

HOW JOURNALISM NOW TRANSCENDS BROADCAST

Nowhere is the transition of the presentation of information away from broadcast more dramatically illustrated than in the global media. When Michael Jackson died in 2009, many people heard about it through conventional news broadcast media, but Twitter users got the news first, and it exploded all over the Web. Similarly, when protests broke out in Iran, there was no centralized news organization to inform the populace and the world of the breaking events. Instead the technology of the Internet and again mainly Twitter galvanized the country and the globe against the violence perpetrated by the government on its own people.

Today, anyone with a digital camera, a PDA, or a cell phone can receive *and provide* instant information, and once information is online, it can explode virally, making the individual who discovered or reported on the event as powerful as any broadcast journalist. Obviously in this environment the issue of credibility becomes significant—if just anyone can say anything, who is to be believed?

With a one-time news story, when someone happens to be in the right (or wrong) place and snaps photos and reports on what transpired in a blog post, discussion, status update (on Facebook), or a tweet (on Twitter), there is no real opportunity to build trust. The photos or video simply tell the story, and viewers or consumers of the news must judge for themselves if what they see is to be believed. But in the world of social media, information providers have the opportunity to build a track record and a following built on trust. So-called citizen journalists can transcend their individual roots and become mainstream.

These days, the technology for reporting an event has become literally child's play. Just a few years ago, digitizing a video and putting it online took hours, if not days, and some real high-tech know-how. Now, if you capture a video with an iPhone, there are simple applications (like Tubey) that automatically handle the transfer to You Tube.

As the old media begins to wither on the vine, many consumers get their news online. While they may visit traditional news sites like CNN or the *New York Times*, the trend is toward the power of the real-time immediacy of status updates and sites that take advantage of the entire community to filter and comment on the news. For example, Digg.com uses the opinions of its user base to rate the relative importance of news and information posted on its site. As users "digg" a story and send its link to the aggregation site, the story's ratings improve, it moves higher in ranking, and more people see it and perhaps digg it to improve its ratings. Users have the option of burying stories with a negative rating if they find them irrelevant or if the stories contain broken links.

Michael Arrington was just another guy who liked technology when he started a small blog called TechCrunch; today it's one of the most powerful sources of information on new Internet products and companies. It has grown into an entire network of sites dedicated to technology news and commentary, with a large staff and significant advertising revenue, as well as a well-attended conference in San Francisco. Unlike an iReporter on CNN who happens upon a single story, Arrington blogged on technology using a voice to which readers responded, built a reputation for insight and integrity, and established a broad-based media platform for those hungry for information on technology.

Could Arrington have created a consulting practice that he promoted with a series of lectures using a PowerPoint presentation and a projector? No doubt—but in today's environment he probably would have fallen short of his goals for any number of reasons, even if his PowerPoint slide shows were inspirational and he had the speaking skills of Barack Obama. Instead Arrington had grown up with the Internet and realized what communicators in all fields are coming to understand: he built a relationship of trust with his audience using no investment or overhead except his time and his intellect. Through his blog he exchanged information that allowed others to learn about new technology in ways they had not previously, and he gradually was able to add to a staff of experts who had similar mindsets.

Like any good blog, TechCrunch stimulates threads of comments and discussions so that the consumers of information also become passionate participants in the process of communication. The presentations of today are becoming conversations.

Of course the level of attention that a participant commits depends upon the blogger's credibility, and in the case of Arrington (or perhaps a blogger on an established technology site like CNET or InfoWorld), there are experts at the top of the information pyramid. But today's experts are eschewing the broadcast scenario entirely. The most successful "presenters" in the broadest current definition of the term are now *facilitators*, and whether they are professors in front of students with PDAs and laptops or sales professionals delivering in a boardroom, they know that they have to include the audience before, during, and after the event in order to be successful.

Mack Collier, a well-respected social media expert and blogger, may be conducting the quintessential modern presentation on Twitter (@MackCollier) every Sunday night with his #blogchat. (The # is a hashtag, a feature we cover in more detail in Chapter Five on Twitter.) With the #blogchat hashtag as the filter, a conversation ensues among a worldwide group of participants on a topic of Collier's choosing (he actively solicits topics from participants). Interspersed with the irrelevant ("How is everyone?" or "Come to my site, buy my product" [spam]) are personal experiences and insights about the social media topic at hand, often a technology that enables marketers to track results of their strategy and calculate return on investment of time or resources.

Could Collier deliver a traditional presentation or post it online and get an audience that would value his expertise? Probably so.

Since he is a consultant, I am sure that he continues to present and inform in person and online to earn a nice living, but the information and relationships he has garnered through his popular blog (www.moblogsmoproblems.blogspot.com) and social online activities like blogchat provide much of the basis for his content and continue to build his personal brand.

REAL-TIME EVENTS IN A WORLD OF SOCIAL MEDIA

The fact is, however, that gathering a group of people together in a single physical or virtual location at a given time is still the best way to present most types of information effectively. (If you wait for information consumers to visit your Web site or blog, even if you have a powerful brand and strategy for driving them to your venue, in most cases it is not nearly as effective as giving a personal presentation.)

But even a traditional information event has dramatically changed in today's climate.

At a recent meeting of the Social Media Club of Los Angeles (admittedly a group that is in the vanguard of the trends covered in this book), as a panel of experts spoke on the topic at hand, what was projected on screens above them was not PowerPoint but a live Twitter feed of questions and comments from the audience. This represented an effective use of the backchannel of instant real-time commentary and input. The event itself was promoted heavily on Facebook, Twitter, and various blogs, and the speakers were recognized from their online activities and the relationships that contributed to the enthusiasm and interest of the audience. Compare the energy in such a room and the retention of information by the audience with the dreaded "Death by PowerPoint" presentation that any of these panelists might have delivered a few years ago in a more traditional training or educational venue.

But very few such real-time events remain one-time occasions that one might miss if one cannot attend—at a minimum, they become archived as video. In the case of the Social Media Club event, the Twitter thread was available online. In most cases, video of the speakers at an event and even any PowerPoint would be available in a merged format (generally some kind of video) that someone who could not attend the event could download or access directly online.

Or, the entire event could take place online using a Web conferencing or webinar program that allows participation and learning across all time zones simultaneously. (We discuss Web conferencing programs in detail in Chapter Seven.)

Real-time Web conferences can be very effective for training, sales, or any kind of important communication, but they pose their own challenges in keeping the audience attentive; after all, if someone is watching the event through a browser on a computer, she can access her e-mail or go to other Web sites in the very next window.

The preconference activities—both traditional promotion and invitation through databases and, in today's climate, the online social activities of the organizer and speaker(s)—will directly affect *the size of the audience* and *the extent of its retention of the information provided.*

Today's Web conferences feature the voices of the speakers, with graphics as the visual component, and in many cases the visuals are still a PowerPoint-type of slide show. But the programs for Web conferencing also support a shared desktop, so that any Web content or software demonstration can be shown to an audience, along with polling, annotation, and other tools. There is an added aspect of instant community in a Web conference, particularly if chat or voice is used effectively for questions and answers and commentary during the event, and if the content itself keeps the participants from checking their e-mail.

While a Web sales conference might still have a traditional close or call to action, many marketers have found that doing a more educational event that provides value for the audience is the most effective use of this medium. In the social media world, this is encoded in a saying: "Don't sell the dog food—teach people something important about their dogs."

And, in fact, the most effective Web conferences build on relationships with their audiences both prior to and subsequent to the event. After a conference, this can go beyond the simple rating or evaluation of the event or the information provided and stimulate more conversation among the audience and the speakers.

If the event is really successful, the participants will be blogging and commenting in ways that will virally distribute the information to an even wider audience.

INFORMATION ALWAYS ACCESSIBLE IN THE CLOUD

Imagine this scenario: you're sitting in an airport lounge when you strike up a conversation with a colleague. Your colleague expresses an interest in your ideas on performance evaluation, and you discuss various ideas, including the concept of metrics. You know that you have several slides with key graphs, but you don't have your laptop. However, you have an iPhone (or some other PDA with a Web connection), and you've posted your slides online using a hosting program like SlideShare or AuthorStream that specializes in PowerPoint. Even though your PDA can't run PowerPoint, you still have access to the vital information in a visual format—you can bring up the Web page with your presentation and click through it as you go through the material with your colleague.

Certainly the screen size is constrained, but with the graphs displayed you can support your ideas effectively. (Or you might be using one of the new "pico" (pocket projector or mobile) projectors that connect to a PDA, iPod, or iPhone.) At the conclusion of the presentation, your colleague thanks you and says that he wishes that he could have written down and remembered all of your points. You simply get his e-mail address and send him a link to the presentation with your audio narration that he can review at his convenience.

What you've just done is to take advantage of one of the major buzzwords and trends in the social media environment: the cloud.

As we'll see, there are innumerable advantages (as well as some pitfalls) when your data is hosted and available online. Depending upon the scenario and the type of data, there are many ways to communicate important information or learn about new concepts and processes during a small or large conference or in an "asynchronous" way (so that people can access the material when it's most convenient for them, not you). Our success in communicating in this new age is built upon strategically and creatively using the many facets of this rapidly changing technology. Perhaps the key feature of these new programs that empower training, learning, and sales is that they have *democratized* the distribution of information. There has been a dramatic shift toward participation, from the authority figure at the apex of any power pyramid to the ability of any of the pillars or stones that support the structure to voice their own ideas, opinions, and suggestions, exert their own influence, and gain their own followings. In some ways this is the ultimate nightmare for the traditional presenter. It's like suddenly everyone in the audience is a potential gadfly or heckler. But for the communicator with an important message, well crafted and prepared, and in alignment with what she has already discovered through a dialogue with the audience, such a process is only enhanced by the new technology and ethos of the coming information environment.

HOW SOCIAL MEDIA RAISES THE STAKES

When a person writes an angry letter to the CEO of a company, the letter is generally answered by someone in the public relations (PR) department who may or may not take steps to address the writer's concerns. If the writer continues to be dissatisfied, she may be able to appeal to a trade organization or Better Business Bureau, but unless she has access to the media, she generally has little additional power or leverage. (Obviously if she is a business writer or celebrity, the PR department will pick up on that, and her case will get more attention.)

But now, take the case of young Dave Carroll, the guitarist for a band called the Sons of Maxwell. On a flight from Nova Scotia to Nebraska, while the plane stopped in Chicago, according to Carroll his $3,500 guitar was broken by the United Airlines handlers. Since he and his band were unknown, his attempts at reimbursement were ignored by the airline. But Carroll had some social media skills, and he recorded a song and created a video called "United Breaks Guitars." The video "went viral" on YouTube, with more than 3 million views and more than 15,000 comments, causing United a public relations nightmare even a top celebrity could not match. Not only did the song and the underdog-against-Goliath campaign that Carroll waged turn him (briefly) into a rock star, it garnered compensation from United Airlines, which Carroll suggested the company donate to charity.

The viral nature of the online event is illustrated by how the guitar manufacturer, Taylor Guitars, jumped on the bandwagon. The company's video on YouTube pops up when users watch Carroll's music video, and in the company video Taylor shows how it stands behind its product and conveys the quality that Taylor Guitars represents. This is an advertising bonanza that the small manufacturer in El Cajon, California, could never otherwise afford, and no number of sales presentations would have the effect of the company's link to the story on the Internet about United Airlines breaking a musician's guitar and the song that made him famous.

SCENARIO: A SHIFT IN TRADITIONAL TRAINING

Jane Monroe, HR director for CelluLink, a software company for applications for PDAs and cell phones, was extremely worried. Consultants had come to the firm and convinced management to make sweeping changes in implementing a new social media strategy that would have a major impact on customer service.

Jane's major task is to conduct training sessions for her customer service representatives on the nuts and bolts of CelluLink's product and to learn various routines that enable them to answer questions and also move on to the next issue, whether on the phone or online. Now Jane is worried that as customer service becomes the domain of a social media policy, many of her staff will be let go because the Internet will deal with many of the issues.

But as the consultants meet with Jane to begin to implement the changes they envision, Jane begins to realize that many of her fears are unfounded. In the plans for implementing social media, there is a large commitment of time and energy on the part of experts in CelluLink's products to build the community that the consultants recommend. In addition to creating, monitoring, and participating in a new social network on Cellulink's Web site, where users can join and share their experiences and help solve problems, there will be a continuing need for employees to create content, provide solutions, and interact with the new social network members. A large effort will be required on Twitter, Facebook, YouTube, and a host of other venues to create a buzz and drive membership to the CelluLink social media network.

Smiling to herself, Jane sees that while some of her staff may have to leave, many will need to be retrained and motivated in the effort to promote and administer the new social network that will address the customer services previously handled by the call centers and online response team. This will enhance their current skill sets and promote engagement with CelluLink's customers, as well as provide new opportunities in the training and development area.

RESULTS OF IMPLEMENTING SOCIAL MEDIA

As Jane realized in the scenario, effective use of social media doesn't happen by magic. In addition to the resources need allocated by CelluLink to develop the new social media strategy, CelluLink employees will need to train in and implement the new strategy.

David Armano is one of the founders of Dachis Corporation, an Austin-based firm that offers social business design services. On his blog at Harvard Business Publishing, Armano points out that the real investment in a social media plan is harnessing people skills, not just using and launching technology. Armano writes, "Being social means having real live people who actively participate in your initiatives. It's difficult to automate and a challenge to scale, but it can also help move your business forward in ways that produce leveraged outcomes such as new/better products or services. The economics of using social media in business require the participation of people to fuel it. It is not simply enabled by technology that maintains itself."

He breaks down the process into three steps, which he calls seeding, feeding, and weeding. *Seeding* is the preparation of the "ecosystem" in terms of resources—information, ideas (insights), and innovative concepts—that will attract and keep members of the community. The *feeding* component involves the continuing production and editorial management of content and maintaining relationships with users. Depending upon the nature of the social solution in place—internal, corporate, or public—a certain amount of inappropriate, irrelevant, and unproductive content will need to be *weeded* out. Armano also suggests that much unnecessary expense and troubleshooting can be avoided if the social strategy is thoroughly planned prior to the launch of the technological components.[6]

Natalie L. Petouhoff, PhD, an analyst at Forrester Research, published a study on "The ROI of Online Customer Service Communities"[7] (social sites like the one contemplated by CelluLink, Jane's company in the scenario). She discusses several companies that implemented such communities, including AlterPoint, DIRECTV, Intel, and Verizon, and found that these companies generally enjoyed significant return on investment in "a short period of time while delivering better customer service experiences."

Petouhoff estimates in the study that a company with half a million customers with 30,000 calls per month would need to invest about $1.2 million in building and using an effective social network over the first three years. Included in the investment are the startup costs for design, maintenance of a social media

Web site, integration with other departments, and oversight and analysis. The Forrester analyst suggests that a payback of double the initial investment is feasible in the first year, taking into account the fact that many issues handled by customer service representatives will be handled by "superusers" or influencers in the community.

Petouhoff states that users in a laptop community found the information from superusers superior to that provided by ordinary tech support or customer service reps. This is hardly surprising; many customer service reps have no hands-on experience with a product, while superusers are contributing to a social network based on their own discoveries "in the trenches." A secondary benefit of such a community is the expansion of the company's knowledge base through the contributions of actual customers, taking information beyond the resources provided by technicians and software designers.

In the case of technical products, in particular, Petouhoff's study says that the longest support calls address the more than 90 percent of issues that are completely new and unanticipated by tech support—but on a social network, presumably someone else may well have had and solved a similar problem, leading to a resolution that is far more efficient for everyone.

THE REAL WORLD: BLUE SHIRT NATION

Blue Shirt Nation is the internal social network for Best Buy electronics stores. It started as a way to check out advertising copy and learn about how customers felt about the stores, and it ended up as a dream internal company Web site that jump-started motivation and proved a boon for both marketing and human resources.

Many companies recognize and try to reward employees who contribute tangible insights into the way their functions work, but Best Buy found that a social network empowered their workers to become motivated to share ideas. One critical element was that all tiers of employees were included and listened to each other with no pecking order, making it possible for anyone to be heard and make a significant contribution. For Gary Koelling and Steve Bendt, the two advertising specialists who designed the site, what started out as a way to learn from Best Buy employees about the customer experience as a research mechanism turned into a way for the company to learn from everyone's experience and foster trust and clear communications throughout the organization. One very positive result is lower turnover among the users of the internal network; only 8 to 12 percent turnover in contrast to 60 percent in the organization overall.[8]

The turning point for Blue Shirt Nation was four months after launch, when the site got the blessing of management and funds were made available for Koelling and Bendt to travel to 130 Best Buy stores, interview employees, and learn what employees wanted to see on the site. While there was little enthusiasm among the rank and file for spending time with the two admen to help them develop their copy, employees did open up dramatically when asked about their personal experiences, gripes, suggestions, and opinions.

Koelling and Bendt got the idea that an effective site would be about stories and listening and learning from the experiences of others. The site was broken down into groups talking about their own areas of interest—cameras, video, audio, and so on, each sharing their unique perspectives and expertise. For example, a sales associate got a meeting with middle management by sharing his ideas for innovative ways to market video games in the stores. One employee posted a picture of a display case he thought was too big for his department and solicited opinions; higher-ups quickly realized that the display case in question was the incorrect size and exchanged it. The photo had a significant meaning and a clear message—two vital elements of any successful communication, corporate or otherwise. Another employee started a conversation that convinced management that e-mail should be supported during working hours to communicate internally and with customers. Management listened to the stream of arguments and agreed.

The upshot is that Best Buy employees know that management is listening, and they can advance through honesty, creativity, and innovation.

Koelling and Bendt encoded the principles behind the site in a slideshow available on Koelling's blog. The three goals for participants are "Be believable," "Bring people together," and "Try things."[9] The Blue Shirt Nation grew because it was bottom up, not top down, making it a trusted platform among Best Buy's rank and file. It profited from open-minded management that supported the project in its infancy and who showed a willingness to listen to all of the users' opinions and ideas. Concepts hatched on the network were implemented, further motivating the rank and file to participate openly. Finally, the dialogue is ongoing and not sporadic; there is always a conversation happening, with comments and results.

As management saw the results of Blue Shirt Nation, they tested the social media waters as well; Barry Judge, the chief marketing officer, accumulated nearly 3,000 Twitter users as followers in a matter of months. This opened the door for customer comments about the brand, some good, some not so good. Judge took the Twitter feed in the direction that Koelling and Bendt had originally conceived: he test marketed some commercials from an upcoming ad campaign and asked his followers to comment.

For human resources and marketing, as well as other silos within Best Buy, the Blue Shirt Network provides a wealth of in-the-trenches information, gauges the mood of employees, and fosters a sense of community that only the new Web experience could provide. Compare this to the old "teamwork" presentation delivered by a chief executive officer to the minions, with generic PowerPoint slides of one hand shaking another.

Bear in mind that a social network, or any blog or Web site, can take advantage of a large range of media including audio (podcasts), video, photos, slides, animation, and everything that one might have wanted to pack into a conventional PowerPoint presentation not so long ago. Just as presentation experts frequently advise PowerPoint presenters not to use gratuitous animation or overwhelming effects—but rather to focus on the core message—so too is it important that content on a proprietary social network serve a specific purpose and be posted in the context of conveying useful information.

Now imagine what a research goldmine Blue Shirt Nation is for the internal and external communications efforts of the company. Stories about all aspects of the company, from sales to fulfillment, are available throughout the site for use in advertising, training, and any other areas that the company needs to sell, motivate, inspire, or teach. The content can be repurposed in seminars, online Web conferences or webinars, or in print or video, online or via broadcast. The nuts and bolts of Blue Shirt Nation constitute a best practices (and a what-to-avoid) bonanza for human resources to use in preparing training materials and for supervisors to use in less formal situations ("Did you see what so and so wrote on his blog about handling a difficult customer?").

How does a company or organization launch such a dedicated social network? You can hire a team of consultants and programmers, or you can use a Web-based program like Ning (see Chapter Five) to build it with generic components, configure, design, and customize it, and then invite members and promote it internally or, if desired, externally.

The following pages go into more detail about strategically taking advantage of this new participatory dynamic and describe the emerging technologies that support it. But becoming acquainted with new programs like Facebook, Twitter, or YouTube is not enough—we need to understand and integrate the new ethic of participatory information exchange (PIE, everyone gets a slice) to transcend the broadcast presentation model. When we ride this wave of intellectual democracy, our traditional tools for communication—text, slides, video, graphics, conferencing, and so on—will become enhanced and broadened in their efficacy. There will be a place for PowerPoint, but as it moves from the projector to the Internet, complementary Web sites and new competitors will emerge that are also well suited to the task of presenting online and stimulating participation, discussion, and collaboration.

As we are empowered to present from our desktops to anyone on the planet, new challenges emerge to maintaining attention and interacting in a meaningful way. As we meet these hurdles head on, we find ourselves liberated from the constraints of setting up a projector, getting on an airplane, or being otherwise limited by geography or even physics.

Similarly, as we meet other communication challenges by tapping the resources of community, we will see new opportunities for solving problems and encouraging participation on the part of our colleagues, customers, associates, organization members, and others. As our entire world opens and expands, we will profit from enhancement to education and information exchange as well as from the ultimately more meaningful improvement to the depth and quality of our lives and relationships.

As we've seen, the nature of how we communicate is forever changed. No individual or organization can feel confident just disseminating a lonely message. Every presentation today is part of an ongoing conversation that reflects on both the messenger and the members of her audience.

QUESTIONS TO PONDER

1. How do you feel about sharing the spotlight as a communicator? Do you see yourself as an authority figure who is above challenges from an audience? If you were to participate on a panel in your area of interest, would you share information willingly or tend to try to outperform or outshine your fellow panelists?

2. How will you address the issue of the back channel? Is your audience likely to be online during messages that you deliver? Can you become comfortable accepting their input and interacting with them?

3. Do you see commentary as a potential threat or support for your endeavors? Are you aware of the various blogs, communities, and groups on Facebook, for example, that are influential in your area of interest or expertise?

Notes

1. Tony Jeary, *Life Is a Series of Presentations: Eight Ways to Inspire, Inform, and Influence Anyone, Anywhere, Anytime.* New York: Fireside, 2005.
2. Chip Heath and Dan Heath, *Made to Stick: Why Some Ideas Survive and Others Die.* New York: Random House, 2007.
3. Charlene Li and Josh Bernoff, *Groundswell.* Cambridge, MA: Harvard Business School Press, 2008.
4. www.speakingaboutpresenting.com/wp-content/uploads/Twitter.pdf. See also Cliff Atkinson, *The Backchannel: How Audiences Are Using Twitter and Social Media and Changing Presentations Forever.* Berkeley: New Riders Press, 2009.
5. www.theconversationprism.com.
6. David Armano, *Debunking Social Media Myths*, June 29, 2009, http://blogs.harvardbusiness.org/cs/2009/06/debunking_social_media_myths.html.
7. Natalie L. Petouhoff, PhD, with Chip Gliedman, William Band, and Andrew Magarie, *The ROI of Online Customer Service Communities*, www.forrester.com. See also Joe McKendrick, *Study: Payback Can Be Quick for Social Media*, www.smartplanet.com/business/blog/business-brains/study-payback-can-be-quick-for-social-media/1132/.
8. www.businessinnovationfactory.com.
9. http://garykoelling.com/node/442.

Engaging with Social Media

chapter
THREE

As we discussed in Chapter Two, the nature of presentations has changed from being one-time events, generally with a single purpose, to being integrated parts of an ongoing conversation. Rather than a broadcast or data dump given by an authority, a presentation now must include interaction and dialogue with a community of interest.

In the old paradigm, a presenter would generally begin creating a project with a significant goal, for example:

- Making a sale
- Teaching a concept
- Motivating a team or group of colleagues, constituency, or congregation

Instead of planning an overall strategy, a conventional presenter might jump right into PowerPoint and perhaps use a prepackaged template that provides common themes or content. A more polished presenter would spend time researching her audience and then go through a planning stage with one or more goals in mind. She might gather stories or anecdotes to use as analogies or metaphors, charts, and graphs if numerical proofs or substantiation was needed for the message, and attempt to address the needs of different learning types: visual, kinesthetic, auditory, and so on.

These are all viable strategies that in the past worked with varying degrees of success in environments in which the audience expected to passively receive or consume information.

Today, even if a presenter could enter a meeting or conference carrying the mantle of expertise and simply dispense a set of ideas, attempt to sell an audience on a product or service, or convince them of anything, that presenter would be operating at a distinct disadvantage. For one thing, a significant portion of the audience would not be coming to the event without previous knowledge. Even in a corporate setting, where they had no choice but to attend, audience members would be comparing notes among themselves and online in a backchannel, perhaps even as the presenter opened with a charming story or anecdote.

The fact is that many members of any audience today participate in a large range of online sites on which others pay attention to them and respond according to very new and precise rules and assumptions. For one thing, difficult as it may be for many people to accept, no one is assumed to be more credible or important than anyone else.

Consequently, as great an expert or authority as you might be, or as powerful as you might be within an organization, you are *competing* for credibility and attention in an environment in which the current norm is that anyone of consequence has already interacted with the community in an exchange of information and ideas. For example, it is inconceivable that the head of a corporate division who was addressing his staff with the idea of implementing a new strategy or launching a product wouldn't have prepared the ground with prior communication of some kind—although that might well have been the case just a few years ago.

Participation in social media is not merely about learning a new set of tools. It constitutes a new attitude and mindset that is pervasive among today's consumers of information.

In the world of social media, any executive would have already created a *communications identity*—a personal brand that was developed over time and had forged relationships with others at her level in the hierarchy, above, below, and within and outside the organization.

On the most basic level, on many social sites you will create a specific profile for that application, although it may be called a bio or ID. The cumulative effect or identity that forms the public persona you project online, including these profiles or bios and your participation and reputation, constitutes your total online identity.

All of your online actions and interactions, both professional and personal, reflect on this identity and serve to establish a reputation based on your behavior and the perceptions of others.

EARNING A REPUTATION AS A "TRUST AGENT"

In their book, *Trust Agents*,[1] Chris Brogan and Julien Smith provide a comprehensive overview of the strategies that result in social media success, mainly in the field of marketing and brand recognition, but applicable also to training, education, public relations, nonprofits, and other areas of organizational communications. The model Brogan and Smith use emphasizes the concept of "social capital," which is accumulated over time by building relationships with potential customers rather than directly selling. To these authors, social media is a long-term investment that allows an entity to break through the hurdle of getting attention on the Web in three stages: awareness, reputation, and trust.

Brogan and Smith say that their book is not about tools (although they do provide some examples of programs that they use with their clients), but rather about the mindset of those who effectively build layers of trust through social channels. Since their main focus is on brands and marketing, they reiterate the point that selling overtly or not establishing a relationship of trust before attempting a marketing effort is in the current environment a huge mistake. The entire premise of *Trust Agents* is that Web users have a built-in barometer that filters out "news-speak," press releases, or celebrity testimonials and focuses on individuals and organizations that have built credibility by providing value at each stage of the communications process—identity building, content delivery, and aftercare.

Because of the singular value of credible information in today's competitive environment, the process of marketing many products or services is best implemented by combining it with training and learning; for example, potential users of a new medical treatment may no longer blindly trust the pronouncements of the manufacturer. In addition to the patient, other stakeholders (family, hospital, community) will want to be educated on a full range of issues and actively participate in every aspect of the caregiving process.

In Brogan and Smith's terms, a Web user becomes a trust agent when she provides and shares valuable information beyond what her own interests might ordinarily dictate and/or retains a level of independence throughout her efforts to listen to, inform, influence, and educate others.

This same trend is continuing in many areas. As students use Twitter in a classroom, or employees are provided training in an organization, there is massive competition for their attention. Attention spans are shorter than ever. Communicators must provide value at every stage of the process—in establishing their credibility as part of an identity, in delivering their messages effectively with the most appropriate audio and visual tools, and in maintaining the connection with their audiences after an event or class has ended.

In essence, all communication today is a massive competition for "mindshare." The trend that began in movies and mass media, where the lines between content and advertising have become blurred, is continuing on the Internet. It is impossible to tell who may be sponsoring an individual, blogger, or Web site. The inevitable result is that the lines separating marketing, education, and training are frequently difficult if not impossible to distinguish—so that today's consumers of information have learned that providing significant value by creating a more thorough understanding of any subject is the main vehicle for building trust and credibility.

THE NEW RULES OF ENGAGEMENT

According to the authors of *Trust Agents*, successful communication in the modern era comes down to six strategies:

1. Make your own game: Standing out
2. Be one of us: Belonging
3. Use the Archimedes effect: Leverage
4. Become an Agent Zero: Developing access
5. Become a human artist: Developing understanding
6. Build an army: Developing mass

Standing out is about attracting attention, but without the old-school shout of mass marketing or public relations—"Here I am, here's what I do, buy my product or service or learn and accept what I am putting out there." As we've discussed, success in social media involves creating value and making a contribution.

Brogan and Smith suggest that communicators not assume a superior (broadcast) position and instead act approachably in appearance and language. Both authors and most experts in tech and social media eschew suits in most settings and speak in plain, no-nonsense tones.

Since relationships in social media take some time to establish, once a reputation is established, one can begin to intelligently leverage connections made. Brogan and Smith use Madonna as an example; early in her career she connected and supported young artists before they were successful, and later on their loyalty boosted her to greater heights.

The process continues, according to the authors, building and maintaining more and more significant connections (their "Agent Zero" concept refers to locating or becoming the hub of a social and/or real-world network). This is not accomplished in a manipulative way, but naturally and through human interaction and mutual support (being a "human artist"): facilitating connection, helping others, and increasing your "social capital."

Finally, you may end up with what Seth Godin calls a "tribe"[2]—and what Brogan and Smith call an "army"—a powerful network of supporters who will lift your ship higher as you keep connected to them and serve their various interests in a sincere fashion.

Trust, for Brogan and Smith, is the essence of the new currency—social capital—which, according to their premise, when properly invested results in the growth of influence and one's network online through links, traffic, and increased social "proof."

In *Trust Agents*, Internet gossip columnist Perez Hilton is mentioned as one of many examples of someone who "made his own game" not by becoming a shill for the entertainment industry but rather by using a unique voice and perspective to deliver his message.

TWO ALTERNATIVE SCENARIOS

Malcolm Cornwell has recently been hired as the chief technology officer of Pomona PetroChemical. Now he's about to address his IT team about a decision made at the executive level to entirely revise the network configuration that controls manufacturing in a way that he believes will increase efficiency. No one knows much about him except that his biography has been posted online, and he's done a brief talking-head video of self-introduction in which he said things like, "I have a commitment to transparency." He has done no other ground work to establish a connection with his team other than to send out a series of e-mail memos to set priorities.

The following is a more modern alternative.

Denise Sturgess has the same task, but she has established an active blog on the corporate network in which she's explained her intentions to change the server software, laid out her reasons, and responded to comments and alternatives from others within the company. Denise has also become active on various internal and external social networks through which she has interacted with colleagues on a personal level, exchanging stories about her passion for scuba diving and photography, posting pictures of her vacation with her family, and reaching out to fellow employees in organizing a Fourth of July picnic at a local water park. She has been active on several professional networks, like LinkedIn and Plaxo, where she has contributed ideas and answers to questions and referred colleagues for other positions, some of whom now have friends or are in the networks themselves.

Although Denise is armed with a PowerPoint slide deck to make her case, she has greeted a number of people she knows personally prior to the presentation, and during Q&A, she calls on them by name and can respond substantively to their concerns based on their comments on her blog and items she has read on their Twitter feeds.

Finally, she promises the assembly that as the change in network configuration is being implemented, she will have her main troubleshooting team monitor a filtered comment feed from throughout the organization to address problems within minutes of their occurrence. In addition, archived minutes of all status meetings will be available in a searchable format to begin to build a wiki or knowledge base to further support implementation of the changed network architecture.

Guess whose strategy for changing an important internal process is likely to succeed?

Of course, the personal strategy that Denise has implemented cannot be put into place overnight. Her blog may have followed her from her previous position (and might well have been one of the reasons she got hired by her new employer). And she wouldn't have suddenly appeared on social networks like Twitter and Facebook, or business networks like Plaxo or LinkedIn, when she began to craft her presentation. Denise had already built a reputation for credibility and had forged relationships of trust before she needed to deliver the challenging speech. She had established a personal and professional network that let her know the concerns of her staff prior to the talk and address them in her formal presentation and during Q&A.

Knowing that there would still be hurdles and resistance to any mass change in the organization, she had developed a communications profile of trust, according to some of the principles outlined by Brogan and Smith, that would give her space and goodwill as the process unfolded. Beyond spouting a platitude like "The channels of communication will remain open," she had demonstrated her commitment to make sure that open communication occurs, and she had plenty of channels available to garner and respond to the concerns of those affected by her decisions.

WHO SHOULD PARTICIPATE IN SOCIAL MEDIA (AND HOW)?

Although participation in social media today is a reality among many information consumers, there is divergent opinion on which members of an organization should actively participate in one or more channels for social media. Some experts maintain that everyone should have a voice, and certainly on internal networks like Best Buy's Blue Shirt Nation (introduced in Chapter Two), that makes sense. But are you comfortable with anyone speaking for your brand on the Web as a whole and posting tweets on Twitter or commenting on Facebook? This is a matter for some strategic thinking and decision making, but certainly if you are a key communicator in your organization, and someone who already uses conventional tools such as PowerPoint to distribute a message, you need to investigate and explore social media.

On his blog, smallbusinessnewz, Shel Holtz identifies six concepts of how social media should be handled in an organization:

1. By public relations, public affairs, or communications departments
2. By those who champion it
3. By project teams and those with specific needs
4. By specialists (who will emerge with their own boxes on the org chart) due to its complexity
5. By HR and training departments as natural proponents
6. By everyone—it's beyond anyone's control

Holtz makes the comparison between the emergence of social media and the beginning of desktop publishing, when those who mastered the technology were turning out newsletters and graphics that were unreadable—until the communications specialists in the organization became involved in the content.

He points to the example of "brandjacking"—the incident of an ExxonMobil employee with no authority posting on Twitter on behalf of the entire company. Unfortunately the employee's posts were taken as official communications by the investment and media world; it took ExxonMobil several days to end the practice. Ironically Holtz had been to ExxonMobil as a consultant, touting the benefits of social media to their public affairs office, only to learn that they had not done any tweeting and that they were in the process of trying to figure out who had put a Twitter stream in the company's name online. Apparently the logo for the Twitter ID was a giveaway, since the company was in the process of divesting their service stations and the employee's answers to questions by her many new Twitter followers indicated a lack of public relations acumen. (In response to a question about the Exxon *Valdez* incident, she replied that though it was a disaster, it did not rank among the top ten such occurrences.)

Holtz uses this example to argue against the notion that social media can be everyone's responsibility.

Taking a different approach, Charlene Li, the coauthor (with Josh Bernoff) of the best-seller *Groundswell*,[3] argues in "Engagement Ranking the Top 100 Brands" that "one recurring theme throughout [these] case studies is that engagement cannot remain the sole province of a few social media experts, but instead must be embraced by the entire organization."[4] Li's comment suggests (and this is one of the key tenets of *Groundswell*) that it is the very freedom that motivates and encourages social media users and makes the new communities of passion such a wellspring for effective and meaningful communication. Indeed, it was the spadework done by the creators of Best Buy's Blue Shirt Nation that convinced the early adopters and participants that their ideas were valued and that management was on their side, which led to the social network becoming a valuable asset to the company. Of course, again, the Best Buy network is internal, but the same principles of trust and freedom apply in the proliferation of the successful case studies in Li's paper.

The differentiating factor for Holtz is that those involved with social media should be clearly aware of and aligned with the *social media goals* of their organization. He cites the Technographics Profiling Ladder in *Groundswell*, which identifies different social media types. (You can find this tool online at www.forrester.com/Groundswell/profile_tool.html.)

Holtz argues that "it's clear from reviewing this data that not everyone is a content creator; similarly, not everyone may be inclined to comment on existing content. A lot of people are collectors or joiners. Others are spectators and many continue to be completely inactive."⁵ Holtz seems to agree with Li that you can't control social media, but he believes that coordination in an organization under a clearly conceived set of goals is a critical element of success, along with making sure that a member of any team involved in the organization's online communications efforts has social media "chops." Holtz salutes social media champions as integral to early adoption efforts (like the one at Best Buy) but suggests that they often do not have the "big picture" perspective that the organization needs for a successful strategy. Holtz says that, contrary to being the natural stewards of social media, training departments should do exactly that: become responsible for training all departments in the most effective use of social media for whatever their tasks may be. Since so much in the area of social media and all organizational communications is about shaping the message, Holtz concludes that public relations (PR) or public affairs will become the de facto administrator of social media in most cases.

He cites the opinion of social media "explorer" Jason Falls, who writes in his blog piece "Social Media Is the Responsibility of Public Relations" that "social media is a method of communications. Social media tools facilitate these communications. To be effective in social media, whether as a marketer or just an ordinary participant, you must, first and foremost, communicate well. . . . Yes, social media tools are mostly driven by technology. But they are driven by technology to deliver a message. You don't trust your IT department to layout your print ad. Why would you trust them to run your blog?"⁶ Not surprisingly, Falls, the president and cofounder of the Social Media Club of Louisville, is a public relations professional by profession.

Holtz expands on Falls's opinion with the example of Microsoft, where program teams with expertise engage in an ongoing dialogue with their clients and customers on technical issues beyond the control of the company's PR department.

Holtz concludes with a list of social media responsibilities:

- Ensuring that all employees are aligned with the company's plans, goals, and objectives; that employees know the company's position on various issues; and that employees have access to resources to help them communicate whatever it is they want or need to communicate

- Coordinating the development and communication of the company's social computing guidelines so every employee knows exactly what his or her obligations and responsibilities are

- Overseeing the selection and deployment of tools employees can use to engage in social media both internally and externally
- Monitoring the social media space in order to identify new channels and alert the organization to the implications of those channels (for example, the need to claim key trademark names for Friendfeed rooms before somebody brand-jacks your identities)
- Ensuring appropriate social media engagement occurs where it supports the business (for example, identifying a gap in a product team that is not employing social media as part of its efforts when social media would be an appropriate channel)
- Coordinating the use of social media for the business's authoritative statements of record
- Working with other departments, such as HR and training, to ensure employees at all levels know how to best and most responsibly use these channels as representatives of the company
- Identifying social media champions from throughout the organization so the company can take advantage of their passion and expertise
- Monitoring all of the organization's social media efforts to ensure that they all serve the interests of the organization and support its reputation
- Reporting the aggregated results of the company's social media efforts to the company's leadership
- Counseling leadership to ensure that good decisions are made (for example, don't shut down a blog the first time a negative comment appears)
- Identifying and deploying the best monitoring resources in order to get apples-to-apples results from across the enterprise
- Serving in a consultative role for any department or team that wants help
- Identifying best practices and ensuring those using social media are aware of them
- Ensuring channels exist that allow employees to contribute based on their technographic inclinations (creator, critic, sharer, joiner, and so on)
- Building links between traditional communication and social media (for example, helping advertisers use their channel to drive customers to conversations)

- Using social media tools to support the company's social media efforts (for example, social networks that allow employees to share successes and ideas for social media applications with one another)

Depending upon the nature of your organization, this can be a complex undertaking or become the province of communications managers who implement an overall strategy and serve as a sounding board for the various departments that blog, tweet, or post on YouTube. Or in the case of the small business, it may just be a set of important issues that need to be considered by a single individual: you. This brings up the reality that emerged in the presentation field when PowerPoint became ubiquitous: the people that manage disruptive technologies and make them work become key players.

In the real world, here is how it often happens.

SCENARIO: NEW HORIZONS FOR AN ADMINISTRATIVE ASSISTANT

Rita Masters is the harried, overworked human resources director for Amalgamated Financial Services, based in the main office in New York. She is continually creating presentations, generally in PowerPoint, to communicate needs assessments to management, manage the efforts of her staff, and drill down to the various departments where training efforts are underway in the areas of software, customer service, financial analysis, and accounting.

Lucky for Rita, her administrative assistant Glen Baker is a PowerPoint whiz with excellent writing skills who also maintains an excellent relationship with the graphics folks from advertising to keep Rita's presentations looking sharp.

But lately there has been grumbling about how HR is handling its responsibilities—that some of the training material has become outdated and irrelevant, and management has felt that Rita's budget should be slashed or other initiatives undertaken. Rita and Glen discuss this situation, and Glen mentions that he's become active on Facebook where there are any number of groups that discuss financial matters and comment about how the industry is performing. He asks for permission to join some groups, do some research, and come up with some ideas. Rita trusts Glen. She figures there is little to lose and gives her okay.

Within weeks Glen has joined several of the finance groups on Facebook, posting on their threads and meeting other professionals in the industry. From this he has gotten links to many of their Web sites and particularly their blogs, where he reads their content, comments insightfully and with regularity, and also surveys the comments of others, particularly the consumers of financial services. He begins to document some of the ratings of the competing firms and the specific stories and complaints from their clients, and writes them up in memos.

Then he talks a couple of the firm's top analysts into starting their own blogs, using the content he has seen in his research to stimulate their own discussion of their philosophy of wealth management and investment. He promises and delivers on promoting their blogs on Facebook and Twitter. On Twitter he creates user IDs for the two bloggers and uses the microblogging site to promote the content they are working on. In addition, he maintains an active search on Twitter for comments about Amalgamated Financial from its clients and has the bloggers respond, stimulating more interaction and conversation. He advises them not to confront disparate viewpoints or critics, but to engage them in dialogue and actively listen to their concerns.

As the buzz builds online, Glen brings the wealth of new research on client comments and complaints, the practices of other firms and trends in the industry, as well as new ideas for handling issues in the various departments to Rita, who is able to present them to the various departments. Upper management takes renewed interest in her innovative initiatives, and one of the senior executives asks about traffic on the two analysts' blogs. In the ensuing conversation, the social media efforts undertaken by Glen come to light, and the executives note that both of the analysts who blog and whose Twitter accounts Glen has managed are among the top producers for the quarter. Rita's department is connected with Corporate Communications and tasked to develop a social media strategy for all of the company branches worldwide. She requires a crash course in the technology and hires some assistants quickly, because Glen is being transferred to the executive suite where he will head up a social media effort for the CEO and of course create the CEO's PowerPoint presentations.

THE CROWDSOURCING PHENOMENON

Crowdsourcing—taking advantage of the know-how of your customers, colleagues, associates, employees, or other online community members—is one of the most powerful ways of using social media in organizations that have a need to solve problems with limited resources or who need to conserve resources in training and customer service. A great example is the turnaround Dell made when it created user forums in which computer users helped each other rather than having people call outsourced support lines with disinterested personnel reading scripts. Microsoft has similar forums in which the most active participants who help the most people become MVPs and earn trips to Redmond for recognition and rewards.

Other examples include Proctor & Gamble, who listened when customers discussed and suggested a replacement for the dustpan and mop or broom; the result was the Swiffer WetJet product and its myriad accessories. Similarly, after listening to its customers the company created a mouthwash that did not contain the burn of alcohol. Best Buy's Blue Shirt Nation, described previously, is another example of crowdsourcing, with Best Buy tapping into the expertise of its employees and through them getting more insight than ever into the experience of its customers.

But you don't have to have a formal internal social network to incentivize or reward passionate users for their input, advice, or solutions to problems. For example, a cell phone marketing director could move her social media efforts to the next level on Twitter by running a contest for "The Most Annoying Thing About My Cell Phone," promising a free year of service or a new phone for the best solutions or tips to handle common cell phone issues. This discussion could also be moved over to her blog, and she might invite the best participants as a panel during a Web conference to which all of the contest entrants and visitors are invited, and where a grand prize is announced. Most good collaborative meeting tools also have polling—imagine the excitement if the winner was the recipient of the most votes in a real-time, instant poll while everyone was in the conference together. (There is always a need for "real-time" events; there is often no alternative to getting key stakeholders and parties of interest together. In fact, problems that were shared among a number of cell phone users could be addressed using an ad hoc "Meet Now" scenario using a Web conferencing tool, with the parties providing the solution during the impromptu meeting getting some sort of recognition or reward.)

Some have raised ethical concerns about the exploitation of users in crowdsourcing. However, if you keep the value proposition of "Everybody wins" in the forefront of such an effort, and perhaps also bring the participants together in a real-time conference or webinar, where there is no overt selling but useful education and information being distributed, it can add cohesiveness and loyalty to your brand or organization.

WHY SOCIAL MEDIA IS A WOMAN'S WORLD

The changing nature of communications in the world of social media is perhaps best understood by contrasting the general attitudes of men and women about communicating, solving problems, and learning.

BlogHer, the women's blog network, found that 42 million women in the United States (roughly 53 percent of the 79 million adult women in the United States who use the Internet) participate in social media at least weekly. That shouldn't surprise anyone, because the more familiar you become with how social media works, the more you may be reminded of conversations with women and about women. Effective use of social media is frequently a matter of evolving or adapting to a different mindset, particularly for men. Men's main focus online has generally been goal oriented—to get things done. Most corporate Web sites have really been brochures to attract clients, and despite discussions of community, they have been mainly geared to dispensing information for direct sales.

In their book *Groundswell*, Charlene Li and Josh Bernoff refer to a group of consumers highly valued in our economy: the "Alpha Moms" who control a majority of American households' buying power. According to Li and Bernoff's Social Technographics Profile Tool of social media participants, Alpha Moms generally start off as critics but can be turned into loyal champions with useful information.[7]

To reach this highly cherished group, companies have created social networks that promote the notion of women helping and supporting each other in their purchase decisions; in the true spirit of social media, the company becomes the facilitator of the exchange. For example, a grocery chain offers ideas on a blog run by an Alpha Mom for getting the family to spend time together over dinner (instead of trumpeting the features of its stores or even the benefits of its offerings). Social media really took off when the Alpha Moms got involved, exchanging information and providing personal experiences to one another through blogs, comments, dedicated social networks, and of course Facebook and Twitter.

As a friend with an online mall pointed out, women shop differently from men—in her words, women shop for *entertainment.* They might peruse an online store with a social site before they can reasonably afford a product, to learn more about how it looks and fits into their lifestyle for the time when they will be able to acquire it. They love to get the lowdown from other shoppers on their experiences and exchange stories over a host of social media: Twitter, Facebook, blogs, or the social site of a smart company that hosts a blog or social network to facilitate such discussions.

But if you think about entertainment value, what could be better than a group of like-minded female consumers brought together for a special event online, in the form of a Web conference or webinar, with a panel of their peers or a well-respected blogger or expert, where they can gather information and ask questions of each other in real time?

My friend Carole and her colleagues fill their eBay and online stores and malls with used merchandise. Carole is currently planning a webinar on how to shop in thrift stores, and she will have an eager audience who has followed her on a well-attended blog, where she conscientiously posts and responds to comments and keeps it interesting with personal stories and images. Her plan is to build excitement through the blog and on Facebook and Twitter and even help plan the event through feedback from her followers. Through her frequent blog posts she intends to post images (which will also be in the PowerPoint presentation at the webinar) that give a taste of what the online event will offer, with accompanying text in her warm and informative voice.

Like her many female blogging colleagues, Carole is interested in long-term relationships, not one night stands.

The result of Carole's preparation will be a webinar in which participants will get great tips on buying pre-owned merchandise, have lots of fun hearing each other over the conference phone line as they banter and ask questions, and Carole's online mall will get a boost in traffic and sales. It is experiences like these that are solidifying the trend of humanizing the interactions within organizations, and between large companies and their customers, and using the "fun factor" to connect and build relationships.

CONSIDERING THE SOCIAL TECHNOGRAPHICS LADDER

To help in planning a social media strategy or initiative, in their book *Groundswell*, Li and Bernoff create categories for the consumers, participants, and creators of social: the Technographics Profiling Ladder mentioned earlier.

> *Creators*: Write blogs, upload video, music or text, generate content
>
> *Critics*: Respond to the content of others, posting reviews and comments on blogs and participating in forums
>
> *Collectors*: Organize content for others, using social bookmarking, RSS (Really Simple Syndication [subscription]) feeds, tags and voting on sites like Digg.com
>
> *Joiners*: Connect in social networks like Ning, MySpace, and Facebook
>
> *Spectators*: Consume but don't participate, taking advantage of information in blogs, video, podcasts, forums, or reviews
>
> *Inactives*: Are still on the outside looking in

What is significant is that these types both inform the content of other communications in social media and in more conventional presentations, webinars, or any other medium, and they also comprise the audience—something to consider when researching a communications initiative.

For example, suppose you were creating a training program of some kind for IT professionals on your staff, and you wanted to appeal to the most basic nature of many of these individuals. Without overgeneralizing, you would probably identify them as participants online in two ways, as collectors and critics, and approach them accordingly. To reach and motivate these technology professionals, you might well direct your content to their sense of order and organization and show them the benefits of new and existing tools that can help them serve their very complex environments more effectively.

Li and Bernoff suggest in *Groundswell* that organizations use this profiling tool to evaluate their target—whether it is a market segment, interest group, constituency, or any other potential pool of users for social media. They point out that if, for example, you create a community and then abandon it because it was poorly conceived or implemented, you pay a price in your online reputation. To avoid this and to determine whether a particular niche lends itself to a social media strategy, they urge their readers to research their targets; for example, if most of the people with whom an organization communicates are found to be inactive, then a social media strategy is ill advised. And if the targets are merely spectators, they have the potential to be reached through blogs and other means, but it will be more difficult to engage them.

Bernoff and Li emphasize at every turn that regardless of the strategy, it is imperative to first connect with your constituency as *people*—not as customers, clients, or prospects. A great example they cite is Procter & Gamble targeting young girls for their feminine hygiene products without ever mentioning the product itself (a tampon) but by creating a community in which young girls could discuss dating, love, and sexual issues. As that community gained in usage and energy, the benefits for the company's marketing efforts evolved naturally.

With the blurred distinctions today between what constitutes marketing and what is training, education, or support, it is helpful as we examine strategies for using social media in communication to look at our first set of tools, which help to evaluate the extent and success of our engagement.

THE NEW ROI: RETURN ON INFLUENCE

There is certainly no shortage of tools available to evaluate the impact of communication on the Web through statistics like click-throughs for links and unique site visits. Google Analytics and tools like Compete.com can provide anyone with a wealth of statistical data on how many people have visited a site, from where and who they were, where they went and why they came, and so on.

If you are a public company or perhaps a nonprofit or fund-raiser, your tendency may be to measure the success or failure of a social communications strategy purely in terms of profit or contributions.

It is thought that "return on influence" as opposed to the old-school ROI (return on investment) originated during a panel on podcasting in 2006 when Michael Goeghegan introduced the concept. As Brogan and Smith point out, trust is a fragile commodity, which is why companies today are monitoring social media so closely to see how their brands are viewed by ordinary people and what stories are being spun that they may need to address. One might also consider the fact that "good will" is factored into corporate reports and balance sheets, which is why powerful and effective public relations firms are so active in social media for their clients, particularly for "emergency response." Today anyone with a Web connection can have influence. And influence isn't always measurable in tangible ways. It's qualitative, not quantitative, because it is dealing with human issues and not dollars and beans. And return on influence often has to do with the *potential* of a particular initiative or communications channel, recognizing that the effectiveness of social efforts takes time to bear fruit.

Proponents of return on influence evaluation consider it a change in mindset toward brands, ideas, candidates, entertainers, and so on. Return on influence recognizes that traditional distribution channels of media do not have nearly the power they once had. When Michael Richards (Kramer on *Seinfeld*) revealed a darker side when he used racial epithets on stage, and the video was shown worldwide, the tangible results were not so much in his earnings thereafter but rather in the change in how he became viewed by a public that had previously thought very highly of him. Richards's video was shown on YouTube after it was shot in low quality by ordinary people attending his show. This speaks to the fact that social media is not controlled by "the usual suspects"—major studios, television networks, or conglomerates.[8]

As Seth Godin has written in *Tribes*, and Brogan and Smith discuss in *Trust Agents*, anyone can become influential by virtue of his or her behavior online—by gaining the favor of an audience based on a different kind of socia l currency. If you think of it in terms of sales, and consider the notion of continuing the dialogue and aftercare, auto salespeople (the good ones) have known this for years. They follow up with customers to see if they are satisfied, *they stay in touch* with birthday and holiday cards, and then they contact customers when they might be ready for a newer model. They continue the conversation.

SCENARIO: NEWHOPE—TRADING IN A HUMANIZED CURRENCY

Allie Powell had always had a social conscience. Since college, she had volunteered in soup kitchens, homeless shelters, and halfway houses to help the less advantaged in her community. Along the way she had noticed something that few others seemed to understand: that while money and resources were important, what many homeless people really craved was attention. Not only that, the public frequently had a one-size-fits-all mentality with respect to helping the homeless. But, especially since the economic collapse of 2008, there were all kinds of individuals and families who had fallen through the safety nets of society and ended up on the streets.

As Allie continued her work, she noticed that many social networks and groups on Facebook or Twitter were trying many different strategies to help in this area, with disparate results. Without any real goal in mind, Allie decided to use the new online tools to test her ideas on how the homeless might really be helped—both by addressing the individual needs of those she worked with and by educating and inspiring the public into more effective responses to the problem.

Allie started with a simple blog where she would matter-of-factly tell the story of a specific individual or family that she encountered in her volunteer efforts. At the same time, she was active on the blogs of many volunteer organizations, in aid groups on Facebook, and following key volunteer agencies and individuals on Twitter. At one point, a local philanthropy wanted to help one of the people she had interviewed, but the person could not be located because the person had no phone or address.

At this point Allie realized that there was one way that she could connect people she had met on the street with aid providers—if she got them e-mail accounts and taught them how to log in. In Los Angeles, the public library system still had free Internet access available, and many homeless and disadvantaged people were using it, but Allie decided to make the process more systematic. Instead of just interviewing a homeless individual or family and telling the story, Allie told the story while focusing on a specific need: housing, job, medical care, food, counseling, and so on. Then she put pictures to the story by photographing her subjects and telling their story online using Whrrl.com (see Chapter Five). With each story she provided a gmail (Google mail) address for the person whose story was told in pictures and on the blog. Within days, people and agencies with resources specific to those highlighted in stories contacted many of the subjects and changed their lives. Eventually Allie was able to give a class on Twitter to groups of homeless people, who used it to connect with others and alleviate some of the isolation in their lives, and tell their own stories themselves.

As Allie's reputation and visibility increased, a camera crew started following and telling some of the stories on the local news, with the e-mail addresses being shown on screen. Other agencies started similar programs, particularly in the retraining area, and as results became publicized, corporate sponsors and philanthropic organizations joined Allie's campaign, which she called "NewHope." With her fellow bloggers in the field, Allie put on a NewHope webinar, "Listening and Attention Inspires Solutions," in which the success stories of some of her subjects were highlighted and a panel of solution providers needing resources participated on a panel, including a food bank, shelter, medical clinic, counseling center, and placement service. The conference convinced the many attendees that there were solutions possible and available, as long as someone was actively paying attention to individual needs. After the conference, national groups got involved, and more money was raised among the webinar panel participants.

Of course, at the same time, more success stories were generated and were described on Allie's blog, which had grown dramatically in readership and commentary. Volunteers came forward from all over Los Angeles, and Allie trained them in two processes—first in the active listening phases that gained the trust of disadvantaged people who had resisted aid or had not been reached. And then, most important, she emphasized the need to continue follow-up with those who had received aid, to tell their stories but also to make sure that their isolation and alienation did not abruptly return.

With her new volunteer staff and financial contributions, Allie reached more and more people. From an individual she had formed a Tribe, based on her commitment to human values and her effective use of social media tools. As NewHope grew, so did scrutiny and attention to how it conducted its business. When some volunteers were accused of using their video equipment for commercial ventures, Allie responded quickly through her blog and Facebook and Twitter accounts—to protect her reputation and preserve the social currency she had so carefully accumulated.

PLANNING YOUR PROFILES

There are two dimensions to the face you show to the world through the Internet: the facts and information you put out about yourself, and the nature of your activities and how you conduct yourself. Both require forethought.

The bio portion of your profile on any social site is the main way that most social media users will determine, ultimately, whether they will follow, friend, or otherwise maintain a link to your content—after their initial impression of your comment, blog post, status update, tweet, or other manner in which your paths may have crossed. In marketing terms, this constitutes your "personal brand," along with the impression you give through your other online activities, but it is just as relevant in any area of communications because it directly affects your credibility and influence. Depending upon the purpose of your communications, the photo on your profile or bio is also very important. Humor, insight, warmth, and creativity can all be manifest in a good photograph, while in a corporate environment something low-key and more formal might be appropriate. Other elements to consider are your username, keywords for search engine optimization (SEO), and links. The more interconnected you can make your various profiles and sites, the more people will learn about you and the more visible you become.

For SEO purposes, by the way, links should preferably not be to direct http: addresses (URLs) but to "anchor text" where possible, using a keyword or image to click on with a reference to the desired URL. For example, the phrase "middle management training" might be a good anchor for a link to another page or site about that concept. Don't think about SEO as only a sales or marketing issue. Anyone in the communications field, from a clergyman to a trainer, wants online visibility in order to participate fully in the new Internet.

In his blog ducttapemarketing, John Jantsch provides the following list of "must have" adds for small businesses; some or all of these sites would be relevant to any social media effort that supports a comprehensive and effective communications strategy. Explore these sites with the idea of expanding your online presence or profile:

Mixx: A site that allows you to submit and vote on content.

LinkedIn: You can add links with your own anchor text through the "other" selection for your links in your profile.

Flickr: Images are showing up right and left in search results making this Yahoo-owned photo sharing site a great place to optimize images. You can also add links on your profiles.

MyBlogLog: This is a real-time blog tracking tool that is used to monitor any link activity to a site. This a Yahoo-owned site and you can add several URLs.

Business Week Exchange: These links get redirected, but high-profile media sites can be very valuable.

Google Profile: Google's personal profiles are showing up in Yahoo searches and allow full-follow anchor text list of links.

Twitter: Twitter profiles are showing up very high in Google searches, so get the links there and let surfers find you.

Facebook: You can still add a number of URLs to your contact information in your personal profile.[9]

MONITORING YOUR STANDING IN THE SOCIAL WORLD

Once you have developed a presence and reputation in the new Internet world and your organization is thoroughly committed and ensconced in numerous networks that reflect what you've been doing, you may feel confident that you're on the right track and that just continuing to build and nurture your network through your current activities is sufficient.

But is that enough?

After all, United Airlines didn't need to be particularly vigilant to know that a young musician's video on YouTube had gone viral and trashed its reputation (Chapter Two). But the company certainly could have discovered the potential public relations nightmare much sooner. In many cases what is being said or written about your organization may not be readily apparent, even if you have a staff of social media professionals. After all, their main focus may well be to comment on blogs (where they may get a hint of how your brand, product, service, or concepts are being received), and for the most part they'll be busy creating content.

If you are a small operation, the chances of your social media efforts randomly turning up significant references to yourself, your company, or aspects of your organization may be very slim. You may have thousands of followers on Twitter, but an influential individual whom you are not following, and may not even be following you, could post an opinion that you would like to address but you remain unaware of its existence until it may be too late.

Using Google Alerts and Google Reader

The first step to getting timely alerts when important comments or information vital to your interests appears online is setting up Google Alerts (www.google.com/alerts). After setting up an account (which is free), you can get alerts by e-mail or through RSS feeds at designated intervals about any reference to a specific word or phrase in News, Web, Blogs, Video and Groups. (See Figure 3.1.)

Once you've entered the parameters and click Create Alert, the information will either be sent to your e-mail or delivered by RSS feed. If you've chosen

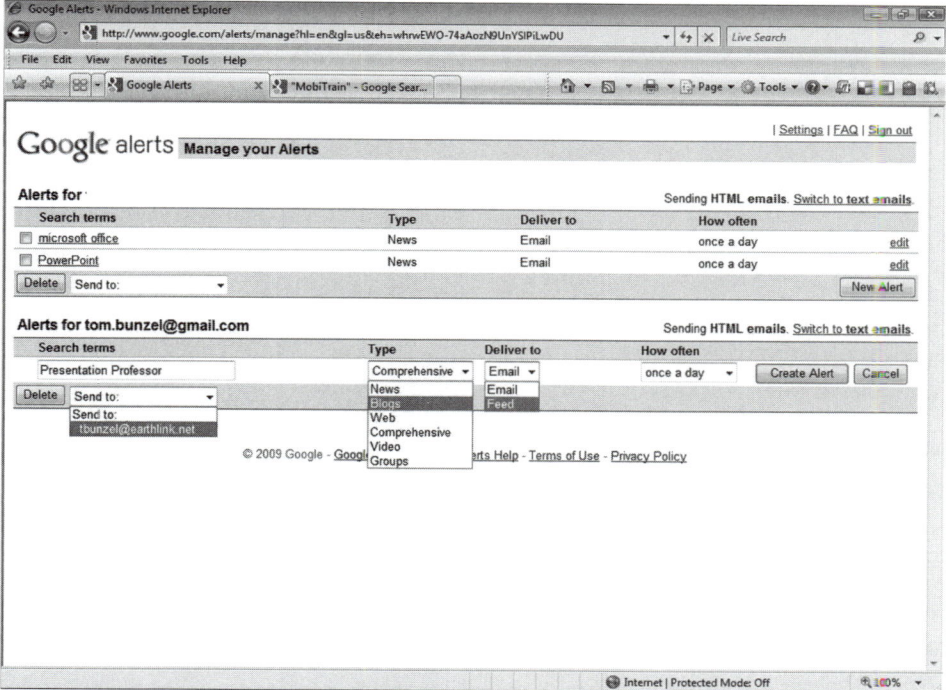

Figure 3.1 Google Alerts is a good starting point for staying informed about references to key terms or names in various parts of the Internet—particularly those relating to your profile.

Feed for the delivery option, you can also click to send the subscription directly to View in Google Reader. (See Figure 3.2.)

Google Reader is an aggregator for RSS feeds to which Google Alerts will automatically send alerts once a

Figure 3.2 For immediate updates. Google Alerts can create an RSS feed that can be read in Google Reader.

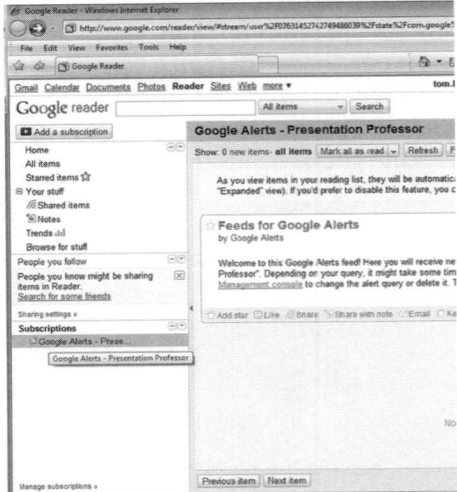

Figure 3.3 After selecting View in Google Reader, a new subscription is added in the Google Reader application from which you can monitor the feed online.

subscription is enabled by clicking View in Google Reader within Google Alerts. (See Figure 3.3.)

If you've set up RSS in Outlook, clicking the little orange RSS symbol on the Web browser menu in Google Reader will give you a chance to subscribe to all your Google Reader feeds elsewhere (in Outlook, for example). (See Figure 3.4.)

RSS is a good alternative if you don't want to have an e-mail inbox cluttered with Alert results; you can also set up most e-mail programs to filter mail so that all your Alerts could be sent to an e-mail subfolder.

Monitoring Twitter Feeds

While search.twitter.com is a great tool for locating tweets with specific references, how often do you want to do that? (The Advanced Search under Twitter—http://search.twitter.com/advanced—is particularly effective.) Some third-party tools like TweetDeck support

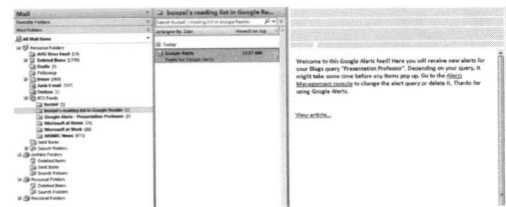

Figure 3.4 If you've already set up RSS feeds in Outlook, you can subscribe to an individual Google Alert or all feeds in Google Reader to monitor results in RSS Feeds in your Outlook folders.

alerts from Twitter, but two tools you can use to search Twitter specifically and alert you to references you value are filtrbox.com and twilert.com. Filtrbox is more for heavy corporate users and promises "real-time market intelligence" in its paid subscription version. Its free version offers five filters with a daily update and keeps fifteen days of history. Twilert is a basic and straightforward solution with a Twitter-like interface that you can use for alerts based on key phrases.

Since Twitter is such a powerful tool in the social media world, it's important to know what's going on beyond your own followers, no matter how many you may have.

Using Reputation Management Tools

Since monitoring your identity or reputation online is so important, particularly as your influence and visibility increases, you can use Web sites devoted to the process, including socialmediaanswers.com. In their Reputation Management section, Social Media Answers goes well beyond Google alerts or simple Twitter tools to monitor how you, your brand, and/or your message are being viewed and received.

For blogs, a key resource, also mentioned in Li and Bernoff's *Trust Agents*, is Technorati.com. This is literally a blog among blogs about blogs with an advanced search capability to find references in the "blogosphere." Blogs are broken down by categories, and you can join the Technorati community or just use it to read and search within a universe of blogs. An alternative or supplement to Technorati is BlogPulse (www.blogpulse.com), which covers blog trends and metrics as well as offering a search capability. For blog comments, www.backtype.com is a useful search tool that shows hot topics and features what it calls a "conversational search engine." A comprehensive search tool that covers blogs, microblogs (Twitter), and bookmarks is www.socialmention.com.

The Social Media Answer site also has some other recommendations:

- Boardreader.com for message boards
- Twingly.com for microblogs (Twitter)
- A comprehensive reputation management solution that includes alerts (via RSS and e-mail) and custom filters, Trackur.com, that starts at around $18 per month[10]

Andy Beal, the coauthor of *Radically Transparent*,[11] offers a comprehensive list of resources in this field:

Manage Your Identity

claimID.com: Works along with OpenID to verify your identity on multiple Web sites

FindMeOn.com: Links all of your networks together and verifies your identity so people know it's your profile

FreeYourID.com: Uses name address to sign you up for sites

Garlik.com: Searches the Web looking for mentions of you that might involve identity theft

MyOpenID.com: Uses one username to verify your log-in on sites that use OpenID: great for sites where you might otherwise have multiple log-ins

Spyshakers.com: Identity management system allows users to access their Web sites and passwords remotely

TypeKey.com: Another provider of the OpenID standard

WordPress.com: Sign up for a free account and use as OpenID

Manage Your Reputation

Naymz.com: Sign up and invite people to write reviews about you and your work

Rapleaf.com: Look up your reputation, rate others, and they will be invited to rate you in return

RepVine.com: Combines reference and reputation management

ReputationDefender.com: Helps you get things being said online about you removed

TrustPl.us: Ranks reputation based on trust scores

BoardReader.com, ForumFind.com, Big-Boards.com, BoardTracker.com, iVillage, Yahoo message boards, MSN Money: Message board tracking services

Yahoo groups, AOL groups, MSN groups, Google groups: Places to find groups to track

Monitter.com: Allows you to monitor and track keywords over multiple search engines

Keotag.com: Allows you to search for tagged blog posts across multiple blog search engines

Manage Your Online Profiles

Comwat.com: Puts your online identities in one place to make it easier to show and find profiles

onXiam.com: Lets you link all your online identities into one account, making it easier for people to find you across the Internet

OtherEgo.com: Displays your online profiles

ProfileBuilder.com: Very function-heavy profile builder shows off the parts of your profiles you select

ProfileMat.com: Pulls all your profiles together and allows commenting on your ProfileMat page

SimplifID.com: Creates one ID for all your online profiles

SocialURL.com: Simple URL shows all your profiles

Venyo.org: Lets you add all of your online activities, including blogs and comments, to one page

Zoolit.com: A landing page that shows all your social networks

QUESTIONS TO PONDER

1. How frequently do you go online specifically to research issues in your field? Have you searched Google or Twitter or used any monitoring tools to see how your area of interest or organization is perceived or view comments about it online?

2. Where might you find users of like interest that could help you or your organization solve problems or address issues vital in your field? Can you identify significant parts of your audience on the Social Technographics Ladder from *Groundswell*? What about you—what sort of social media user are you now, and what would you like to become in order to communicate more effectively?

3. How comfortable do you feel sharing your own valued information or insights with others? Do you need to see a payback for everything you share or post? Can you see the value of engaging in a more free-flowing exchange of information and value?

Notes

1. Chris Brogan and Julien Smith, *Trust Agents: Using the Web to Build Influence, Improve Reputation, and Earn Trust.* Hoboken, NJ: Wiley, 2009.
2. Seth Godin, *Tribes: We Need You to Lead Us.* Indianapolis: Penguin Group, 2008.

3. Charlene Li and Josh Bernoff, *Groundswell*. Cambridge, MA: Harvard Business School Press, 2008.
4. www.engagementdb.com/downloads/ENGAGEMENTdb_Report_2009.pdf.
5. www.smallbusinessnewz.com/blogtalk/2008/08/05/where-does-social-media-responsibility-fall.
6. www.socialmediaexplorer.com/2008/07/18/social-media-is-the-responsibility-of-public-relations.
7. www.forrester.com/Groundswell/profile_tool.html.
8. www.returnoninfluence.com.
9. www.ducttapemarketing.com/blog/2009/05/26/social-media-profiles-as-tools-for-links-and-traffic.
10. www.socialmediaanswers.com.
11. www.ducttapemarketing.com/blog—http://bit.ly/ZIFg1.

The New Tools of Engagement

chapter
FOUR

Using technology effectively is always a balance between understanding needs and concepts and learning specific techniques and programs. Now that we've gotten a taste of how training, presenting, communicating, and marketing have changed in the age of social media, it's time to examine some of the specific ways to implement a strategy that leverages these new communities and "tribes" of trust and shared interest.

IN THE BEGINNING WAS THE BLOG

In the first phases of the Internet, many organizations rushed to put up "brochure" Web sites and simple tutorials for online learning or training.

What is it that differentiates blogs from these early Web sites? There are very important distinctions.

First, from a practical standpoint, many blog users avoid the need for a domain name registration, using a popular service like Blogger (Google) that gives them immediate real estate online. When you go to www.blogger.com and fill out the forms to name and launch your blog, a personal URL (Web address) is generated for you, for example, tbunzel.blogspot.com.

More important, a blog includes other interactive features that enhance your message, like a bio, events, archive of past blogs, and of course, *comments*. Comments are probably the most significant attribute of blogs and the feature that really launched the social media phenomenon. It took the blog far beyond chat or instant messaging

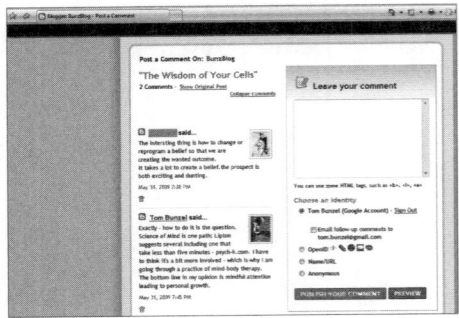

Figure 4.1 The Comments feature of blogs is critical for creating a dialogue with readers.

in providing a back-and-forth thread of information that stimulated the energy that drives the social Web.

Responding to comments on your own blog is obviously extremely important for building traffic; you can do all kinds of promotion, but if you don't post regularly and respond to user comments substantively, you may as well be using a static Web site. (See Figure 4.1.)

Every blogging tool has its own attributes, but as you'll find with many of the applications that inhabit the "cloud" (a buzzword for programs that you access through your Web browser and for which most if not all of the data is stored on a server hosted by the application itself), there are preset options for laying out and formatting the various elements. (See Figure 4.2.)

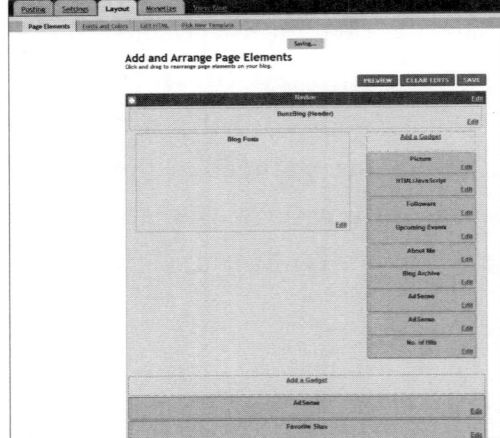

Figure 4.2 You can customize the appearance of your blog on Google using a Layout grid.

You can add functionality through the use of various gadgets, widgets, or modules, depending upon the versatility of the blogging tool you choose. (See Figure 4.3.) By dragging and dropping or moving the elements through the master layout page, you can determine which elements you want and where they appear on the page. Note that for Google there is an AdSense gadget that lets the user place ads on the blog to earn money.

Particularly if you intend to use video on your blog (which will be linked from a hosting site like YouTube), you will want to have some familiarity with the use of HTML (hypertext markup language) and, for other add-ons, perhaps even Java Script. (See Figure 4.4.)

You don't really need to learn these programming languages—you just have to understand the concept of how they work. Most blogging programs have an area

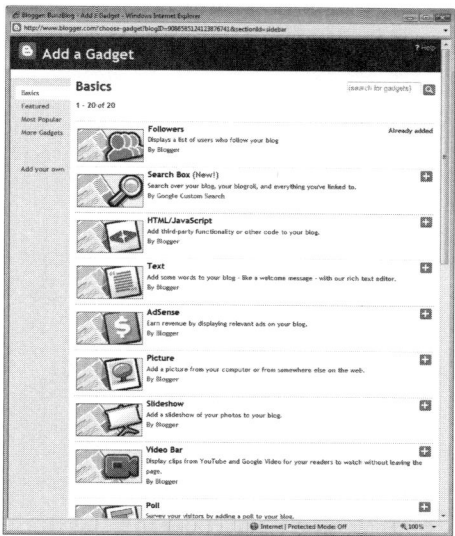

Figure 4.3 You can add features and functions to your blog with gadgets or add-on programs.

for writing or pasting the text for your blog from a word processing program (the Compose area) and another area for entering or pasting code—generally a block HTML text.

If you click on View > Source in your Internet browser, you can see the code that determines how the browser displays the page (see Figure 4.5).

The Edit HTML tab in Figure 4.4 accepts the source code viewed in Figure 4.5. It will become important when you begin to reference other objects around the Web in your blog—for example, embedding a YouTube video into your blog post.

At this point, all you need to note is that there is a form for HTML or other code to be pasted in your blog.

Note that in Figure 4.3 one of the gadgets that can be added to your blog can also contain HTML/Java Script (containing a window where third-party code of this nature can be pasted). While the mainstay of the blog will generally be text-based

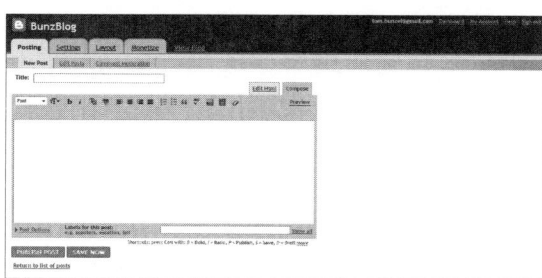

Figure 4.4 The Posting tab of the blogging tool will have general text formatting tools, as well as tabs to paste or type text, and a separate tab for HTML. Note also the Labels field at the bottom where search tags (also known as meta-data or metatags) can be placed.

information, blogging tools like Blogger add the capability to use modules or gadgets to add content from other sources. This kind of repurposing of content hosted elsewhere is sometimes called "mashing."

IF YOU BLOG IT, WILL THEY COME?

Of course, with the millions of blog postings daily, the issue becomes, How do you get online visitors to take notice?

```
<p align="center"><b><font color="000099" size="2"><a href="http://www.professorppt.com/ning_how.htm">Create
Your Own Social Network with Ning<br>
a New eBook by Tom Bunzel<br>
<img src="ningcvr.jpg" width="184" height="247" border="2">
<br>
Available for Download -- 80 pages<br>
Only $12.00:</a></font></b></p>
<p align="center"><b><font color="000099" size="2"><a href="http://www.professorppt.com/ning_use.htm">Participate
in a Ning Network<br>
a New eBook by Tom Bunzel</a><br>
<a href="http://www.professorppt.com/ning_use.htm">Download
for Only $10.00:</a></font></b></p>
<p align="center"><a href="http://www.professorppt.com/ning_how.htm"><img src="wingcvr.jpg" width="184" height="24
<p align="center"><a href="http://www.informit.com/store/product.aspx?isbn=0321423445"><font color="000099"><b><im
<p align="center"><a href="http://www.cio.com/article/101504/Bite_the_Bullet_Improving_Your_Presentation_Strategie
an excerpt from the book</b></font></a></p>
<p align="center"><font size="-1" color="#000099">Contact
the Presentation Professor:</font><br>
<br>
<font color="000099">Email:</font> <a href="MailTo:tom@professorppt.com">tom@professorppt.com</a><br>
<font color="000099">Phone: (310) 286-0969</font></p>
<p align="center"> <script type="text/javascript"><!--
```

Figure 4.5 The source code for any Web page in HTML places the elements of the page in their proper locations for the browser to display. The highlighted portion of code here references an image on a Web page.

You can make the same mistake with your blog that many conventional presenters make with PowerPoint: you can launch your blog and begin to post haphazardly on a wide array of subjects, or worse, make it into a broadcast platform from which you begin to trumpet your achievements, feature a product or service, or just promote yourself or your organization. While controversy definitely stimulates comments, a better way to look at your content is in terms of *creating value based upon your own unique opinion or perspective*. For example, you create training modules that teach your employees how to assemble various manufacturing items. A great subject for your blog would be your direct experience and opinion on various software programs and perhaps a 3D animation program that helps your staff visualize the assembly process. This would be far more likely to get traction online than a description of your training facility, the size of your staff, or other facts that attest to your personal or organizational significance.

One way to attract attention is through the use of metatags or keywords that will enable search engines to find your blog and individual posts. In Blogger, for example, you can add a set of labels to any post that will theoretically be indexed by search engines (as shown in Figure 4.4). Experts have various tricks that they suggest for making your blog more visible to search engines. They will recommend using keywords as much as possible, even in the name of your blog, in the biographical information, throughout the text, and in any hyperlinks that open up referenced Web sites or other locations online. And, of course, these experts have blogs all over the Web, suggesting you hire them to "optimize" your blog for search.

But the real key to communicating effectively is meaningful participation, so the first and best way to get your blog known and truly build your reputation—which is the real essence of your Internet profile—is to participate actively. Rita, the human resources director in Chapter Three, whose two analysts have started blogs, would have been served by having already participated in various social media sites. On Delicious.com, the bookmark aggregator, she could begin to build a reputation for having compiled a significant set of resources for training professionals in similar fields: manufacturing processes. On Twitter and Facebook, she would be active in posting her own ideas and discoveries in the field, linking to the appropriate blog item if relevant, but also contributing information that links to other blogs and resources.

The point here is, it's probably best to begin these activities before you plan or launch your own blog, just to see the landscape online for your area of interest.

A good first step would be to try search.twitter.com (whether you have an ID or not) and take a look at what kinds of feeds are available. (We cover Twitter in Chapter Five.)

Social media expert Chris Brogan, coauthor of the best-seller *Trust Agents* with Julien Smith (mentioned in Chapter One), is on the road almost constantly these days. Nonetheless, among the five key tasks he lists on his blog (www.chrisbrogan.com) that he performs every day are reviewing connection requests and introductions on LinkedIn, dropping in on at least two or three communities and Ning networks, and visiting blogs and leaving comments, posting ideas, and maintaining relationships.

A good technique is to click on any @ references in a Twitter post (@TomBunzel, for example, is any reference to me) and go to a listing of posts mentioning that person. Click on the reference again and go to the Twitter Profile page of that individual; you will generally see a link to her Web site or blog. You can check the bios of any of the people you find on Twitter, and chances are sooner or later you will find other blogs related to your niche. Of course, you are searching conventionally with Google or Yahoo and actively participating in as many online events and signing up for newsletters as possible. Gradually you will locate a set of blogs where you can actively comment. *Commenting is probably the best way to get noticed.*

In many ways the process is like dating, because it's truly a matter of feeling when it is appropriate to suggest that others check out your blog. The best suggestion would be that when there is a specific feedback on something you commented on, and you have relevant additional information in your blog (which you may decide to post based on the comments you've read), then go ahead and promote your content with a link.

It's all about relationships: *Think Oprah!* Don't set unrealistic goals or expect instant results. Women were the prime moving force behind social media for a reason—they generally build deeper connections over time and have the patience to get to know their audience before trying to "close" or otherwise force matters.

The critical elements for participating in social media and in the process building your communications profile and getting traffic to your blog are all the same:

- Don't focus on results (sales).
- Do focus on creating value for yourself and your connections.
- Don't get sidetracked by the latest and greatest technology.
- Do dig deeper in those areas where you are naturally drawn and find meaning.
- Don't join everything and anything that's available.
- Do focus on "passionate participation."

Another key point of etiquette is to never "pitch" someone to go to a Web site or do something until you have established a connection. Many established individuals in the social media field will write you off if you transgress in this way. You need to "earn your chops."

As you test the social media waters, you will see fairly quickly what works and what doesn't. While the number of followers on Twitter is not a perfect indicator (there are lots of services that help Twitter users accumulate unrelated followers, and the key in social media is always quality, not quantity), seeing the volume and caliber of commentary on other blogs, checking status updates on Facebook, and monitoring as many social sites as possible will give you fodder for your own content.

Obviously not everyone is a writer, so getting started can be a challenge. To determine whether blogging is for you, some social media experts recommend writing at least a few blog items as a test before even beginning to think about committing to this practice. A good option is to start on a personal level and find an area of interest about which you're passionate—custom autos, vintage clothes or jewelry, travel to specific locations, extreme sports—and begin to visit and comment on the social sites dedicated to your bliss. In this way your style will evolve naturally, and you can begin to adapt and shift it to your professional or more serious endeavors.

In his book, *Blog Marketing*, Jeremy Wright identifies seven distinct blogger types you may recognize or who can help shape your own efforts at content creation. Obviously there is overlap among these categories, but to the extent that you recognize yourself in any of these profiles, knowing these might help you focus on the kind of blog you want to launch and maintain.

1. *The Barber*: A generalist who has accumulated and shares wisdom based on personal contacts and experience
2. *The Blacksmith*: An insider or company person who "hammers" industry opinion based on his or her corporate perspective
3. *The Bridge*: A person who makes connections and brings people together, using the blog as a networking vehicle; may placate controversies, acting as a peacekeeper
4. *The Window*: A person who works within a company environment but relates more to corporate from outside, following trends in the industry
5. *The Signpost*: An industry commentator and aggregator of useful and cool things of interest (Wright's book was written before Twitter's ascendancy; this type of blogger typically posts many short items and *links* as she comes across items of interest)
6. *The Pub*: A blogger who generates lively opinions and discussions and explores all sides (This function may also be addressed by the discussion forums of many social networks, both public and those hosted by companies)
7. *The Newspaper*: A person who creates a blog that is primarily fact based (rather than opinion, which will invariably be generated) and is particularly apt for technical environments[1]

Besides Google Blogger, there are numerous blogging programs available; one of the most popular for professionals who need a customized interface is WordPress, which has a community of third-party developers contributing and selling templates and conferences for its devotees. Whatever tool you choose, take the time to learn it in depth so that you can take advantage of features like tags, labels, or keywords to enable your readers and Web users on search engines to locate your material. When you link back to your blog from comments you make elsewhere, e-mail, or any other communications you create online, take the recipient directly back to the most relevant post by copying its link from the address bar of your browser. When possible, use a key anchor phrase for the link that establishes the relevance of the information in your comment or post. This may take a bit more time, but it is simply another aspect of creating maximum value as you interact; taking the easy way out and simply linking back to the main blog URL (and the current post) may not be as pertinent for the end user, and she may decide not to search for what you promised and never return. Of course, on many occasions the most recent post is the one you want to promote, so using the general URL will work—until you post again.

A WORD ABOUT WIKIS

Almost everyone who uses the Internet is familiar with Wikipedia, the user-run online encyclopedia with reference information that pops up near the top of many search engines. Wiki, from the Hawaiian word for "quick," is a completely collaborative Web site run, edited, and managed by its users. Many companies now use wikis for internal knowledge management, and *Groundswell* (mentioned in Chapter Two), was written by Charlene Li and Josh Bernoff using a wiki. Authors Li and Bernoff describe wikis as collaborative tools that emphasize community; they remark that while you might think that with everyone able to edit everyone else there would be "chaos." In fact the trend has been toward consensus.

A wiki is probably not the first thing you would consider for a social media initiative, but it is worth noting as a powerful new communications tool that can lay the foundation for the visual and thematic content creation applications covered in the pages ahead. Ironically, or not surprisingly, Wikipedia.org itself has a listing of wiki creating tools at http://en.wikipedia.org/wiki/List_of_wiki_software.

USING A BUSINESS NETWORK: LINKEDIN

While blogs certainly began the social networking phenomenon, it was really business networks like LinkedIn and Plaxo that began to take conventional networking onto the Internet. These business networks became referral systems through which savvy users found that they could locate professionals by skill sets or other attributes and make contact with much less than six degrees of separation. Human resources professionals and recruiters, in particular, gravitated to business networks as a way of filling positions that required specialized qualifications. As a business network, LinkedIn wasted no time integrating with desktop applications like Microsoft Office, which further enhances its functionality. For example, you can locate contacts in

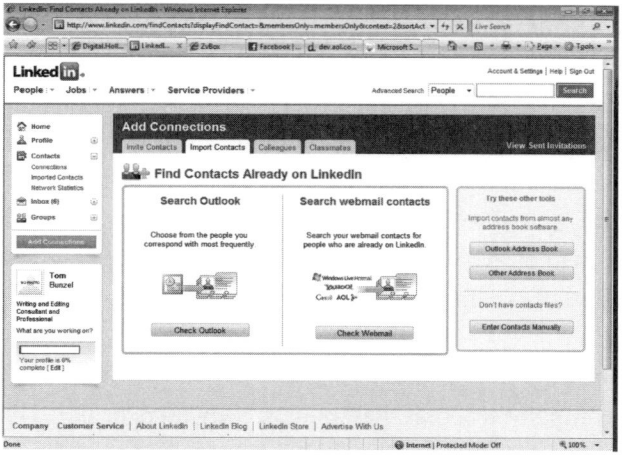

Figure 4.6 LinkedIn is a business (social) network that integrates with desktop applications like Microsoft Outlook to locate and organize contacts with specific attributes.

Outlook whom you correspond with frequently on LinkedIn and import part or all of your contact list from MS Outlook into the social networking environment. (See Figure 4.6.)

LinkedIn scans your Outlook contacts for other members, whom you can import and/or to whom you can send invitations to join your network on LinkedIn. (See Figure 4.7.) You may well find that many of your most significant current contacts already are members of LinkedIn, and you may have already received e-mail invitations to join them on the site; the fact is that so many of these invitations flooded the Web when LinkedIn, Plaxo, and others showed up that people started ignoring them.

You can also download a LinkedIn Outlook Toolbar to:

- Build your network from frequent contacts
- Manage your LinkedIn contacts in Outlook
- Stay connected to your network

LinkedIn lets you take advantage of search engine optimization (SEO) capabilities for finding members and doing research. To take advantage of this feature, you will want to make sure that the URL of your public profile matches your name, so that those who search on Google or other search engines will be able to locate you based on many of the

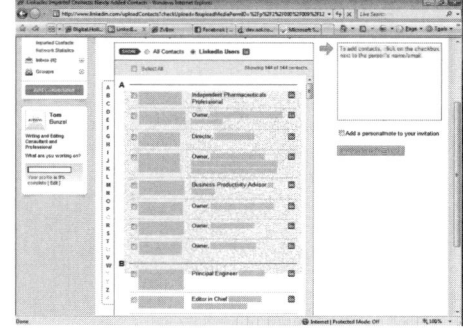

Figure 4.7 LinkedIn has a Web tool that lets you locate people in your existing contact database who are already part of its network.

The New Tools of Engagement

qualifications and attributes in your profile—such as your blog, Web site, company affiliation, and so on. It's important to add significant keywords to the Summary and Experience fields to make them effective as meta-data for searches as well, so that those who might be looking for specific skills and qualifications that you possess, particularly in hard-to-find combinations, can locate you in the network.

Another area to concentrate on is Testimonials or Referrals; if there are individuals who are familiar in your field of expertise and would write a short paragraph describing your skills and talents, this can be a big boost for your online credibility and communications profile.

The Advanced Search window for People (see Figure 4.8) allows you to modify a search for those at a specific company, whether they are currently there or not. This is a good way to get the lowdown on working conditions from former employees and to locate individuals by drilling down using a host of parameters. (You can

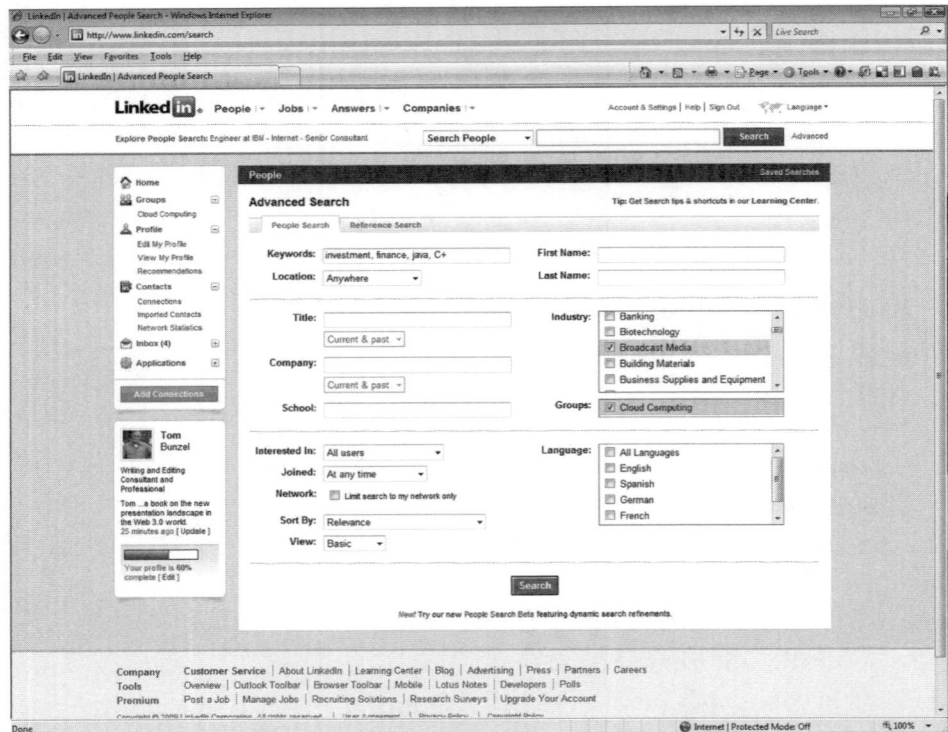

Figure 4.8 The Advanced Search feature of LinkedIn lets you locate individuals with unique combinations of skill sets or very esoteric attributes through the combination of keywords and other parameters.

also find people who worked at specific firms during specific times in the Reference tab.)

You may have to modify the search to find appropriate results; a search for "investment, finance, and Cloud Computing," for example, yielded 252 LinkedIn members. Based on additional information in people's profiles, you could recruit them for a position or invite them to become experts that you can call upon in your research or targets for sales, training, or other goals you may have.

Business networks such as these first dominated the social sphere because of their ability to allow participants to directly interact with other members based on areas of interest or concern. The Answers section of LinkedIn lets you create a question about an issue of importance to you that will generate responses and then an exchange of information on topics that you select, within industries you designate, or across all of LinkedIn.

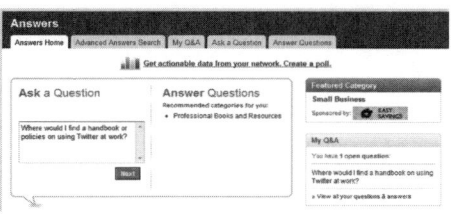

Figure 4.9 Asking specific questions of your LinkedIn contacts or the community as a whole can generate discussion and connections that yield dividends in your ability to communicate with them, their companies or organizations, or others of like interest.

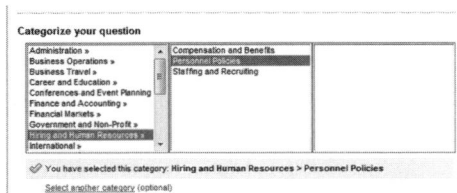

Figure 4.10 You can categorize your query to a specific industry or level of profession to focus the results.

Asking questions and sincerely listening to and caring about the answers is a big part of participating successfully in the new world of social media (see Figures 4.9 and 4.10); it leads to deep connections among people that result in greater awareness and much richer communication at all levels. Once you've established such a connection based on a common interest on a site such as LinkedIn, your audience would be much more likely to pay attention to your PowerPoint slides or not send e-mail during your webinar.

Browsing Q&A from others can also provide interesting insights and lead to dynamic interaction, provide unexpected information, and stimulate your own communication efforts with precise and valuable research and insight. (See Figure 4.11.)

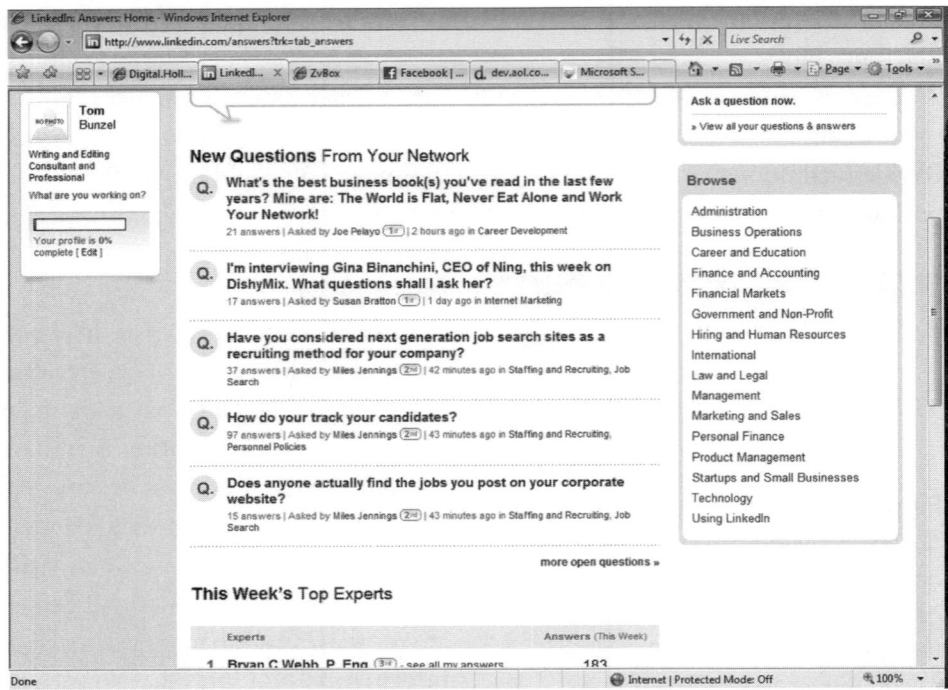

Figure 4.11 As you establish a network that reflects your interests and expertise, browsing through questions and answers in your main Answers area of LinkedIn can provide new connections, research, and inspiration.

LinkedIn also forges connections back to the real world of networking and face-to-face interaction—you can go to http://events.LinkedIn.com to use a comprehensive search page for events by choosing from various lists, entering search parameters, and narrowing your focus down to an area or region. Using the connections of the business network with Outlook, you can easily process invitations and registration through a targeted distribution list for a live or virtual conference and to generate traffic to a Web site. You also might find that some of the experts who answered your question on LinkedIn might be available for a panel at a live event, Web conference, or webinar in exchange for promoting their blogs among the targeted attendees.

As LinkedIn developed, it took on the features it needed to compete with the exploding social networks like Facebook and Twitter, so that today this professional networking environment has status updates and other social features on its home page. It lets you enter your own latest information in a "What are you working on" form that is, once again, a way to let others find you based on your professional interests and projects. LinkedIn currently has tiers of membership for professionals that add features beyond the original free service. For example, by upgrading, you can use a Profile Manager to organize your contacts into folders, add notes, and view a message history for each contact within a set of folder categories.

GETTING PERSONAL WITH BOOKMARKS

For effective communication, professionals know that an all-important first step in any project is *research*. Digging deeper into any topic is the only real way to understand it in depth and then be able to transmit your knowledge and perspective to others. And today a vast amount of research takes place online. One of the most challenging aspects of the Internet is keeping track of and organizing the voluminous amount of information that you accumulate. The first step in this endeavor is generally to assemble a list of bookmarks or favorites, perhaps arranged in folders, but one quickly discovers that the process is cumbersome and searching in the folders is almost as time consuming as searching from scratch on Google.

What evolved on the Web is the process of personal bookmarking, which not only lets you store your Web locations in an organized fashion online but also provides a comprehensive network of interaction (if desired) through which you can see who else is accessing the same information, and get in touch with them. Probably the preeminent application in this space is Delicious.com, which allows you to open an account to store your own bookmarks and share them with others. It facilitates the process by providing a set of icons that work directly in your Internet browser. Using the Tag icon on the Delicious toolbar, you can open up a window where you can Create a Bookmark. (See Figure 4.12.)

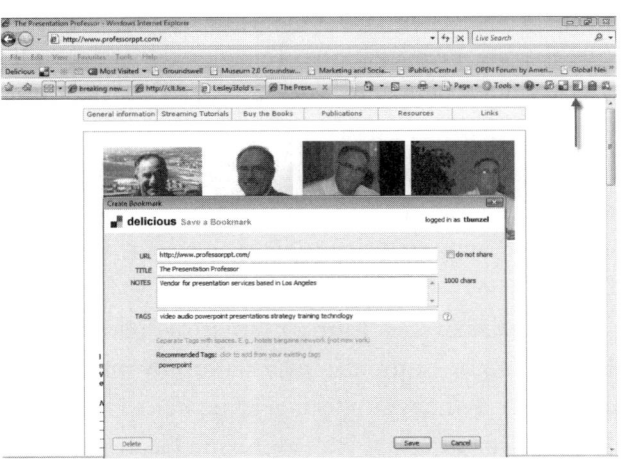

Figure 4.12 The Delicious toolbar in your Web browser lets you add any Web location to your own account and share the tags with others.

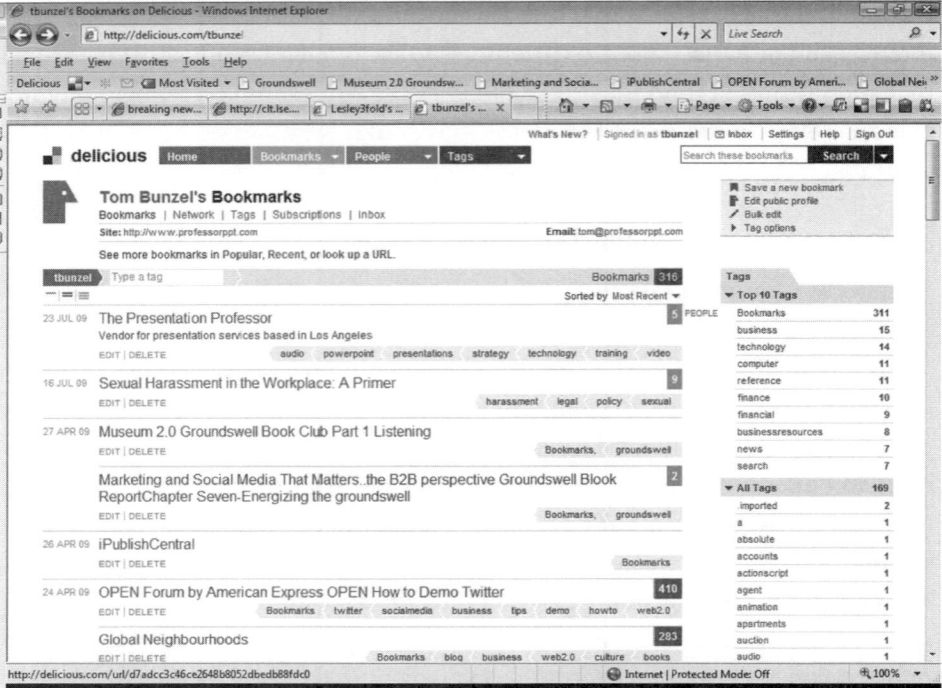

Figure 4.13 In your Delicious account, you can locate others with the same keywords as tags, add them to your network, or join one of their networks.

In your account on Delicious, the new Web location is catalogued for you, with a list of the tags for each URL and a column with your Tags and All Tags arranged on the right. By clicking on the drop-down arrow for People, you can quickly see who else on Delicious bookmarked this page and their other tags. (See Figure 4.13.)

For any Delicious user, you can see their bookmarks, add them to your network, and sometimes get profile information with their Web site or blog. (See Figure 4.14.)

Seeing other peoples' tags and the sites they found in their own Web travels is a terrific way to build your own catalog of topical information by research. As Bernoff and Li point out in *Groundswell*, tagging is a very powerful tool in its affect on a profile or brand. Seeing, for example, that someone has tagged your new application as "bug-ridden software" or "flawed" can be an eye opener and wake-up call for an organization. If that description spreads through a site like

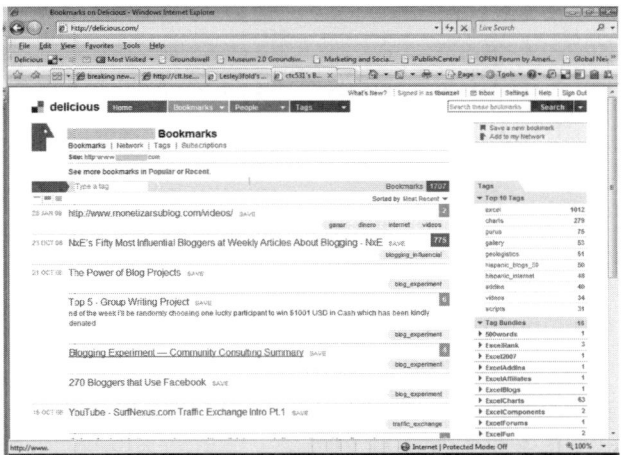

Figure 4.14 Other Delicious users who share their bookmarks can be located through their tags, added to a network in Delicious, and sometimes contacted through their profile information.

Delicious and eventually goes viral through references on Facebook and Twitter, it can become a serious issue to be addressed.

The University of London published a case study on social bookmarking with Delicious.com in 2008 as a tool for librarians to make Internet sites available to students in their research endeavors. They found that social bookmarking, as an enabler of shared resources between students and teachers, offers a "flexible approach to maintaining lists of Internet resources."[2]

SCENARIO: SOCIAL BOOKMARKS AND HIRING THE RIGHT PEOPLE

Eleanor Davis is a corporate headhunter—but she calls herself a recruiter and frequently works with human resources departments. She has created a network on Delicious to which she invites individuals she locates online who have bookmarked sites with tags that correspond to the qualifications she is searching for. For example, she might be looking for a presentation expert with qualifications as a strategic thinker who also specializes in video. While her Google search might hit the page shown in Figure 4.14, her Delicious network may soon comprise other individuals with similar skills and qualifications or people who work with or can refer such talent.

As she builds her network on Delicious, she gathers contact information when possible and frequently gets the @ Twitter ID for her new connections. As she follows them on Twitter, they follow her back, and she begins to build a relationship based on their key areas of interest and may glean some personal insight into how they feel about their current positions. Rather than cold-calling executives, she begins to accumulate information until her new contacts feel comfortable talking about their work situation with her, or she finds new prospects through personal recommendations, referrals, or other people in the various networks she discovers.

In many cases the target individual has a blog, Web site, or Facebook (and/or Twitter) account, which yields more background information, both professional and personal. Eleanor also searches and frequently locates individuals on her business networks such as LinkedIn and Plaxo, which provide her with additional insight on employment history and other relevant information before she ever broaches the possibility of employment with the prospect.

Ultimately, she may share a PowerPoint presentation or video about a current client who is seeking an executive with specific qualifications or invite the prospect and perhaps the human resources contact from her client into an ad hoc Web conference.

Most important, her web of connections is natural and personal as opposed to forced and impersonal, using a fount of knowledge organized first in a social bookmarking account and then leading to more and more professional and personal detail and insight.

SCENARIO: SMALL BUSINESS AND ENTREPRENEURS

Karen Sawyer, a health foods distributor, searches the Internet for detailed information about a particular kind of ginseng that she is thinking of promoting to her retail outlet. She bookmarks a Global Ginseng site on Delicious.com and sees that there are 568 other users who have bookmarked the same site. By clicking on the number, she gets immediate access to all of the 568 Delicious users who have publicly shared this bookmark, along with the other tags or keywords that indicate more about their interest in ginseng: herbs, stress control, anxiety, stomach pain, and so on.

She could click on any of these tags in her tag list and find the top bookmarked sites for any of these subcategories, which may be helpful, but by clicking on a few other users that share keywords like *herbs* and *stress*, she stumbles upon a network in Delicious that aggregates bookmarks on herbs and stress management (natural healing). She joins that network and begins to contribute her own tagged bookmarks and subscribes to a feed that sends her new bookmarks tagged ginseng, stress, and herbs. As she finds new users with similar bookmarks, she invites them to the network in which she's active on natural healing.

When she has a critical mass of natural healing members on the network, she offers an educational webinar on the uses, types, and benefits of ginseng. During the webinar she shares her desktop to use her Web browser to conduct a "world tour" of ginseng, describing its various flavors and properties, and makes the URLs of the tour available in a handout to attendees. She promotes her own blog, Natural Serenity, during the webcast and makes connections with a few retailers who agree to stock the ginseng she has imported from Korea.

Her sharing of knowledge about the herb resonates through her Delicious network, her blog, and other social media sites, enhancing the cache of her Lotus Ginseng line, which she continues to support by responding to comments on her blog and on the network on Delicious. Through her continued aggregation of new Web sites and interested users on Delicious, she stays active and keeps educating new people and expanding her brand presence. The webinars become a monthly event, and she cross-promotes them with other health-related natural products.

While marketing is a big part of organizational communication, we have seen that consumers of information are now more likely to trust each other than an institution or authority, and they are looking for the value inherent in any message—something truly informative and educational. This makes the integration of training and storytelling principles into all corporate and organizational communications of paramount importance. When combined with effective technology, training and storytelling become a powerful combination in direct organizational learning and facilitation. Effective implementation of desktop tools with social media can keep communication open among management, employees, partners, or colleagues and focus resources on the human aspects of the latest technology.

FACEBOOK MAKES IT PERSONAL

There is no question that the big leap in social networking happened when Facebook came on the scene, as not just a program, but a platform people can use to stay in touch on a human and personal level. (You can make the case for MySpace, and both Facebook and MySpace began with college and high school students, but Facebook remains vibrant and has been widely embraced by adults and professionals.) (See Figure 4.15.) There are a number of factors that set Facebook apart as a phenomenon that crosses over from social interaction into business and all facets of life:

Figure 4.15 Facebook provides an open platform for social and professional interaction that lets third-party developers create branded applications and members connect in groups and subnetworks.

- Tight integration of multimedia and images
- Cohesive connection among members of groups and networks within Facebook
- API (programming capability) that allows for expansion by third parties with applications

Larger and larger organizations found their way to Facebook through its focus on the essence of social media—connection through personal interests and exchanges—and the platform became a place where many users created their communications profiles. Stories proliferated about professionals whose employment offers were rescinded or who were terminated because of their activities or revelations in their profiles on Facebook (and also MySpace). This focused further attention on these platforms as the means by which individuals connected and formed bonds of trust based on "talking about dogs" as opposed to selling dog food. As Facebook grew, those who openly sold or promoted were quickly avoided as connections, while those who participated, explained, contributed, and enlightened built solid connections with "friends" who responded to status updates and comments and exchanged information. Organizations got busy on Facebook, and many large companies began to form their own internal networks to create a sense of community and foster communication between tiers of management and the rank and file. Because of the burst of energy provided by the trust engendered by social interaction, as distinct from sales or conventional networking elsewhere online, Facebook raised the awareness on the part of organizations that social media would be a key to their success and effectiveness in the world of social media.

For many companies, it probably began in the marketing departments, where the younger staffers were already active and alerted their peers that consumers no longer trusted the official spokespeople for corporations and were taking their buying cues from "influencers" on social sites like Facebook. Rather than being excluded from organizational environments because of gaffes in their profiles and their tendency to personalize their interactions, experienced Facebook users began to staff significant positions in the enterprise and were sought after by recruiters and human resources departments. They themselves became adept at hiring and enticing the best prospects to join an organization because of the connections they could forge by foregoing formal contacts in favor of interpersonal connections. As organizations realized they needed a viable social media strategy, it was the Facebook "expert" who was called upon more and more to come up with processes that would drive traffic to a Web site or foster cooperation among employees and team members through online efforts on Facebook itself and elsewhere.

Companies, schools, and other institutions that embraced social media began to need IT and network experts in the social space (and the cloud) to build branded applications and integrate the initiatives and processes that were put in place to leverage the cohesiveness and effectiveness of connecting with individuals and groups through their passions instead of as ciphers. With the growth of internal and external networks, the need developed for those who had cut their teeth on Facebook to staff the social media efforts of organizations by creating content and providing the interaction between the organization and those who sought knowledge, information, feedback, and connection through its social media efforts.

Finally, those who had mastered the concept of social media as a means to create community and knew their way around the tools and technology became heads of social media departments and directed the efforts of organizations, interfacing with human resources, finance, administration, marketing, and other departments to improve communication and performance.

This explosion in Facebook confirmed a number of important trends:

- Social media was growing rapidly and would become a key source for research and information in any organization's internal and external communications efforts.
- Social media users were becoming key players in the communications space.
- Awareness and competence with social media tools were going to be key competitive advantages for corporations and significant skill sets in all institutions going forward.
- Mastering the various tools and creating a communications profile that fostered true social interactions would set the bar for those organizations that survived and thrived in the world of social media.

Like Glen, Rita's assistant in the scenario in Chapter Three, many Facebook or social media experts happened into this space and flourished due to their natural abilities to form and nurture relationships of trust and create value for their connections. Facebook (and Twitter) allowed them to participate on a more personal as well as a professional level and build networks based on both worlds.

While blogs used for organizational communication can be technical and matter of fact, Facebook is an area in which you can join the social media conversation as a fully rounded person, discussing personal issues, giving a wide range of opinions (without being tied to a company or institution), and combining true friendship with business relationships. Commenting on Facebook is similar to commenting on a blog post, except that the potential audience is generally wider and the subject of the content, again, tends to be more "human" than specialized or targeted (as in a blog), stimulating far more interaction. Responding to a Facebook post can be as easy as clicking the Like thumbs-up icon, thereby adding your opinion to the stream (and sending a short message about your opinion to the person who posted the update and to everyone else who commented). For example, if you click a Like link beneath a friend's video, it will be noted beneath the video that you liked it, a story will be posted to your Wall that you liked your friend's video, and your friend will get a notification that you liked his or her video. It's easy to imagine how information and opinion posted and responded to in this manner can explode exponentially.

Facebook and Twitter both are being expanded by applications that work on their respective platforms to provide even more communications options. At the moment there are at least four applications working on Facebook that let you access your Twitter account and read or add to your Twitter stream.

Mashable.com, one of the premiere sources of social media information on Facebook, will add many updates to your page and also provide a wealth of information about this evolving world. Visit Mashable.com and TechCrunch.com regularly, but try not to become overwhelmed by the sheer volume of new programs and concepts.

SCENARIO: PUTTING TRAINING ONLINE: A SOCIAL MEDIA SOLUTION

Emily Porter, Head of Training for Capital Payroll Services, had a serious problem. The IT department had convinced management to move the entire company, including the sales force, from Office 2003 to Office 2007. She knew that the sales team was mostly nontechnical and they "just wanted to know how to point and click." She had finally gotten them up to speed using PowerPoint 2003 effectively, and she knew that the new version, with a brand new interface, was going to cause a lot of resistance. Worse yet, her superiors wanted her to arrange a series of training seminars and put together a handbook based on PowerPoint presentations to be given by whomever she hired to teach the new version of the PowerPoint to the sales team. But Emily knew that the sales professionals did not have the patience to sit through a series of training sessions and that they would never read a handbook. They would monopolize her help desk staff and call her directly as soon as they hit snags in using the new software.

She arranged a meeting with Chief Operating Officer Keith Monroe, who she knew had been looking into social media but had not yet put together an internal social network. Emily requested and was granted permission to launch a Ning network (see Chapter Five) to test her new training concept. She explained to Keith that the network would be kept essentially private; she would initially invite only the sales staff and one or more PowerPoint training professionals. These training professionals already had blogs, text, and video tutorials online that they could link to from the Capital Payroll Ning network, but more important, they would participate in the forums and discussion areas and sometimes use chat to answer specific questions.

Emily drove home the point that by setting up a model social network and then, using tools like Twitter to create energy and stimulate conversation, and Flickr to host images that showed sample presentations and training materials, she could educate the sales staff in this exploding new area. Many members of the sales team wanted to use Twitter and Facebook but didn't have the go-ahead from management. This would give them a way to get their toes in the water.

Keith was sold and liked the concept because he would not have to approve a travel budget to bring in any trainers. Emily emphasized this point by suggesting that they could use the Ning network to schedule and support a series of Web training sessions (webinars) for the sales staff.

Keith was on board, but he still waffled on the issue of the handbook. While he liked the idea of an interactive set of tutorials that could be put on the Ning network and supplemented by discussions, he still wanted something tangible that would hold the staff accountable for certain standards and skills. Emily agreed to begin the program by putting together a "What's New" handbook for the sales team using screenshots of new PowerPoint features and would use those same images in online tutorials on the new Ning network. The training team would use blogs and discussion forums on the Ning network along with Facebook and Twitter posts to get the staff excited about this quick way of learning and getting their questions answered without sitting through long training sessions.

The key to the program she envisioned was interactivity—she intended to urge participants, both students and trainers, to share their experiences and stories and not just focus on the details of learning the new Office programs. While she needed to get everyone up to speed on the program's functionality, she knew that as they integrated the new software into their daily tasks and issues came up, the discussions about solutions would form the basis for an entire training community. As a seasoned training professional, she looked ahead to a library of success stories and experiences that would help her staff achieve a level of comfort and adapt more quickly.

Capture and Annotate Screens with Snag-It

Emily wanted to create a short introductory set of tutorials for her staff. She knew that she could provide a good overview of the new PowerPoint features by quickly capturing a series of images in TechSmith's screen capture utility, Snag-It. In the past, she had used these images in slide shows or training booklets, supplementing them with step-by-step instructions and annotations. What Emily loved about Snag-It was that it had both a comprehensive Capture Module, through which she could set her own profiles to capture screens in a variety of different ways, and an Editor that she could use to make annotations and edit and reedit the images. (See Figure 4.16.)

To bypass the Editor entirely, Emily used the Properties options to set a filename and extension for output files that would be appended for

Figure 4.16 Snag-It's Capture program lets the user set up a series of profiles that can be used to save screens directly to a file or first annotate them in an Editor.

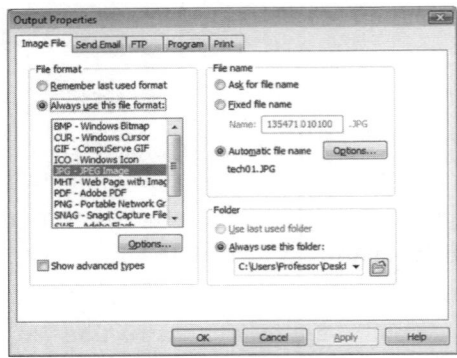

Figure 4.17 Snag-It lets the user set the file output options for name, file type, and location.

each capture (see Figure 4.17) and choose a hotkey for automatic capture and saving (see Figure 4.18).

By using the hot key feature, Emily captured a set of screens from the new version of PowerPoint that demonstrated its new features. She opened the destination folder for the capture files to make sure that it worked before continuing. (See Figure 4.19.)

For more complex concepts, she brought the image into the Snag-It Editor, where she could add arrows or other annotations to the image when creating the handbook or putting the images online. At the bottom of the Editor she was able to access a gallery of recent images to reedit or reuse. (See Figure 4.20.)

Figure 4.18 By right-clicking on a profile, a hotkey for automatic capture can be set up.

When Emily had compiled some screenshots, she decided to post them to her online image hosting service, Photobucket.com. (Numerous other similar sites are now available, including Flickr, Posterous, and TwitPic, for Twitter specifically. Posterous has the additional ability to Autopost to Everywhere or "mash" your content.) The important issue for Emily was that she would have a large number of images to organize and keep track of, so she used the batch utility of PhotoBucket to add descriptions and tags to each image before uploading. (See Figure 4.21.)

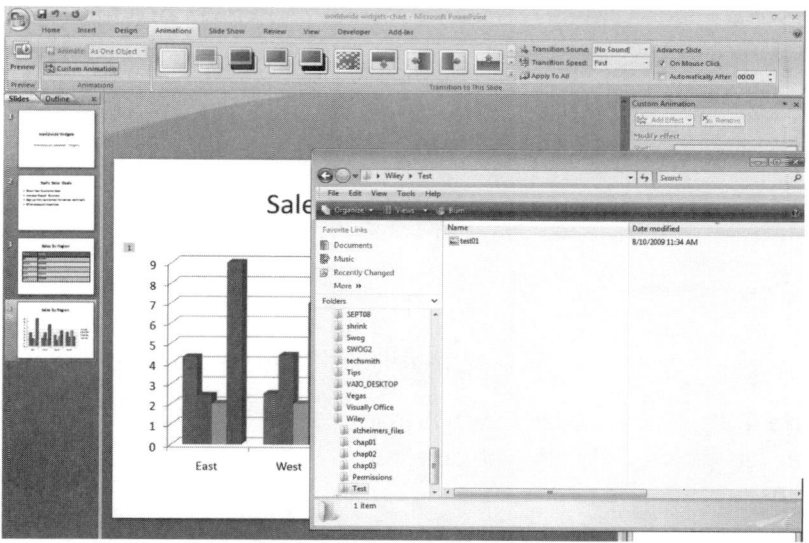

Figure 4.19 By using Snag-It's Automatic Capture, Emily could quickly and efficiently compile a folder of screenshots.

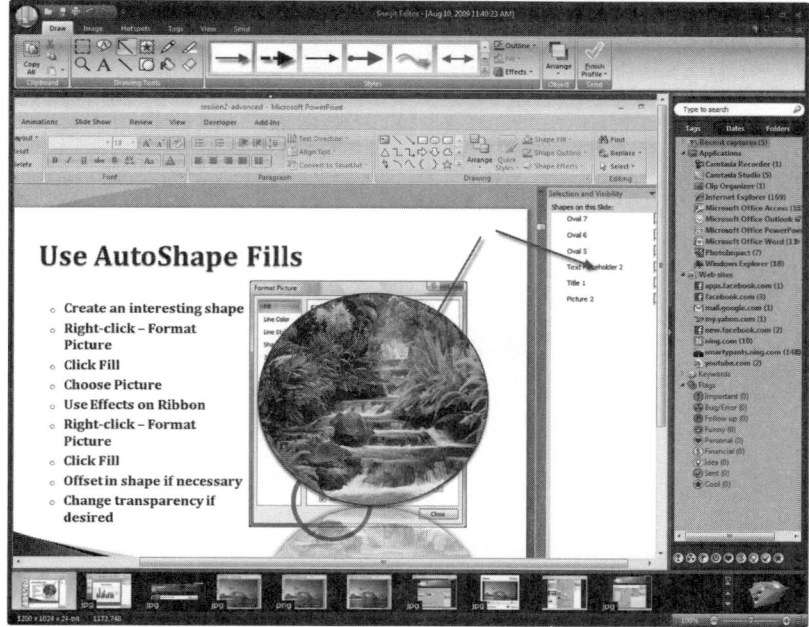

Figure 4.20 Snag-It's Editor gives the user the ability to annotate and change images before they are saved or after reopening them later on.

Figure 4.21 PhotoBucket's batch upload feature lets the user add tags and descriptions to multiple images (to facilitate search) before they are saved and uploaded.

Emily organized her PhotoBucket account into a series of "sets" to keep the PowerPoint images separated and then opened one of the images and clicked Share to get the embed code to use in the new Ning network. (See Figure 4.22.)

Emily decided to let one of her PowerPoint trainers introduce the new PowerPoint 2007 feature in his discussion thread on a new Ning network. She posted a message explaining the feature and

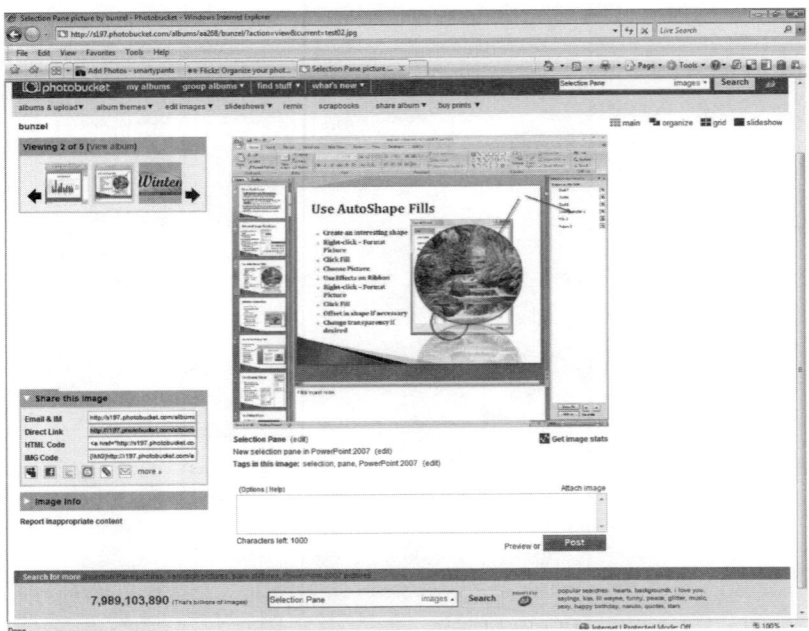

Figure 4.22 Opening an image page lets you access the Link and Embed options in PhotoBucket to copy and paste the URL or embed code into a blog or other Web page.

Tools of Engagement

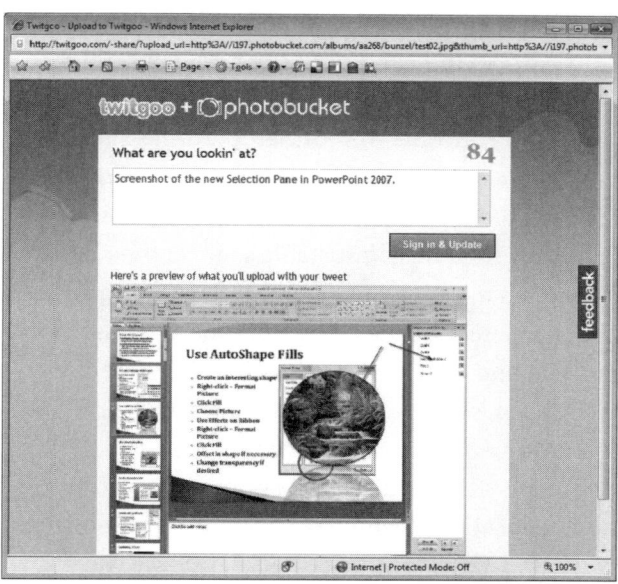

Figure 4.23 With an image hosted on PhotoBucket you can use the TwitGoo application to send it directly to Twitter.

pasted the URL for the image that was hosted on Flickr into the Add an Image panel.

The PowerPoint trainer would use these images in a training presentation to be uploaded as a video or linked from YouTube. The PowerPoint trainer wanted to let his followers on Twitter see the new PowerPoint 2007 screenshot and later on, when more content was available, invite them into the Ning network. He clicked on the little Twitter icon in PhotoBucket and opened a TwitGoo page that let him enter Emily's tweet directly to Twitter. (See Figures 4.23 and 4.24.)

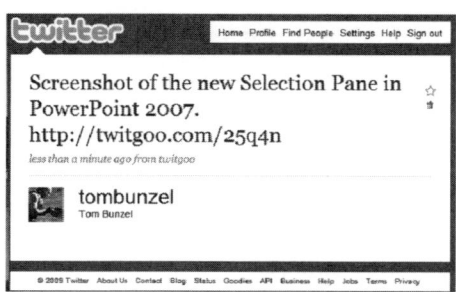

Figure 4.24 The Twitter post or "tweet" can let the user click the link to view a picture on PhotoBucket.

Emily eventually compiled a series of dozens of screenshots of the new version of PowerPoint using Snag-It. She put together a handbook fairly quickly by inserting all of the images at once into a PowerPoint presentation by using the PhotoAlbum feature of PowerPoint in the Insert tab of PowerPoint 2007. She had her staff and the PowerPoint trainers add explanations to the images, and then she output the handbook in PDF format and posted its link on the Ning network.

The New Tools of Engagement

Part of the assignment for the PowerPoint trainers was to actively post and then respond to comments on the Ning network discussion threads, using images where appropriate, and also to blog twice a week on important "in the trenches" tasks and concepts that came up during the training. Tweets were used to send invited members to the Ning network when they saw items that concerned them directly. The trainers' responsiveness energized the workforce as they became comfortable sharing their experiences and getting quick answers to questions about their pressing issues, so that they could remain productive through the upgrade process. Emily collected stories, both positive and negative, and discussions were generated on the Ning network about issues such as that charts in Office 2007 now used Excel rather than Microsoft Graph for a datasheet.

Eventually other departments at Capital Payroll Services wanted access to the Ning network, and several of the newer clients whom the sales team won over saw that getting important information quickly was facilitated by the social network. They were invited to join.

Entirely new channels of training that she had never anticipated were integrated into Emily's Ning network. There were screenshots of Payroll Service's Web forms; tax information was a hot topic in the forums in the spring; other Capital employees used the network to communicate with management about customer service issues and get solutions by "crowd-sourcing" other employees' experiences.

The experience went full circle when the IT department, which decided to train the staff on PowerPoint 2007 in the first place, was charged with the task of moving the Ning "test" network to a private network on Capital Payroll's own servers.

SCENARIO: BUILDING RELATIONSHIPS WITH VALUABLE INFORMATION

Gary Williams was one of the PowerPoint trainers that Capital Payroll Services brought aboard to get its sales team up to speed on the new version of PowerPoint, but he was more of a strategist than a graphics specialist. Gary convinced Emily, who was now head of human resources, that Capital should begin using Twitter and other social media tools, along with content and resources that the company already had available, to market more efficiently.

Gary and Emily met with Carl Taylor, Director of Marketing and Communications, who was already chomping at the bit to use the new Capital social network to generate sales. He bragged to Gary and Emily that many of his sales professionals were already active on Twitter, Facebook, LinkedIn, and FriendFeed (a filtered network that Facebook had acquired).

Carl took out his BlackBerry and showed Gary how he had already begun blogging on LinkedIn. The title of Carl's blog was "Capital Gains Pay Dividends with Payroll Services for Small Business." In the piece, Gary saw that Carl had spelled out all of the features of Capital's offerings and a few of the benefits. Then Carl showed him how he had posted a YouTube video of a sales presentation he had made earlier in the month and embedded it into the blog.

"You tech guys aren't the only ones who know how to do this stuff," he proclaimed proudly. He wanted Gary and Emily to watch the entire video to the end because "That's where we close these guys," Carl said.

Gary sat back in his chair in the conference room and sighed to himself. He had come to understand that using the new social tools wasn't about conventional marketing or using the latest and greatest tools—it was about building relationships. He studied Carl and tried to think of a way to persuade him to consider this kind of approach.

"Carl," Gary asked, "have you had much in the way of comments on your blog? What kind of traffic are you getting?"

Carl got a bit defensive, responding that the blog had only been up a few weeks. He added that that was why they needed to put together a strategy for using Facebook, Twitter, and some of the other tools "to drive some traffic to the blog and our Web site."

Emily stepped in and told Carl that she and Gary had been studying social media for a while, participating in several online networks geared to the financial services industry, and watching how some of the more successful professionals in the field conducted themselves on Twitter and Facebook.

"I follow all of those folks," Carl said when he saw the list of people that Gary had studied in the financial social media space.

"Are they following you?" Emily asked cautiously.

"Not yet," Carl replied, repeating once more that he was still new to the game.

"Okay," Gary said, "I've compiled a series of blog entries, Facebook status updates, and Twitter posts from these individuals and put them into a PowerPoint presentation." He turned on a projector and ran through the series of slides, spending perhaps ten seconds on each. Then he asked Carl, "What did all of these entries have in common?"

Carl was scratching his head, considering his answer. Emily decided to frame it for him.

"Carl, there was no selling in any of these posts. They were all contributing to a conversation, offering professional opinions, and providing valuable resources on financial matters."

"Are you saying you want my guys to give away our expertise?" Carl asked incredulously. "That's our competitive advantage!"

Emily met his eyes and said, "We want to test a new strategy. Are you ready to hear it?" Carl nodded, unconvinced.

Gary projected another slide, explaining that he wanted to propose a six-month plan with the phases shown in Table 4.1.

Table 4.1
Capital Payroll Services Social Media Strategy Plan

Task	Content	Tool
Listen	Focus on subject matter and opinions of experts and end users	Blogs, LinkedIn, Facebook, Twitter
Learn	Watch how the most effective experts use social media and give credit to others	Social media conferences and bloggers
Contribute	Take advantage of Capital resources to inform and add value to discussions	PowerPoint, AuthorStream, SlideShare, SlideRocket, Audacity (podcasts)
Engage	Maintain interactive discussions and commentary with customers, colleagues, and experts	Blogs, Twitter, Facebook, and new emerging tools

Carl stroked his chin as he studied the chart and nodded. "We've stressed the listening thing in a lot of our sales training sessions. What we do is try to find the pain points for any prospects and then target them in our attack."

"Sounds like a war," Emily murmured.

Gary stuck up for Carl on this issue, saying that many presentation experts suggest that it's important to establish what's at stake for any company considering hiring Capital to handle its financial affairs. "What's the main value proposition in a particular situation? Is it just efficiency and cost cutting, or keeping key employees with a retirement or health plan, or making sure that accounts are paid on time?" Gary said that the key to any successful presentation is knowing the audience by doing research about what matters most to them, not just generally covering the features and benefits being offered. In fact, Gary added, this is precisely where the social media effort would pay off for the company, by identifying trends and issues that would help nail down the company's key benefits *from the customer's perspective* when the sales team went out to present to prospects.

He put up another set of slides, explaining, "Here are some Twitter posts you may not have seen. We did a search for 'payroll' and 'Capital,' going back a few months and came up with these." The slides showed dozens of comments about Capital, and its competitors, from satisfied and dissatisfied customers. One tweet directly stated that a sales rep from Capital "tried to sell us some modules we told her we did not need, but she persisted and tried to package them in anyway."

"Ouch," Carl said. "I'd like to know who that was!"

Emily suggested that Carl, or someone in the department, engage that customer and, instead of trying to convince them of anything, find out more specifics about their needs and address them through the blogs and other posts. She pointed to the last item in the table: take advantage of Capital resources.

"What we've decided to do," Emily said, "is to create teams between your sales reps and some of our trainers, so that your people can build relationships based on the knowledge base that the company already uses to train its customers." Carl thought that might slow his team down; they had quotas to hit. The social media effort was going to take resources and time.

Emily shook her head. "Keith Monroe has already approved this plan," she told him, "at least on a limited basis. We've identified six of our top value propositions and customer support and training staff who are proficient in each of these."

1. Payroll tax administration: Calculate liabilities, taxes, and file returns.
2. Workers' compensation: Assess workers' comp costs.
3. 401(k) and retirement services: Select the most appropriate retirement plan, investments, and comply with recordkeeping requirements.
4. Health insurance: Compare group rates and benefits among numerous carriers.
5. Time and labor solutions: Implement a time and attendance system to maximize productivity.
6. HR outsourcing solutions: Support hiring, staffing and compliance efforts.

"We've got white papers, PowerPoint presentations, and video content that address each of these issues," Emily told Carl. She said that as his sales team created connections through blogs and posts, when any of these issues came up in online conversations, they would be able to link to some of these resources.

"Plus," she concluded, "the customer service and training individual assigned to each sales rep will help frame the responses to address the concerns raised in the blog or discussion."

"Isn't that going to cut into the time that they have allotted to support our customers?" Carl asked.

Emily explained that part of the program also called for discussion forums on the new Capital social network in which customers and clients would suggest ways of using the Capital services more effectively. After all, Emily said, each of their clients had a unique set of experiences with its own customers, vendors, and staff that could be beneficial to others, and the company was going to encourage that kind of crowdsourcing.

Another aspect of the initiative that Gary wanted to bring up touched on doing research on prospects for sales presentations and on engaging individuals contacted through social media through insightful questions and knowledge of their backgrounds. Gary handed Carl a social media checklist and said, "These are the items you and your team should be researching for each client prior to sales calls and social media interaction. The information provided can be used to easily generate themes and discussion points."

Social Media Checklist

- Bio and head shot (on blog or Web site)
- LinkedIn profile
- Facebook profile
- YouTube search
- Google search
- Read "the book" (for an expert or authority)
- Read "the blog" and establish relationship with comments[3]

"So when do we call the prospects and set of up sales presentations?" Carl wondered.

Emily replied that they would create a database of the various decision makers and key contacts that became visible through the social media initiative, and Carl and Gary would consult to determine at what point they might be contacted directly. But before any of that happened, Emily added, they wanted to make sure that all of their connections were actively engaged with the sales team without any hard selling. "The key element is building trust," Emily said. "And that will take some time. That's why we've set aside about six months for the initiative, and be aware that you may not see a tangible return on investment for up to a year."

Carl did not like that.

"But if you take a look at some of the case studies on Twitter's Business Site," Gary said, "you'll see that the level of customer satisfaction among companies that are using these tools grows significantly much sooner than that."

Emily said that there would be one other phase of the program that would be initiated once a critical mass of followers and connections was achieved through the new campaign—Web events to which they would invite their new connections to learn about the latest issues in the field through online conferences and meetings.

"Great," Carl said. "We can use a Web conference to follow up on those leads."

Maybe, Emily agreed, but she again reminded him that this would happen on a case-by-case basis, with consultation with Gary and some other team members.

"But my sales professionals will be giving some of these webinars, right?" Carl asked.

"They can be on the panels," Gary agreed, "but we're going to try to get respected key influencers, the most well-respected financial bloggers in the field, to participate in these webinars. Management has provided us with a small budget to test it out."

Emily added that by using well-respected independent consultants and experts in the financial industry, many of whom had thousands of social media connections of their own, Capital would establish credibility in the webinar programs and also add these participants to their own database once the participants registered for the events.

This finally got Carl excited. He reviewed a list of potential speakers and realized that any of these would certainly attract key decision makers among his potential prospects. He began pairing up his sales professionals with the company's trainers to take advantage of the trainers' content and expertise in the blogs and online posts.

"What about these other items," Carl asked. "What's this SlideRocket and AuthorStream?"

"We're going to teach you those tools as well," Gary said, explaining that the IT department would help post the training and informative content on the new Capital social network so that it could be accessed from the company's BlackBerries, iPhones, and other mobile devices. These new tools meant that a presenter did not have to always use a laptop and projector and go through a complicated setup procedure—the content was available on the Web and accessible through any browser. The Web conferencing solution also meant that once Carl's staff got up to speed, they could reach prospects around the world without leaving their desks. Now Carl got really excited about using the social media tools with some new hardware and software to reach even more potential customers.

Emily told Carl that the Web conferencing solution that the company was considering also supported quick ad hoc meetings, so that when an important issue came up with a prospect or customer, the sales or customer service staff could quickly invite that individual into an online conference where solutions were explored and offered in real time.

Capital Payroll Services integrated social media applications with its presentation and training capabilities in such a way as to satisfy its customers and its own employees. Not surprisingly, other payroll service companies were forced to emulate this scenario to compete with Capital, and for her efforts Emily Porter was promoted to an executive position at the firm. In her new position, she began looking ahead to plan a series of webinars for both clients and employees to leverage the content that was on the new internal social network for the company.

Posting Resource Material Online

As Capital's social media initiative took shape, the company's communications department found that it needed the help of IT to get up to speed on how and where to post significant content so that it could be leveraged in the campaign. The company needed to catalog and index its resources within the main topics based on various value propositions, such as health insurance, time and labor, workers' comp, and so on. Within weeks the staff had amassed a wealth of images, PowerPoint presentations, and documents like white papers that were organized by subject area, topic, author (with bio), and location on the company network. The information was entered into an Excel spreadsheet and distributed to the individuals charged with participating in the social media initiative. When a specific item was identified that added value in answering a specific question or in response to a discussion on the social network, it was posted online in the proper location and format.

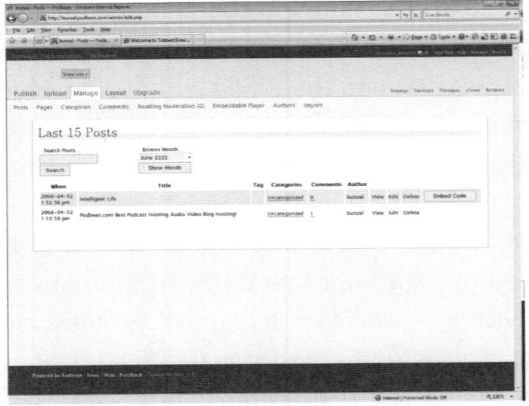

Figure 4.25 An audio hosting site like Podbean.com can let you post MP3 audio files with descriptions and keywords as podcasts, which can be aggregated in an MP3 player (iTunes) and subscribed to as RSS feeds.

Enabling Subscriptions (RSS) for Podcasts

To enable the users of social media to subscribe to receive content as they might a magazine subscription, Steve Gilbert, a social media expert that Emily brought in for technology training, explained how RSS (Really Simple Syndication) can bring content on a regular basis into a feed reader or an e-mail program like Outlook. (Refer to Figure 3.4 for a look at Google Reader.) He demonstrated by narrating an MP3 file in Audacity and uploading it to a free audio hosting site (Podbean.com) (see Figure 4.25). (Audacity, an audio utility for editing MP3 audio, is covered in Chapter Six.)

Steve explained that a properly configured hosting platform is required to get the series of podcasts into a subscription format that will work in a program like Outlook (to manage subscriptions; see Figure 4.26) or iTunes (to download and listen to the podcasts and subscribe to the feeds; see Figure 4.27). A savvy Web developer can post a folder on a server, with a URL like http://capital.podbean.com/feed, where Podbean is the host and Capital has created a feed from a series of uploaded MP3 files (with description in an XML format). A hosting service like Podbean automatically generates the XML for its subscribers, but for a company like Capital Payroll, the IT department could host the podcasts on its servers and create its own XML scripts and feed URLs.

Posting Documents, PDFs, and White Papers

Capital Payroll indexed a large number of reference documents, help files, and how-to tutorials in Microsoft Word and PDF format. Steve suggested that they use a site like Scribd.com to host the documents they wanted to

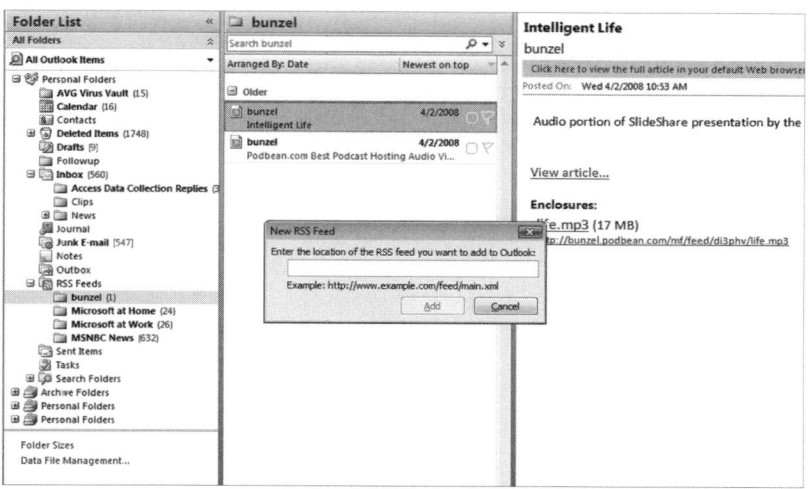

Figure 4.26 An RSS feed can be managed from Microsoft Outlook or used to bring the content directly into an MP3 player. Use a link from the standard RSS symbol icon or use a Subscribe link to get the feed URL.

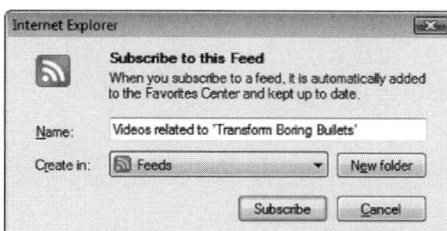

Figure 4.27 Users can subscribe to an RSS feed from Internet Explorer by clicking the RSS symbol, going to the feed page, and clicking Subscribe to this feed, giving them a subscribe dialogue box that lets them rename the feed and add it to their favorites (where Outlook or iTunes can access the subscription).

make available with links in social media posts. They could also take advantage of Scribd's community and search features: for each document there is commentary, description, and tag (keyword) functionality on the site, making it ideal for inclusion in Capital's social media presentation strategy. (See Figure 4.28.)

At this point Capital Payroll Services had some cogs in place for its social media initiative. It had educated its sales team on how to participate and build relationships on social sites and the social network it had created for that purpose and by making video, slideshow, audio, and documentary content available, searchable, linkable, and embeddable for use and distribution online.

Figure 4.28 A document repository like Scribd can host supporting reference material for linking and embedding and sustain an active community around your content.

MASHABILITY: EXPANDING THE NETWORK

Mashability is the ability to use content on one site through references in another. When you embed code from YouTube to play a video in a blog or Web page, or when a program like SlideRocket (see Chapter Seven) enhances its presentation capability by directly accessing content from Google Docs, it is an example of "mashing." This capability has expanded dramatically as many applications are exposing their API (application program interface) to others, making the copying and pasting of code unnecessary and automating the process. Mashing makes expanding a network and continuing the conversation from a meeting or webinar out through a growing community easier than ever.

For example, for her blog, Allie, the founder of NewHope, the philanthropic community introduced in Chapter Three, used WordPress, a professional blogging tool that comes with a number of plug-ins that allow for immediate distribution to other social sites. These plug-ins include Add to Facebook, FriendFeed, and Digg Digg. Digg Digg offers voting buttons for your blog, including TweetMeme, ReTweet, Yahoo Buzz, and Submit to Reddit, in addition to a Digg button. Instant Highlighter lets the user select portions of your blog to share on Twitter, Facebook, and other social sites. WordPress also has a Social Bookmarks plug-in that lets you send bookmarks to social bookmarking sites like Delicious. Not surprisingly, there are two plug-ins directly to Twitter: Twitter Friendly Links and Twitter for WordPress.[4]

Because of the sheer number of pictures Allie needed to edit to post on the blog and on Whrrl.com, she decided to try an online image editor: Picnik (www.picnik.com). While Picnik is not as robust and feature laden as desktop programs like Adobe PhotoShop, it mashes or connects directly with MySpace, Flickr, Facebook, PhotoBucket, and other Web sites and programs. Picnik has many of the important features Allie needed, like cropping, with additional options to save images locally or them it directly Twitter or Flickr (see Figures 4.29 and 4.30).

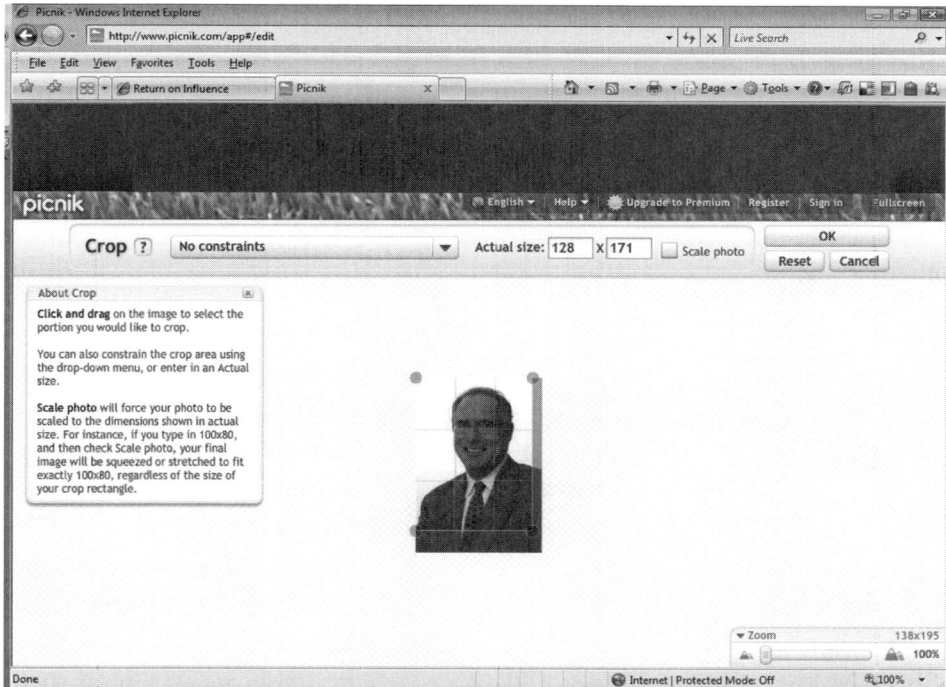

Figure 4.29 Picnik has the most common features of an image editor but lives entirely online, and it's free.

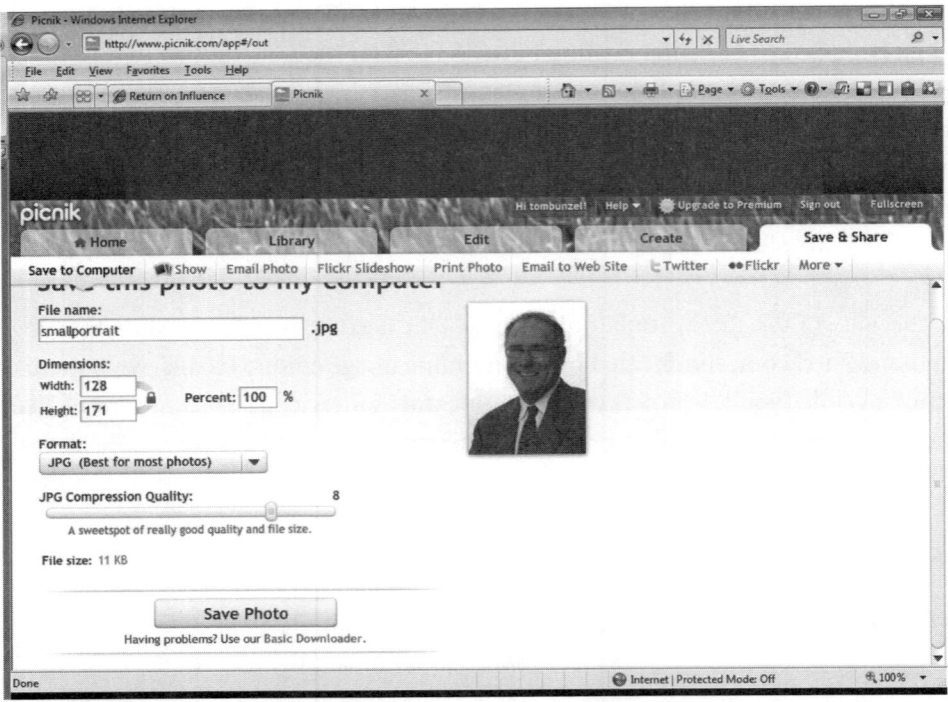

Figure 4.30 Picnik lets you save the image file locally or send it directly to Twitter, Flickr, and other Web sites.

Figure 4.31 With the image on Flickr, it can be shared in an e-mail by using its URL on the Flickr site or sent to a blog.

With the image on Flickr, Allie was able to reference it in her blog and include it in her Whrrl visual stories (see Figure 4.31).

Finally, after her successful webinar, Allie worked to continue the conversation about NewHope on Twitter with her growing set of followers. She had learned about how effective hashtags on Twitter could be specifically for nonprofits and foundations from a blog

Tools of Engagement

by Beth Kanter.[5] Her followers quickly recognized the #NewHope hashtag, and the blog became a rallying point for a community built to help the homeless using Allie's listening and attention process and the gmail accounts that had been given to the disadvantaged.

Allie moderated a miniconference or chat on Twitter on Tuesday nights, at which volunteers, agencies, and even some of the homeless shared stories and links. The sessions were free floating: each tweet simply used the #NewHope hashtag and community members saw and responded to it. During these sessions and on her blog, Allie shared other important hashtags for the nonprofit and foundation community and its affiliates. In specific instances, Allie combined the NewHope hashtag with another term to filter and distribute information for an emergency or event—like #NewHopeFooddrive. To get more information, she participated in a Sunday night #blogchat on technical issues moderated by Mack Collier (introduced in Chapter Two).

In this way Allie was able to "make her own game," in the parlance of *Trust Agents*, and she stood out without intending to by creating immense value and making significant contributions in the area of aid to the homeless. She began by sharing her stories, leveraged her media resources, and built a following with webinars. She continued the conversation, and her contact with those individuals who had gotten off the streets thanks to her, using Twitter.

TOOLS FOR SHARING BLOG CONTENT ON OTHER SITES

As you read blogs and comments, you will find that many content creators make it easy to "mash" or share their content with others. Two services that make this easy are sharethis.com and addthis.com. (The steps taken in ShareThis, shown following, are typical of how such a process works. Mashing services use a similar model, allowing visitors to a site to distribute content that they find of value to their colleagues and associates around the Web.) With ShareThis, you create an account, and on the welcome screen, in the area for Publishers, you can enable sharing by choosing to Get the Button. See Figure 4.32 for specific options.

When you click Get the Code (if you've chosen Any Website), the process will be similar to embedding a YouTube video. (See Figure 4.33.)

Depending upon which Web site you want to share (for example, Blogger), you will paste this code into the HTML panel or area for that page. (Refer to Figure 4.4 for how to use the Edit HTML tab of Blogger, for example, to paste

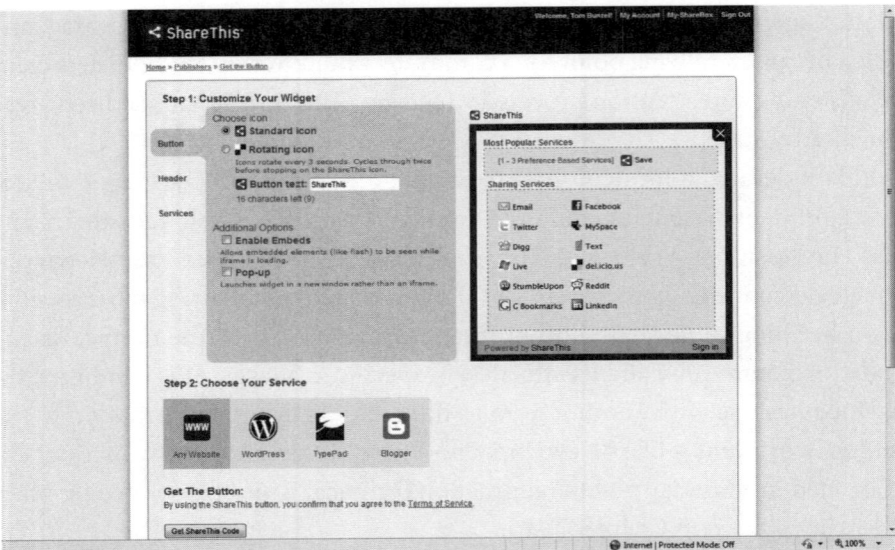

Figure 4.32 In the Get the Button screen, you can choose a style of button, which services you wish to distribute content to, and whether you want code for any Web page or for one of three major blogging tools: WordPress, TypePad, and Blogger.

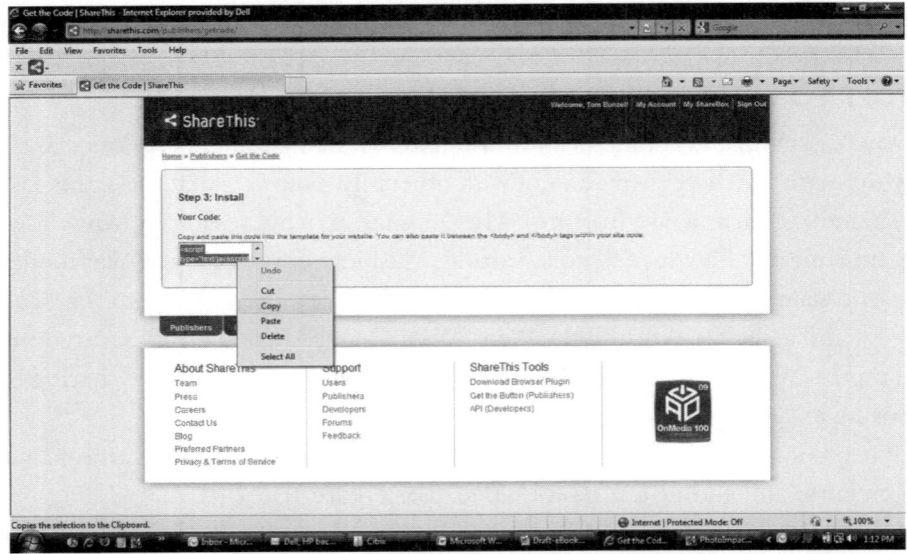

Figure 4.33 In the Get the Code window, select the code and copy it to your clipboard.

Tools of Engagement

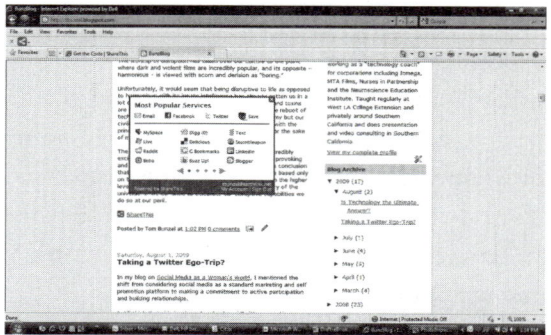

Figure 4.34 The ShareThis widget on a Web site or blog lets the visitor share your content, by e-mail, on popular sites and other blogs.

this code into your blog.) This snippet of code with specific functionality is sometimes referred to as a "widget." When you enable a widget like ShareThis, visitors to your blog can instantly distribute your content to any of a number of social media sites. (See Figure 4.34.)

Your account under ShareThis has a ShareBox where you can track what's been shared, by whom, and to which location (see Figure 4.35).

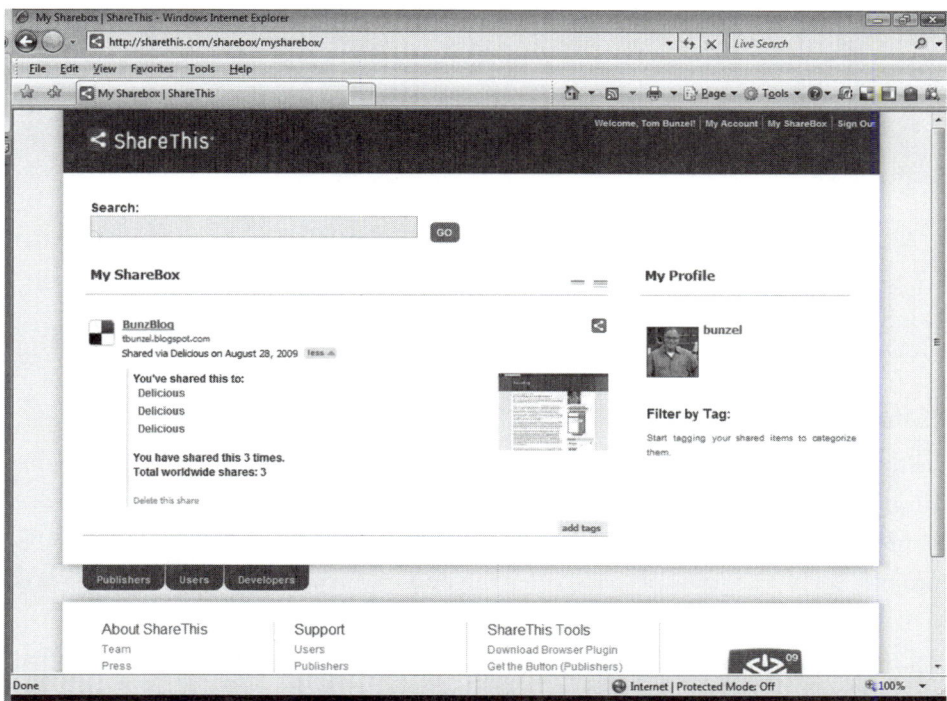

Figure 4.35 This ShareBox lets the account holder track the sharing history of the widget she has created. (In this instance I shared my own blog to Delicious.com.)

The New Tools of Engagement

In addition to pre-set widgets like ShareThis, you can use other services to create customized widgets to distribute specific messages.

Another tool for sharing other kinds of content, like pictures, audio, and video, is Posterous.com. You can start without a Posterous account and just send your content to post@posterous.com. But when you've set up an account, Posterous features a bookmarklet that allows you to instantly send any Web content to Posterous. It also features an AutoShare capability that distributes content from Posterous to any number of sites, including:

- Facebook
- Twitter
- Flickr
- Tumblr
- Blogger
- WordPress
- TypePad
- MovableType
- LiveJournal
- Xanga

All that you need to do is to set up your account with your options (similar to ShareThis), and whatever you post to Posterous is distributed to the Web sites chosen.

USING CUSTOM WIDGETS TO STAY CONNECTED

Custom widgets are eye-catching snippets of code, frequently animated or containing video, that users can easily copy and paste into their blogs, Web pages, or profiles on social sites that visitors can click on to spread the word about valuable content. Social media sites vie to offer the best and most creative widgets to link back to them and gain traffic and traction in the market.

J. A. Jones, author of the Speak Media blog and a social media consultant, has been a "big fan of these fun little tools for many years. They are increasingly popular with web savvy consumers. (According to eMarketer, widgets are used by 43.5% of adults and 77% of the teen Internet population.)"[6]

So what are widgets and how can you use them effectively? In her blog, Jones describes a widget created for a pet supply company that had an animated cat or dog scratching when its flea collar needed a replacement. Taking this scenario a step further, if you were the client and were offered a webinar on battling your pet's pests, the same widget could bark or meow to prompt users to sign up for the event and then remind them of when the event occurs. In addition to helping an organization stay in touch with its audience, clients, or employees, a widget like this could be particularly effective in counteracting a big problem with Web events: no shows. Many users are inundated with webinar invitations; they sign up, but when the event occurs, they forget or are otherwise occupied. A widget with a link to the registration page and then to the actual event can make people remember to log in and participate, or it could direct them to the video archive afterward. With a video playing within the widget, it could even be a trailer for the archived webinar.

An online resource for making your own custom widget is Widgetbox.com, which lets you create a widget in Flash or HTML/JS (Java Script), use a remote widget, get a blog feed, or import a Google Gadget to create a tiny app to stay connected online. Using Widgetbox (see Figure 4.36), an eBook cover can be combined with a description that takes the user to more information, in a widget that can be placed in a blog or Web page in a manner similar to embedding a video (see Figure 4.37). All that is required is to copy and paste the code generated by Widgetbox.

To create a widget in the program, you begin by using the sample widget—a simple "Hello World" textbox—and revising it, testing it, and finally publishing the widget.

We've covered in this chapter a lot of different programs, representing the ways in which content can be posted, distributed, and referenced

Figure 4.36 Widgetbox is an online tool for creating, distributing, and tracking widget applications.

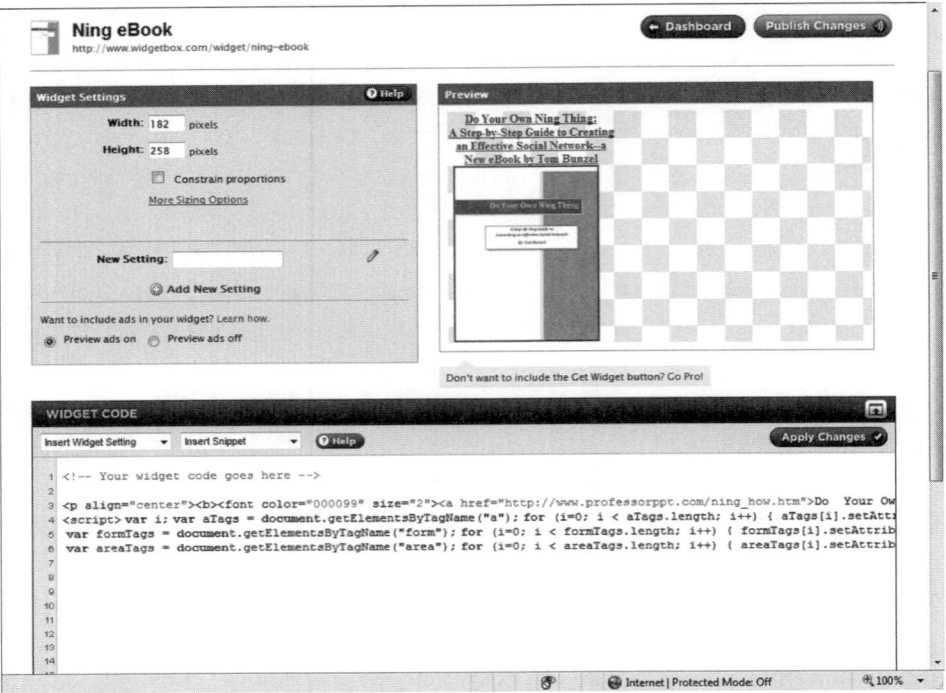

Figure 4.37 Widgetbox has a visual interface for creating a widget in a set size and generating code.

and shared online within blogs, social bookmarking sites, business networks, and other similar communities. In Chapter Five we look in greater detail at two online social networks that are currently extremely popular and growing: Twitter and Ning.

QUESTIONS TO PONDER

1. Have you participated in the commentary on any blogs, your own or in areas of interest in your field? Have other people responded? Where did it lead? Have you posted content using the Web 2.0 mashup features?

2. How might asking questions and more active participation on a business network like LinkedIn benefit your networking in your field and provide you with useful information, resource material, and answers to important issues?

3. Do you waste a lot of time trying to relocate important online information? Could you benefit from an organizational tool like social bookmarking? How might it help to see what others in your field are finding and how they react to it?

4. How might you best expand the reach of your area of expertise online? Could sharing your content in some way benefit you and your audience and build community? What kind of content might you share—text, images, video, audio (podcasts)?

Notes
1. Jeremy Wright, *Blog Marketing*. New York: McGraw-Hill, 2005.
2. http://clt.lse.ac.uk/Projects/Case_Study_Two_report.pdf.
3. Susan Bratton: http://talkshowtips.com.
4. Don Reisinger: http://bit.ly/cRAix.
5. Beth Kanter: http://bit.ly/1960az.
6. www.speakmediablog.com.

Major Social Networks: Twitter and Ning

chapter
FIVE

Now that we've begun to see how some of the new social technologies are changing the realities of communication and blurring the distinction between training and marketing, it's time to take a closer look at dedicated social networks or online communities.

Twitter exploded onto the scene seemingly from nowhere; it is now a major source for real-time information, constituting a continuous stream of communication like one giant conversation among a huge community of users and followers.

Ning is less well known, but it hosts 1.8 million communities with 37 million users. We cover it here as a representative model for conceptualizing and implementing a dedicated online community for specific purposes, such as shared interests, training, education, and marketing.

THE VIRAL POWER OF TWITTER

In early 2009, a young woman who was seeking a job had a successful interview. Here is what she "tweeted" on Twitter: "Cisco just offered me a job! Now I have to weigh the utility of a fatty paycheck against the daily commute to San Jose and hating the work."

Oops.

Someone from Cisco noticed the post and did some digging, alerting the hiring manager; not surprisingly, the offer for the position, which the woman later said was an internship, was withdrawn. The incident became known online as "Cisco Fatty" and presents a classic warning, particularly to online job seekers (but really to anyone) that good sense must extend to online activities, particularly to "conversations" such as those on Twitter.

Twitter is a so-called microblogging tool that is geared to the short attention spans and quick-change mentality of today's world. Newcomers often scratch their heads as they see post after post that describe how someone put their kids to bed or where they had dinner that night, and wonder, "How can this help me to communicate, particularly in a professional way?"

According to Human Resources Online, Heather Gardner (@heathergardner), a Silicon Valley recruiter, says she uses Twitter extensively as a networking and referral tool. The recruiter, who is on the list of the top fifty recruiters on Twitter, uses her tweets to attract correspondence and interest from potential candidates. "Sometimes it links to useful info, or to a new blog post of mine or a request for assistance, job opening and what not." Gardner considers Twitter a "fabulous branding and knowledge sharing tool." She thinks of it as a form of "speed dating"—or speed networking. The key to her process is mining through the enormous talent pool that has a Twitter presence, using search and referrals.

Human Resources Online lists three ways to use Twitter:

1. *Sourcing*: Using searches, you can identify candidates and their current positions in their profiles.
2. *Referrals*: After you've built an industry network, you may be able to obtain referrals based on the quality of tweets that you send out.
3. *Industry research*: Twitter works great as an informal Q&A for information. From real-time intelligence on your clients, promotions, hires, layoffs, and projects, to asking your network how to answer questions on buzzwords, lingo, and technical matters, Twitter works to give you information more quickly so that you are more interesting on the phone.[1]

Twitter Nuts and Bolts

At the time this is being written, Twitter is extremely hot and is the most significant real-time social media communications tool. "Real time" refers to the immediacy of Twitter's status updates and the responses of followers; because of the brevity of posts, there is almost no lag time between a post and a slew of responses, a viral dissemination of information and opinion.

We saw similar tools take off with MySpace and Facebook, and there are many people who think Twitter may eventually fade in importance. (Doubters cite the emergence of Google Wave as a likely reason; Wave is previewed in Chapter Eight and interfaces well with Twitter, according to its beta users.)

But at the moment, Twitter is an important tool for seeing quickly how social media can affect the outcome of communications strategy, how it comprises a key component of your online identity, and how you interact and are perceived by others. Twitter works equally well in a Web browser or using SMS (Short Message Service, or text) messages from a cell phone or PDA.

If you've looked at Twitter and thought, "Oh my God, what drivel," you are certainly not alone. Jokes abound about the significance of a continuous stream of information about where people had dinner or vacationed, or how they felt when they got up in the morning. As we're discovering, however, there is value in some of this information; a concrete opinion about a restaurant or hotel can trigger comments and be of value to an organization that is truly *listening* in the world of social media. And it can lead to real-world results and change—as we'll see particularly in the area of crowdsourcing—or the solicitation and use of information gathered from a community of shared interest.

But what is really going on with Twitter, and how do you use it?

When you first set up a Twitter account, you create your own user identity, with a Web link, a picture or avatar, and a one-line bio of up to 160 characters. Pictures are key and should represent you or your brand, identity, concept, or strategy for using Twitter, which you should carefully consider before you begin. A good representative picture is considered generally better than a logo or something "cute" unless you are using Twitter only for personal reasons. Keeping the generic picture placeholder on your site identifies you as someone new to the game and unlikely to be followed.

Following and Getting Followers

It has been suggested that Twitter is a return to high school and at its core just a huge popularity contest. Indeed, when Ashton Kutcher beat CNN's Anderson Cooper to a million followers, it jump-started the Twitter phenomenon in mainstream America. For personal brands like celebrities, the number of followers is a key indicator of success. When followers reach a high number or critical mass, the power of Twitter is leveraged, because a single message or 140-character tweet reaches each of them instantly. For mere mortals, however, adding followers is a time-consuming process of being discovered by people who care about something you have to say.

The first step is finding other people to follow: identifying others on Twitter with similar interests. In search.twitter.com, you can type in any search parameters or use the Advanced Search option to fine-tune what you're looking for; the more specific you get, the fewer hits. As you look through the search results, you will notice various features of the individual posts. At the very beginning, before the colon (:) is the username of the entity posting. Within the post, you may get a link to Reply, or more likely you will see a curved arrow that lets you reply to that post. The star lets you mark a post as a favorite so that you can return more easily later. (See Figure 5.1.)

Figure 5.1 Each Twitter post has options to reply to the post or mark it as a favorite.

When you click Reply, you get a new post with an @ before the username of the entity to which you are responding. This means the person will see a post referring to him (if he is following you), as will anyone else following you. This is another way your presence on Twitter will grow. As you see @ references, you will discover more people to follow.

You can also repeat a post by another entity that you find significant by "retweeting": adding "RT" and a space before the @ reference and username, and then copying the rest of their post. This is considered good form, and anyone whom you RT or retweet will appreciate it and probably begin to pay more attention to you. Many Twitter users will acknowledge your RT in a separate post. As you search, post, and respond, you will follow more users, and others will follow you.

Twitter has recently added a Retweet icon to the right of the Reply icon for automatic retweeting; this feature has not been universally accepted by seasoned Twitter users because it does not afford the opportunity to comment upon or add or describe the value of the post being retweeted.

When you have a Twitter username, a Find People option will appear at the top of your window; you can use this as another search option to locate users you want to follow. As you might imagine, many of those who follow you will have ulterior motives (spam) or simply be irrelevant. However, particularly at the beginning, some experts suggest following everyone to begin to build your own following and experience Twitter fully. You will likely find that some users fill up your home page with irrelevant posts; to stop them, you can simply click on them to see that you are in fact following them; then click on the checked button (Following) and you'll be prompted to stop following. They may never notice you stopped following them, but you'll no longer see their posts.

Figure 5.2 Clicking Direct Message in the right column gives you a chance to send a direct post to anyone following you, using a drop-down list or @ prefix.

The right column of your home page is significant. (See Figure 5.2.) A link with @ and your username lets you see posts by people you're following that reference you. Next are Direct Messages you've received, which are different from @ references—they are like quick e-mail messages between you and people who follow you. (You can't send a direct message to someone you're following unless and until they follow you back.)

Favorites let you see the posts you've selected as such. Below your Saved Searches are the Trending Topics, which are the hot issues on Twitter at any moment. This is the "Twitter-verse"; going there, participating, and getting noticed can exponentially increase your following among those who

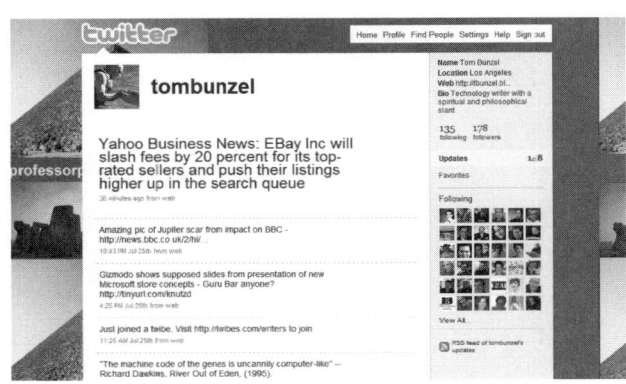

Figure 5.3 The Profile page shows how others see you and also shows your most recent posts.

are interested in that topic. If you want to see all of your latest posts in a window that represents how others see you if they click on your picture, click Profile at the top of your window. (See Figure 5.3.)

If you need to change how your Profile page looks, you can click Settings. Under Settings you will find various tabs that enable you to revise aspects of how you use Twitter and what other users can discover about you. In the Design tab, you will find an area where you can apply various generic themes to your page instantly and change the colors.

Creating Your Own Background Image for the Profile Page

You can change the background image for your Profile page, which is a significant way you can customize your look and representation on Twitter. (By adding text to the background image before you save it, you can supplement the 160-character limit of personal information on the profile you create, but the text will be in a graphic format and not "clickable.") To create a background image in an image editing tool like PhotoShop, you need to create a graphic file in GIF, JPG, or PNG format, under 800K. Your best results will come when you make the width of the image about the same as most of the screen dimensions of your users; in the

Figure 5.4 You can create your own background image for your Profile page on Twitter in any good image editor by saving it in a Web image format. A good procedure is to create a new image in the resolution you want and paste in your elements, saving it as a JPG file.

United States that would probably be 1280 pixels. You can experiment with the height, but keeping the image relatively narrow lets you use the Tile Background option to repeat your design throughout the page effectively. Using one large image will probably make the Tile Background option irrelevant. (See Figures 5.4 and 5.5.)

Figure 5.5 Making your image wide and short lets it tile throughout the page and provides space in the middle for the Twitter content to scroll down.

Having a custom Profile page with a unique background image will set you apart from many other Twitter users and give you a chance to provide more information, like the URL of another Web site you want your followers to check out. At this point, backgrounds are static images without hyperlinks, but that can and will change at any time.

Keeping Posts with Links Under 140 Characters

While Twitter will shorten some links automatically, you can use one of two Web sites to create truncated versions of any hyperlinks to paste into your Twitter posts. TinyUrl.com is the oldest such site; you simply paste in the link and then copy its shortened version for reuse. There's nothing to join, and you can use the link anywhere.

A newer site with this feature is http://bit.ly, which has the added advantage of keeping track of your links once you've created a user ID on the site. You can also see the number of clicks on any of the hyperlinks you've shortened on bit.ly and, for those who want to track who has clicked on links and gather other statistics on the hyperlinks they've posted on Twitter and elsewhere, this is a site to explore.

Organizing with Seesmic Desktop

As your presence on a site like Twitter grows, the challenge becomes keeping up with what's going on, trimming the list of people you follow to maintain some focus on your goals and strategy, and prioritizing your time.

A popular tool among early adopters of Twitter is Seesmic Desktop, which installs on the Adobe Air platform (allowing you to run Web applications on a Mac or PC desktop). (For a listing of the many new apps that work with Twitter for organization and a myriad of other tasks, check out http://twitter.com/downloads and www.squidoo.com/twitterapps.) Seesmic Desktop creates a series of columns organizing your Twitter feed and, if desired, your status updates from Facebook. It's a versatile interface for seeing the entire picture from Twitter at once. Clicking on an avatar brings up a useful submenu that allows you to quickly follow or unfollow users or add them to a custom userlist. (See Figure 5.6.) Creating your own userlist on Seesmic Desktop is a good way to focus on specific groups of individuals and respond specifically to their updates. (See Figure 5.7.)

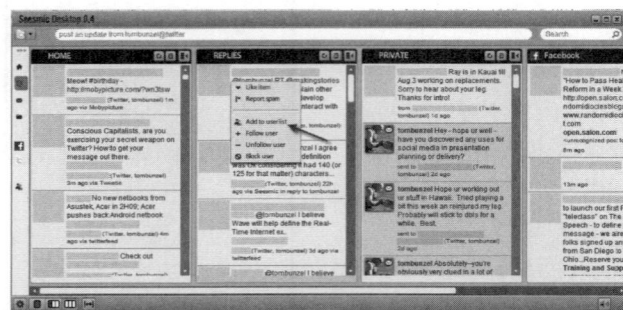

Figure 5.6 Seesmic Desktop lays out your Twitter or Facebook updates in a series of columns from which you can quickly respond, or follow or unfollow other users.

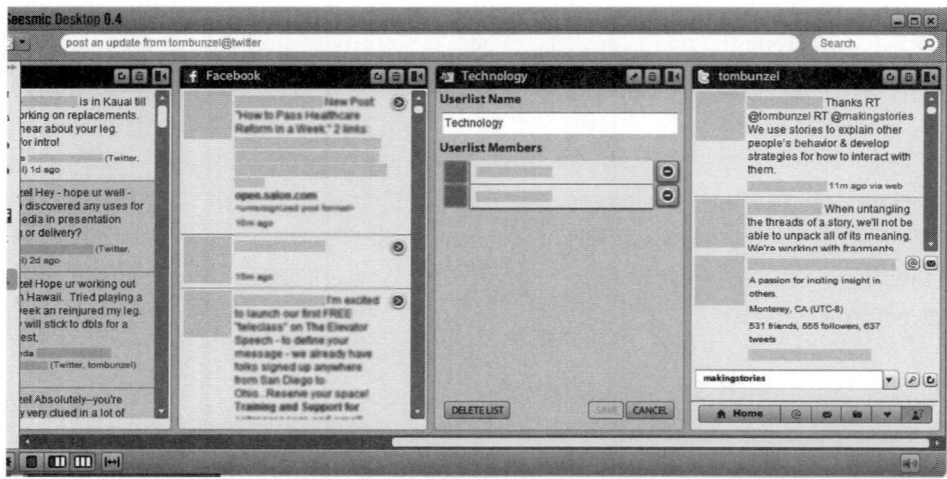

Figure 5.7 Naming a userlist and then adding appropriate people lets you pay attention to their specific concerns and respond quickly and effectively.

There are a growing number of third-party applications forming around Twitter, many for the purpose of organizing and responding methodically to tweets. Another popular tool is TweetDeck, which at the time of this writing is in beta but is in wide use, especially on the iPhone.

CREATING LISTS DIRECTLY IN TWITTER

While TweetDeck and Seesmic have gained popularity among Twitter power users, Twitter came out with its own List feature as this book was written. Users can view any of their lists (after they've been created) and create a new list in a panel called Lists in the right column.

When you click New List, a dialogue box opens to let you name and describe your list, and then click to Create it. Another box opens with a panel to add Twitter users to your new list and search for them, but the easiest way to add a follower to your list is to go to her Profile page and click the drop-down arrow for Lists; then select the list to which you want to add her as a follower. You can also click View All under the panel that shows all of your followers, and in the directory of your followers, you will find a List drop-down arrow to let you add any of your followers to a list you have created.

Giving Online Pictorial Stories with Whrrl

The major distinction between Twitter and Facebook has been the multimedia limitations of Twitter. Facebook shows previews of multimedia links like video from YouTube and has video applications; Twitter is currently supporting only links with URLs. However, the landscape is changing, and from a presentation perspective it's interesting to look at some of the options on Twitter for showing pictures and also video.

In most cases, Twitter users upload their images to hosting sites from digital cameras and PDAs, but more and more there is a crossover out of the consumer area and into business. For example, as users upload their images from a convention or event, interest in that event gradually builds, and more people may show up for that venue or plan on attending in the future. At a recent Comic-Con convention in San Diego, scores of attendees showed pictures of the event to those at home, letting them experience it vicariously or get in their cars and attend themselves. Many of these photos were uploaded into a storyboarding application called Whrrl (see Figure 5.8), which lets you add text and titles and put your pictures into a sequence for viewing online; these can be linked directly from Twitter or Facebook.

What's amazing is that just a few years ago something like this would have required perhaps a couple of hours in PowerPoint, and yet the sample story here took less than ten minutes and could be shared instantly. In addition, there is room for participating and commentary on each Whrrl story, so that a community can build around any event or presentation shown in this manner; if compelling enough, the effect could become viral. While there are none of the bells and whistles of the latest version of PowerPoint, the fact that photos can come

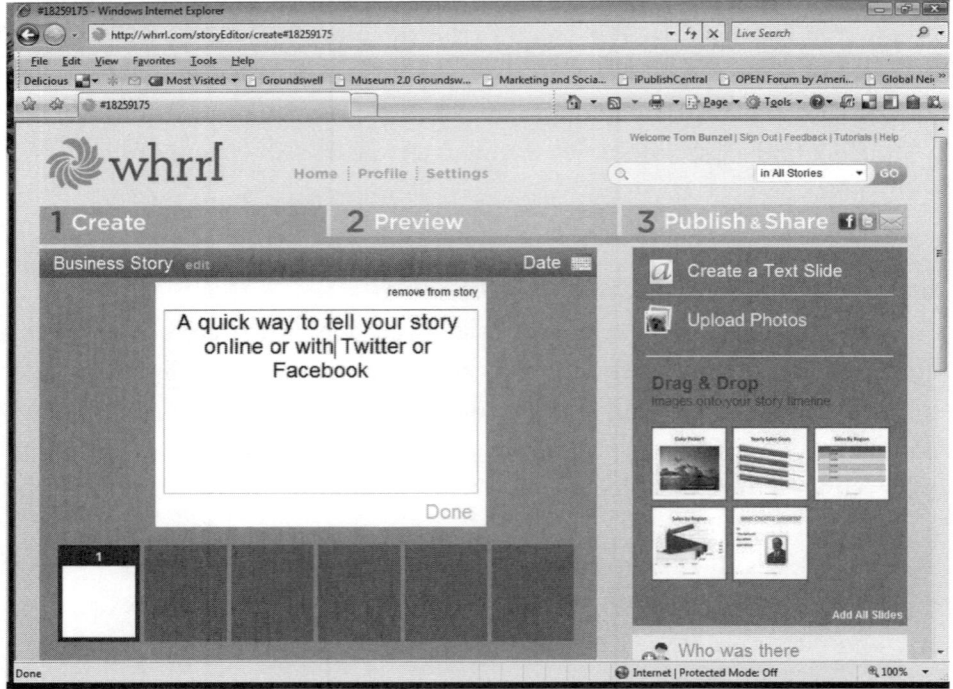

Figure 5.8 Whrrl creates a quick and easy slide show of uploaded pictures and text.

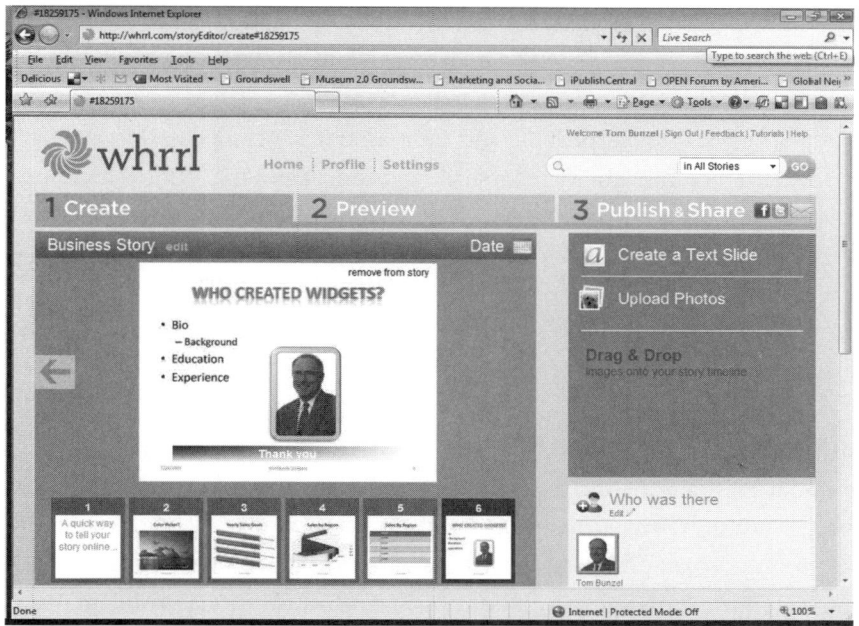

Figure 5.9 The user simply drags and drops the uploaded pictures and creates text slides to construct a story.

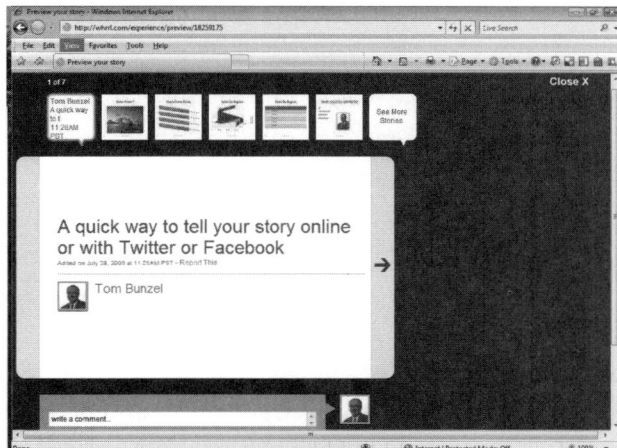

Figure 5.10 The final version is online with a Web link to post on Twitter, Facebook, or in any Web page or e-mail, along with a comment thread that can build viral interest.

from mobile devices and that you can construct a story in minutes puts the technology, which is free, into everyone's hands. (See Figures 5.9 and 5.10.)

Whrrl itself is an active online community, with the best stories featured on its home page to create even more interest. The combination of pictures and text in a storyboard sequence puts this Web technology on the cutting edge of modern communications. While it may not be slick and polished, it can reach anywhere and be seen by millions almost instantly, giving it power that could never have been contemplated just a few decades ago by a presenter with a carousel of slides. More important, and the reason it is included in this chapter, Whrrl is a true social tool in its ability to broaden your impact online. With Whrrl stories you dramatically expand your online profile and add depth to how others perceive you.

Whrrl has changed a bit for mobile social media users by connecting its stories to a specific location. Now, to begin a Whrrl story and upload photos, users "Add a Check-In" under their Profiles and let those with whom they're connected know where the story takes place.

Real World: Twitter Case Studies

The social media add-ons that work with Twitter are a key part of creating an identity online. As we've seen, the kinds of relationships that the new Internet fosters require trust, presence, and participation. With so many brands, ideas, concepts, and individuals vying for attention, a communications profile that is clearly defined and actively pursued is critical to success.

That said, exactly how does Twitter build relationships for businesses in the real world?

For one thing, a simple search for a brand on Twitter can yield surprising results for the purveyor of any product or service. The search results are far more potent than the information gained from any focus group or survey. A marketing manager will quickly see the real comments of users, for better or worse. A manufacturer or retail business can communicate quickly with those same users, and many more if the business can build a following and distribute information, specials, coupons, prizes, and invitations. As users join the thread, they will be instantly connected to others with similar interests and learn from one another about the product or services and its quirks and features.

One of the first major corporations to use social media was Dell Computers. It started by creating user communities to share technical know-how and solve problems. But the Dell Outlet division of the company also got on board, originally starting out with the broadcast model of distributing information. But the Outlet's followers weren't satisfied with coupons and specials; they wanted a two-way dialogue in which they could ask questions and interact with the Outlet staff. As its branded Twitter accounts grew to more than eighty in total (including @dellhomeoffers for system deals and @StefanieAtDell for customer service exchanges), the Dell Outlet booked more than $3 million in revenue as a result of its Twitter presence. Obviously a great deal of time and effort goes into monitoring and responding to messages, but as the community grew, the team found that a great deal of the energy was provided by the users among themselves, sharing experiences and giving advice.

A huge organizational benefit was the new awareness of the Outlet, which had previously been built with conventional e-mail marketing and various search engine efforts. Now the word spread virally as the Dell Outlet realized that reaching out to its customer base could yield amazing dividends in brand loyalty and recognition.

For internal training at Dell, and its outreach to other corporate customers, the information gleaned from these social media initiatives is invaluable, providing real-world experience and expertise in areas that many trained tech support and IT professionals might never have looked.

The experience of JetBlue Airlines on Twitter exemplifies how a company can use instant communications to build customer loyalty. When Morgan Johnston, JetBlue's manager of corporate communications, started using Twitter Search, he got an eyeful of how passengers were being treated and felt about their travel experience.

JetBlue opted for starting slowly on Twitter after Johnston got support from management and soon found that using a conversational tone with users and helping them with their customer service issues began to generate many replies and more and more followers. Johnston realized that directly asking the community about specific issues, like new travel routes, built a buzz because travelers had a new experience—an airline showing a sincere interest in their opinions and ideas. Travelers wanted a voice in how the airline treated them and conducted its business, and that translated into more bookings and loyalty.

As he discovered how many travelers stay in touch with mobile devices while travelling, Johnston used the Twitter account to stay connected when JetBlue's schedules were affected, making sure that his customers remained informed and in many cases keeping them calm.

Johnston currently needs a staff to manage the JetBlue account. In addition to those who work for him, professionals in other departments provide their expertise to address specific concerns that come up on Twitter threads by raising the significant question: "How are we doing?"

A great example of how the personal aspect of human interaction can expand horizons in the social media world and open new channels of communication happened with an Australian boutique winery, Teusner. Dave Brookes, who comprises Teusner's sales and marketing department, happens to be a big fan of cycling, and when he began to follow Lance Armstrong on Twitter, he realized the potential for raising awareness about Teusner.

After searching for other companies with a Twitter presence, he saw that Starbucks was building relationships with customers based on their interest in coffee. Brookes decided that the same principle would work with wine. Like Starbucks, Teusner concentrated on building recognition and relationships instead of sales, by talking about something the customers were passionate about: their vintage. Brookes, in fact, specifically adopts an informal tone with Twitter users and avoids any aspect of sales in his communications, because that it is what he finds builds trust—a key component of Teusner's communications profile via Twitter.

Like Dell Outlet, Teusner has found that the community that has grown around its wine has grown through customer to customer interaction. When a particular vintage (Riebke Shiraz) captured users' attention, it became a hot topic on Twitter, raising awareness among customers and also giving Brookes key insights into their tastes and desires.

Shipping restrictions prohibit Teusner to sell to individuals outside Australia, but Teusner connects with Twitter to its distributors, including @JugShop in San Francisco and @JustinELiddle in Great Britain. Reviews of wines are posted regularly, along with invitations to special events including tastings and dinners that feature Teusner wines. Even without the ability to sell directly to individuals, Teusner has seen its direct contact with those who appreciate its wines result in increased traffic to its Web site and on its tours of the winery.

In San Francisco, a media company was competing with other broadcasters in the political arena. To set themselves apart, Current Media created a Twitter application, using Flash, that would show voters' responses to the debates on a separate feed as the events were broadcast. The application used two levels of filtering: the first to locate debate-related items and vet the posts for inappropriate language or copyright infringement; the second level went through the content selecting the best posts to show on the air. As a result, Current learned a great deal about the role of real-time social media in the new Internet communications world, and the firm received more attention than many of its rivals because it pushed the envelope on traditional broadcasts.

Etsy, an online marketplace specializing in handmade items, at first made the common mistake of using Twitter just to send feeds from its blog, the Storque. When Anda Corrie (who manages @Etsy on Twitter) decided to "just have fun" with the feeds, her followers began to actively discuss creative products on the site, share tips and tricks, and tell one another about important events and promotions. The coolest items on the site are frequently retweeted by the Etsy followers, resulting in greater sales and awareness of those selling on the site. Everyone wins. The key question is always "What's happening?"; but specific queries can ask, "How are we doing?"

Like JetBlue, Corrie made one key discovery on Twitter: the importance of asking *a significant question* that results in a stream of replies from followers who are intrigued and stimulated to respond. On Etsy it could be something like "Which handmade items sell best, and why?"

What these examples share is the realization of the human and informal nature of the social media world. Press releases don't work. Substantive responses and a sincere interest in the opinions and ideas of the followers provide valuable information for training and customer service and build traffic, awareness, and sales—all of the goals that have always driven communications for any organization—but instead of struggling to find an audience, social media can help a company build one naturally.

Twitter is the best current example of this important trend. Whatever the tool or medium of choice, the basics remain the same: Don't sell; build relationships; nurture trust; and build your communications profile effectively over time.[2]

POSTING TO TWITTER WITH SMS

SMS is the standard protocol for text messaging; you can use it to update your Twitter stream.

1. Go to http://twitter.com/devices (you'll need to log in).
2. Add your phone number in the form provided.
3. Follow the instructions provided to verify your phone.

Once your phone is verified, you send updates via SMS by sending your 140-character message to Twitter's SMS number.

> - If you're in the United States, send to 40404.
> - If you're in Canada, send to 21212.
> - If you're in India, send to 5566511.
> - If you're not in any of the three listed, send to the United Kingdom long code +447624801423.
>
> Note: Depending on your cellular plan rate, you may be charged for sending these messages.

Twitter as a New Paradigm: The Real-Time Internet?

Jeff Pulver, the force behind the 140conf (the name is based on the 140-character limit of tweets), a fast-growing conference of Twitter evangelists and cognoscenti (or what he calls "characters") around the world, takes the Twitter "speed dating" analogy a step further.

When asked about how Twitter contributes and informs the content of conventional presentations and other forms of communications, Pulver was very direct in his statement that Twitter represents a complete shift into real-time communications. He doesn't see Twitter as a means to an end—more effective communication in another medium—but rather as the basis for modern communication: a continuing conversation on topics of interest and concern by a community of users. For Pulver, Twitter's real-time power originally concentrated on the fields of politics, media and entertainment (celebrity), and advertising, but he has now branched out to look at Twitter as a platform for organizations that see the new wave of communications taking place entirely in "The State of NOW."

For example, the time and effort of a political campaign's strategic planning and presentation as a webinar or in a conference room would partially be shifted to real-time communications with its operatives and supporters using a microblogging tool like Twitter. (Pulver doesn't like the term "microblogging," since with any blog there is theoretically a delay between the post and the response; he is dedicated to a continuous flow of "now" information.) Instead of using charts and graphs to strategize, the political pros are in real-time communication with the troops on the ground, perhaps getting feedback as the people in the field go door to door canvassing and tweet back what they're hearing from voters. Messages would be shaped with blazing speed as this information flows in and gets analyzed; the next wave of campaign staff goes out and gathers and responds to more real-time information, resulting in a continuous two-way communication with the public—like an endless exit poll. The very nature of polling will likely change. Using tools like Twitter, campaign staff can gather and respond to qualitative information, and statistical polls will become more powerful than ever, compiled and analyzed in real time.

How would this work in more conventional organizations, for example, in the case of training?

While some preparatory presentations or classes would still be a key part of the process, there would be an ongoing dialogue between trainers and students and even among students themselves as they master new technologies, sales techniques, customer service concepts, and so on. The organization of this information will be critical to the effectiveness of such scenarios.

You may recall that a hashtag is the # sign followed by a keyword that, on Twitter, brings up a thread on that topic. For example, the Twitter hashtag, #gastax, would bring up a thread of all Twitter users interested in the topic of governments taxes on gasoline who add those characters to their posts, creating an instant conversation on that topic. A topic like this could become "trending," generating critical mass or viral momentum on Twitter, appearing on every user's screen and prompting many more people to focus on this issue and contribute.

This is how Twitter originally exploded; trending topics like earthquakes and Michael Jackson's death outpaced the response time of conventional media outlets. Print media became almost insignificant in this onslaught of instant information, and only those news organizations with substantial resources could keep pace with the flow of information that became available instantly online from Twitter users. Of course, there is always the issue of how useful or relevant the information in such an avalanche really is. Pulver considers this medium to be in its infancy; particularly in the area of real news and public information, trust becomes the balancing component. But in the organizational space, one or two key experts in a field could monitor one or more real-time threads on topics of interest among their students or colleagues, contributing or guiding where necessary but letting the participants help one another to the greatest extent possible.

Making the Most of Twitter

Zach Braiker, CEO of Refine and Focus (www.refineandfocus.com), a digital media agency, lists "developing a collaboration with colleagues around the world, having access to cutting edge ideas and thinking, and participating in real conversations with prospects and current customers" as the key benefits of tools like Twitter. He also cautions that it is not a way to cut costs for marketing, training, or other communications efforts, because it still requires a commitment to participate meaningfully and provide significant content and feedback in whatever medium you choose.

Braiker uses Trish Karter, the CEO of Dancing Deer Baking Company, as an example of how to use social media effectively. She leveraged her passion for addressing the issue of family homelessness by riding her bike 1,500 miles. Braiker and his team helped Karter implement a social media campaign that encompassed YouTube (video), Twitter (@dancingdeer), Facebook, and an active corporate blog. In comparison to more conventional communication efforts—for example, a presentation by Dancing Deer to potential retailers—it is interesting to now consider the way such a campaign might be leveraged:

- Humanizing the company to those in the audience
- Providing anecdotes, stories, analogies, and metaphors for a session that would set the brand apart from competitors
- Creating content (collateral, video, testimonials, and so on) for a presentation or webinar
- Presenting real-world feedback from customers, clients, and colleagues about the attributes of Karter's products

On a more subtle level, it is likely that the connections Karter created through her social media efforts would have led to meetings and conferences that she might schedule as follow-ups.

It's important to consider that this is not a blatantly manipulative approach but rather a natural outgrowth of Karter's human concerns—her real passion for a subject that forms the basis for others to connect with her, and by extension, with her company. It's quite likely that Karter's connections with her colleagues, vendors, and staff are enhanced through her social media presence; she doubtless has an identity as a caring passionate human being rather than simply a faceless presence in the corporate suite.

Braiker reiterates what others have suggested: simply having a goal to increase Twitter followers or increase the depth and quality of the exchanges with existing connections is fine, but you need to have a clear set of objectives for the campaign as a whole, so that all participants on behalf of the organization run in parallel and not in opposition to the message. Braiker has other tips for Twitter that apply to any social network or medium through which you establish a profile and then create a communications identity:

- Photos are vital to personalize the communicator, and pictures of people (rather than logos or cute avatars) attract more quality and quantity of attention.
- Choosing a username for your entity or yourself is worth some thought. Beyond attracting responses through a search engine, it should reflect your taste, interest, and overall purpose. Keep in mind that you can test more than one username in a limited run to see how each performs.
- The critical aspect to success, according to Braiker, is a distinct point of view. Successful tweets are different from "I had a great breakfast." If you share links, Braiker suggests, make sure you venture an opinion on the topic that stimulates interest and commentary.
- Probably most important, Braiker accentuates that sustaining an account while you "continue to add value to the conversation" is what separates successful campaigns from those that falter. Again, it requires a commitment of time and energy and won't pay dividends overnight. Braiker also stresses the real-time aspect of Twitter as a conversational tool, but of course most conversations develop over time as trust and areas of mutual interest become apparent—and each side *listens* to the other.

Asking questions and soliciting opinions and then acting upon the information creates a level of trust that heightens the energy in any social media campaign.[3]

THE NING SOCIAL NETWORK: A COMMUNICATIONS PETRI DISH

There are any number of consultants and programmers whom you can call on to create a custom social network, but Ning is a community of separate social networks that tests what flies and what crashes in the social media space. (If you are an enterprise and your main concern is marketing and interacting with customers, you might consider the custom social networks that are created expressly for this purpose by Communispace.com.)

When you go to www.ning.com, before you sign in, create a network of your own, or do anything, you can review a preview of popular networks. What is fascinating about social networks like those on Ning is that they combine the traditional media of conventional communications—text, images, video, and audio—with the interactive energy of community, so that just as a petri dish organically nurtures a culture of bacteria, you can grow a network of your own into a successful online culture or learn from your mistakes.

You can use a social network for many purposes. Here are just a few examples and features that might be of importance or benefit to the organization sponsoring the network and of course to its members:

- Business (External-Marketing): Outreach (photos, videos), events, forum, blog
- Business (Internal-Support/Training): Videos (instruction, motivation), forum, events, chat, blog
- Special event: Music, videos, pictures (excitement), events (news), members (attendance), forum
- Special interest group: Members (community), events (news), forum (connection)
- Sports or other team: Videos (instruction), pictures and members (motivation), events (news), forum (connection with community, coach, parents, sponsors)
- Education (Class or Topic): Events (news, deadlines), forum (instruction), videos (instruction, motivation)
- Civics/Government: Events (outreach), videos and pictures, forum (communication), textbox (news)

Everyone also stays informed through e-mail, updates, comments, and the latest activity areas at the center of just about every social network. In addition, Ning's video, picture, and music players allow members to play them outside of their Web browsers to keep them connected to their favorite social networks.

With Ning, all networks exist under the universal www.ning.com URL but can be accessed directly through their own addresses; for example, www.newnetwork.ning.com. Within this private social network there is great versatility in customization of the user interface, page design, and feature set, along with the implementation of various modules (similar to creating a blog) to create a unique social network for virtually any purpose—from complex support and training to promoting an entertainer or movie.

Ning has enabled users to build a multitude of new social networks by dragging and dropping features into a grid and then letting the entity grow organically. There is an excellent searchable Help database available on Ning, and new network creators, in particular, can find additional information on the Ning Network Creators Blog.[4]

A Ning network creator can take advantage of Premium services when a network has reached critical mass; that is, when it has achieved a membership of significant size to be attractive to an advertiser or sponsor. For example, if you have a social network with thousands of skateboarding enthusiasts, you could probably attract sponsors of boards, sports clothes, and other gear, like pads and helmets. You can use a Ning network to try out an idea for a more complex social network application and then let a programmer review the setup before committing to building an application.

As you create your own network, you begin to realize that administering and using a social network in an area that you care about is addictive for the creator, administrator, and the members and various groups. You keep getting inspired by other members, learning new things, and making friends and connections as you exchange ideas and information.

Ning has since eliminated its free networks in favor of a three-tiered pricing system, but the basic features of a dedicated private network are still available at a nominal cost on Ning, and other aspects of using a targeted social network can be learned by trying out Ning networks.

Planning Your Network

While it's okay to just wing it with Ning, it's better to plan your network out first. For example, what's the purpose of the network? Is it for business, for your internal use, for exchanging information and promoting a service or product with clients or customers, or a combination? Which Ning features are the most important for you to use and emphasize? And what will it take to implement them? To help you plan your social network, the following features are available. They can go into the left column of the Main Ning window (see Figure 5.11), on the main menu, or both.

Default Features (Standard in Layout)

Description   Activity

Members   Photos

Videos   Forum

Additional Features (with Drag and Drop)

Events

Groups

Blog

Chat

Music

Notes

Text Box

RSS

Get Badges

Birthdays

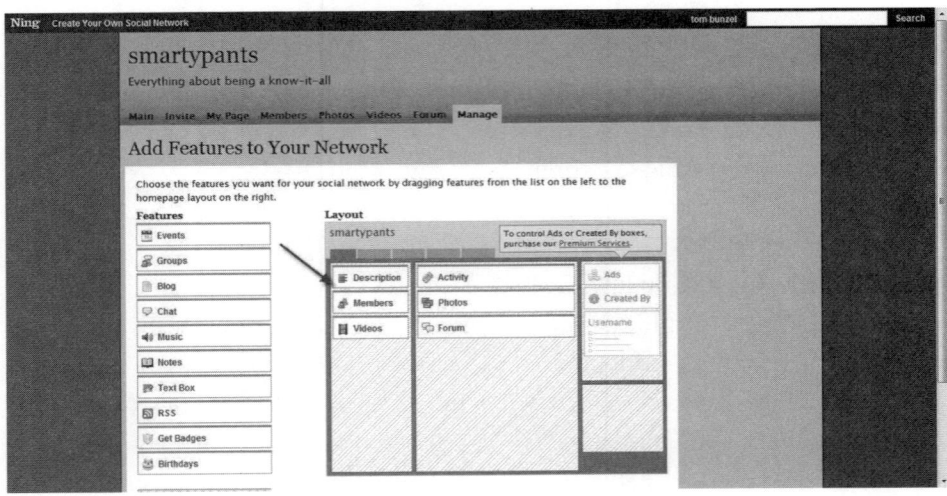

Figure 5.11 The configuration chosen in the layout is reflected in the Main Page that you see on your Ning social network.

The organization panel lets you configure your network once it's launched. You can use Add Features area (under Manage, see Figure 5.12) to make changes to these features and the look of the network. Only an administrator (or other member with administrator privileges) can make these changes. (If enabled by the administrator, members can alter the appearance of their own personal profile pages.) You can change the layout by dragging and dropping features into and out of the placeholders in the Layout grid. The process is similar to the Layout in Blogger (refer to Figure 4.32) with a "palette" of features from which you can drag and drop.

For starters, the four features that you might concentrate on when planning your network would be Members (public or private and respective privileges), Activity (how much you will want to show), Groups (you may want to organize your members), and Forum (probably the most important area for interaction—which topics do you want to begin with and/or showcase)?

As you begin to construct the interface, you'll use the Manage window as your control panel. (See Figure 5.12.)

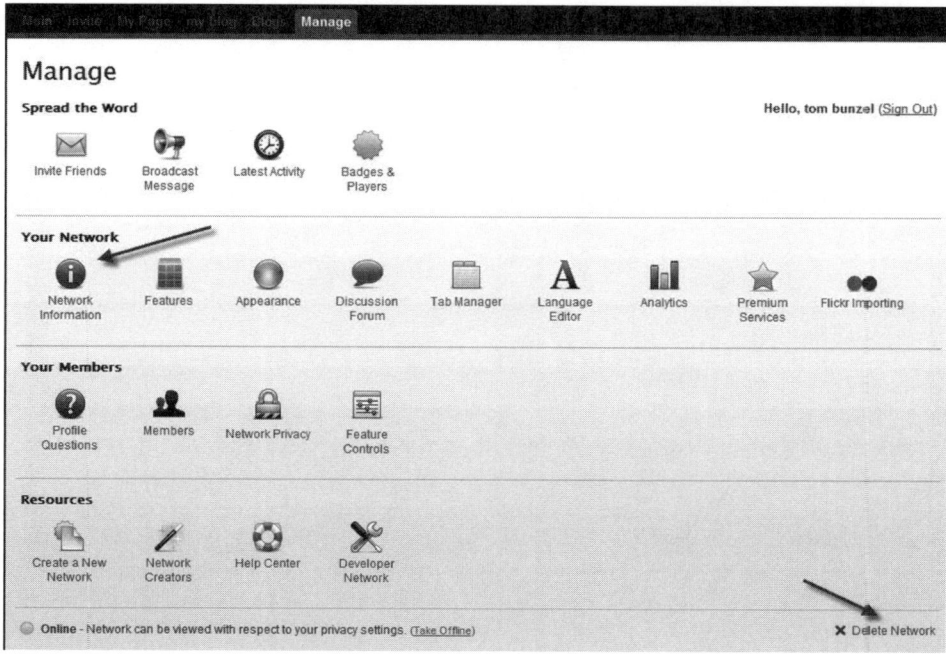

Figure 5.12 In the Manage window of your Ning network, you can open option windows for Network Information, Features, Appearance, and Tab Manager.

In Network Information, you can enter a short description (which can include search engine keywords) along with a separate list of keywords that will serve as meta-tags for the network page. Tab Manager is similar to the Features window (Figure 5.11), but it adds navigation tabs to the top of the network window.

Ultimately you can launch a social network with your own custom banner and use the features delineated here to create a community of like interest for your users. You will want to begin by adding some exciting content in the form of videos, audio, and pictures and then populate your blogs and forums. (See Figure 5.13.)

Some of the content, in typical "cloud" fashion, can be hosted on sites like YouTube (video) and Flickr (images). Both are covered in more detail in Chapter Six.

Figure 5.13 Your new social network's Main Page can be configured with all of the features of popular social networks like Facebook, but it is entirely branded to you, with your own Web address, keywords, banner, and network information.

MAKING A CUSTOM BANNER FOR A NING NETWORK

In your image editing program, save the banner with a 955-pixel width and a height between 150 and 200 pixels. A height of 150 pixels lets the tagline remain visible and leaves plenty of room for the tabs at the top of the window with the theme colors you selected working fine. If you want to create a banner from a large image, set your Marquee selection size (in PhotoShop or any similar program) for the banner size (955 × 150), click to select in the image, and then crop to the desired size. Then add your text on top of the banner, and merge/flatten the image into a JPG file.

If the banner goes all the way to the bottom of the header (200 pixels in height), the tab colors will need to be coordinated with the colors at the bottom of the banner image, by choosing a theme where the tab colors have enough contrast with the theme color to be visible. When you're done, you're ready to add your banner to the Appearance window accessible from Manage.

You may need to add a logo to keep the tagline from interfering with the banner itself. If you don't want to use an actual logo, because the banner is sufficient, create a blank transparent PNG file and upload it as a fake logo to move the tagline down.

Inviting, Welcoming, and Communicating with Members

Once you've created your Ning network with a suitable Main Page, configured the various components where you think they will work best, and made some decisions as to how members can use your network and which permissions they have been granted, it's time to let the world know.

You can invite new members directly from within the network's Invite page in the Manage window (Figure 5.12) and either import e-mail addresses from Yahoo, Hotmail, gmail, or AOL or invite members individually. You can also click Invite Members from the Welcome box on the Main Page (Figure 5.13). If you want to invite members through a desktop e-mail program like Outlook, go into the Network Privacy Page from Manage and copy the URL for your social network to the clipboard. After a new member joins, she sees the social network from her own vantage point and her own main page view and, with administrator permission, can customize her profile page.

Successful Ning networks have active administrators and moderators who welcome new members and respond to comments, discussions, and blogs frequently and promptly. Even on corporate networks or other networks created for formal communications, acknowledging personal events like birthdays or other celebrations is significant, and the administrator, moderator, or staff should regularly take advantage of comments in all of the network windows and explore member profiles to generate interest and learn more about members. Anyone can leave a comment calling attention to their opinion with text, hyperlinks, and images on any photo, video, or blog post on your network or on any member's profile page. Just as you have with blogs and other social sites, you should get in the habit of replying to forum posts and commenting on as much content as you can, and encourage your members to do the same.

A successful Ning or other social network will grow organically as other members get excited and invite more people, but it takes a commitment to staying the course. Successful networks incorporate powerful visual messages, which is the subject of the next chapter.

QUESTIONS TO PONDER

1. Do you have a Web presence (blog, Web page, or other information or educational page) that would benefit from your participation in discussions on Twitter? What sorts of insight could you contribute, based on your expertise, that would build a Twitter following?

2. Are colleagues and associates in your field already using Twitter? (Have you searched?) Are they adding significant value? How might your unique personal and professional experiences add value to others who could benefit from the information you share?

3. Have you investigated Ning and searched for existing communities within your area of interest or expertise? How vibrant and effective are these communities? How might your own field benefit from a community of shared ideas and visual content on a Ning network or similar network created within your company, institution, or organization?

Notes

1. www.humanresourcesonline.net/news/12816.
2. http://business.twitter.com.
3. Vince Thompson, *Social Media Tips for Business—10 Smart Ones for Twitter*, www.smartplanet.com/people/blog/pure-genius/10-smart-twitter-tips-for-businesses-and-social-media/280/ or http://bit.ly/1BviDO.
4. http://blog.ning.com/2009/04/new-network-creator-announcements.html.

Crafting a Visual Message

chapter
SIX

As we explore the rising impact and significance of social media in the world of organizational communications, it is now time to examine how to implement tools and technology that can influence audiences and individuals and most effectively deliver the messages we need to convey.

Clearly social media can help us with research, preparation, and reaching an audience. According to a Reuters blog in early August 2009, among Fortune 100 companies, 54 percent were using Twitter regularly, 32 percent were blogging, and 29 percent had a fan-focused Facebook presence.[1] The influence of social media and the presence of communities of like interest are spreading out into training, marketing, human resources, motivation, and all areas of organizational communications.

But what sort of communication is possible in 140 characters? An ongoing dialogue with customers, clients, or coworkers is energizing and informative, but in most tweets of substance, there is a hyperlink or reference to some other content. A substantive blog piece—even with stimulating commentary and a place in a vibrant social community—is still largely limited in its ability to truly educate, inform, persuade, inspire, or sell.

For all of their power, blogs are primarily text with images (or sometimes embedded video), and in the organizational space they serve mainly to introduce or supplement a carefully researched, structured, and delivered presentation. The tools we cover next can create graphics and video messages that greatly strengthen the impact of a social media initiative.

Successful presentations have always appealed to our emotions as well as our intellects. The most memorable presentations hit home viscerally and tell stories, and they frequently do so with multimedia—images and audio blended together.

Some of the most dynamic presenters and storytellers today can be found on the TED Web site (www.ted.com). TED hosts conferences of the world's greatest thinkers, attended by members who seek to learn and interact at considerable cost; its Web site has a catalog of the presentations delivered by the thought leaders in science, technology, philosophy, business, and other disciplines. The TED Web site allows anyone to join and interact through evolving social media tools, like blogs and comments (as of this writing, no Twitter or Facebook). The TED presentations are lectures by luminaries or authorities that convey the expertise of the presenters with ground-breaking concepts. Most TED presentations also feature extraordinary visuals in digital format and are projected on multiple screens from—what else?—PowerPoint.

It is interesting to speculate to what extent the talks are informed by the participants' use of social media. In many cases the subject matter was probably shaped and influenced by the speakers' ability to interact through their own blogs and online networks with colleagues, students, and the subjects of their research, all of whom now comprise the greater TED community. (Because of the stature and authority of these presenters, there has not yet been a significant backchannel to distract from their presentations.)

After the presentations are given, users can view and comment on them on TED.com; the presentations are frequently referenced with embedded links in other locations on the Web.

Whether in science, philosophy, or other fields, masterful TED presenters use their slides sparingly but effectively, invariably amplifying and explaining key points with visuals whose impact resides in their furtherance of a narrative or a story. The videos of the presentations, along with the visuals and graphics, continue to reach wider audiences when hosted on the TED Web site and distributed on sites like YouTube.

The point here is that in a setting where deep meaning resonates and there is a need for complexity, social media may facilitate internal communication (on the TED Web site), but there is still a need for a well-crafted message supplemented by effective visuals.

SCENARIO: USING SOCIAL MEDIA TO CRAFT A MESSAGE

Karen Engle was on the bubble. As training director for PharmaFriend, her task was to make sure that the company's pharmacists performed their tasks to the satisfaction of customers. But Karen's concerns were not just about customers. PharmaFriend's pharmacists were working in facilities under other companies' brands. Many of PharmaFriend's pharmacies were in large supermarkets or big box stores, and one of its biggest clients, Mel's Grocers, had implemented a new computer system. Many of Karen's employees were scrambling to learn the new system's complexities while still addressing customer needs.

Mel's Grocers had a Twitter account and a Facebook fan page, and "Mel" wrote a weekly blog about specials in the stores and tips on how to eat healthy on a budget. But suddenly, all of Mel's accounts were buzzing with complaints about the PharmaFriend installations and how slow and unresponsive their service had become.

> "Getting my pain meds is a bigger pain than what they are for."
>
> "Reboot PharmaFriend. Staff is clueless on how to serve customers."
>
> "Checked my blood pressure after going to the pharmacy. Through the roof."

These were the kinds of tweets and comments on Mel's blog that the client was receiving and passing on to the CEO of PharmaFriend, who relayed them to Karen. Clearly she needed to take drastic steps to retrain her staff. She had worked with the software provider of the new computer system to create a comprehensive training program for her staff, but her employees would need time to master the new system. The system was very complicated and required an interface with credit card readers and a centralized Web site.

First Karen tried a bit of crowdsourcing. She used PharmaFriend's internal social network and wrote a blog in which she described what was going on: that the pharmacists in the stores were being blamed for the complications caused by the new software. In the blog, Karen requested that anyone on the staff submit her own tips and ideas for streamlining the use of the new software, and she provided a Twitter account through which the employees could tweet immediately when they had a negative experience to report, and particularly if they had a solution. Bonuses were promised for the most effective responses.

In her next blog Karen began a push to reinvigorate the "brand" of her staff in Mel's Grocery stores. The title of the blog was "We're Pharma*Friend*, Not a Computer Company." In the piece she acknowledged the frustration of her employees with the new computer software and empathized with the stress of handling its complexity *and* serve customers in a warm and friendly way. She made it a point in the blog to show that she had listened not only to the customer complaints but also to the feedback from the staff and spent an hour a day responding to comments and taking notes on her blog activity.

At the same time she had gotten busy using the customer complaints in an internal campaign that she rushed through PharmaFriend's advertising agency. The agency created a series of short videos that focused on the customer's experience purely from the perspective of the person seeking to pick up medication. In each video, a customer described his ailment and the medication required, and then a simulation was created that showed two experiences: one in which the pharmacist allowed his or her frustration with the technology to divert attention from the customer; the other in which the pharmacist smiled, listened to the customer, and then did his or her best to manage the computer system and provide the prescriptions.

Harnessing the Power of Hosted Video

The ad agency was charged to emphasize warmth, compassion, and humor in the first set of videos, which were played on the PharmaFriend Web site and then uploaded to YouTube. Mel embedded the videos into his blog for the grocery chain in response to the complaints the company had received; the videos were funny and helpful enough that they started getting hits on YouTube as well. Each video *emphasized that the pharmacists were empathetic and listening to the problems of customers* and *apologized for the issues that had come up*. The videos began to get traction on the channel created on YouTube for Mel's Grocers, where Karen again interacted with those making comments and had key influencers promote the videos on Twitter and Facebook.

One video became so popular that it was shown nationally on CNN and resulted in additional traffic for the pharmacies, and it raised the visibility of Mel's Grocers as well. In the videos a new character was introduced, a "pharmacilitator" who kept his or her eye on the waiting time and length of lines in the store and interacted with customers who were waiting if delays got too long. In the videos, talented actors were hired for the roles, but Karen hired and trained a set of pharmacilitators for the worst stores and used a computer program to note the worst incidents and send new customer service specialists to the right store at the right time.

As a result, PharmaFriend was able to bridge the adjustment period it needed for its staff to master the software and retain customer loyalty at their stores. Mel was so pleased with the positive effect of the YouTube video campaign on the stores that he paid for more videos to be produced, using some of the same techniques to enhance responsiveness in his stores' other departments.

THE POWER OF YOUTUBE

Indispensable to Karen's solution were the use of YouTube as a video hosting service for the spots created by the ad agency and the ability of the various members of her team, and Mel, the head of the grocery chain, to easily reference the files in blogs and other Web pages, respond to comments, and keep the energy flowing on Twitter, Facebook, and other social sites. The content within the videos was critically important, and Karen was smart to hire a talented creative team to produce effective video clips in response to the research she had done.

Once the videos were shot, fast and easy distribution was critical to handle any technical issues involved and to ensure that playback worked seamlessly. While Karen could have put the videos on PharmaFriend's network using a video streaming service, she didn't want to hassle with the IT department and a lot of technology. Instead she created a channel for PharmaFriend on YouTube and began posting the videos. The key advantage of using the video in a YouTube channel was that the files could be easily embedded in other Web pages; they would still play from YouTube, but, like PharmaFriend's stores, they would seem like they were playing in other Web sites. This made the video easy to play everywhere, not just by PharmaFriend but by the visitors to YouTube who found and enjoyed the video and decided to share it.

When a YouTube video is uploaded to the site, it is automatically converted into a Flash format that makes playback almost universal. In addition, a unique snippet of code is generated for a standard Web URL (or address) and to embed the file at a certain screen dimension. (See Figure 6.1.)

What is helpful about blogging tools like Blogger—which we covered in Chapter Four—is that when you compose a new post, that there is a separate tab for HTML (hypertext markup language). By selecting and then copying and pasting the HTML code from an Embed field in a video hosting service like YouTube into the Edit HTML panel (not in Compose), the video's first frame will appear in the Web page, and the video can play through the Web page from YouTube without

Figure 6.1 Videos hosted on YouTube feature snippets of code that let the user embed the videos in any Web page.

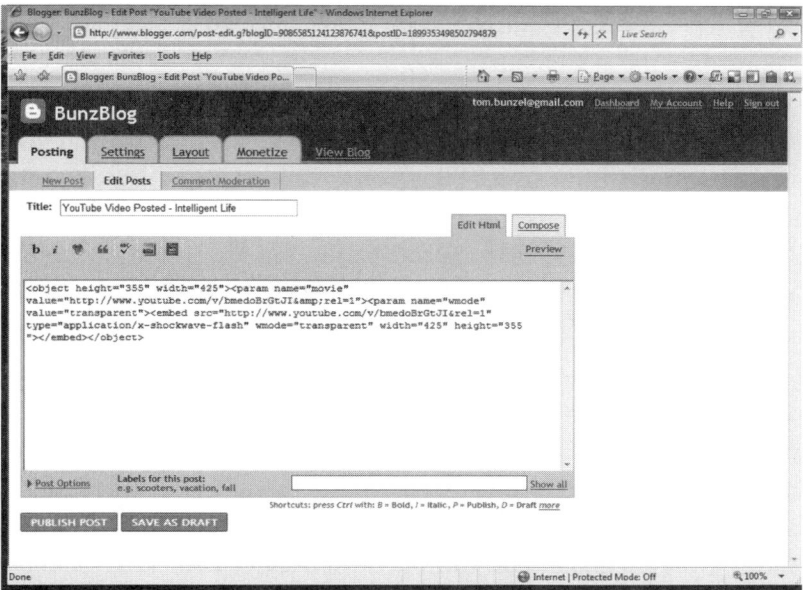

Figure 6.2 Copying and pasting the embed code from YouTube into the HTML tab of a blogging tool will make it appear in the Web page.

any further coding or linking. (See Figures 6.2 and 6.3.)

In addition to embedding the code in a Web page, you can distribute the URL of the video by e-mail or post it online, directing users to the YouTube channel or page of the organization posting the content.

YouTube has many elements of social media, including comments and search capability. When posting a video, if you want it to get as much recognition and attention as possible, you should plan to put keywords in both the video description panel (visible as you upload the

Figure 6.3 The user can play the referenced video from directly within the Web page in the dimensions that the embed code generates in a Web browser.

file) and the Tags area. For example, when PharmaFriend posted its video series on YouTube, someone at CNN may have picked it up in the business section in a search on customer service or even drug companies. But video on YouTube doesn't need a major media outlet to go viral; as described in Chapter Two, an unknown musician who wrote a funny song about having his guitar destroyed by an airline captured the hearts of millions and got airtime for his video and his music.

While YouTube can be the primary focal point for a communications strategy built around video—one can also blog on YouTube, create RSS (subscription) feeds, and more—some of these methodologies or strategies may require the services of a developer who uses the API (application program interface) to program YouTube channels and customize them.

But the real power of YouTube is its simplicity and the popularity of the site itself. Millions of users watch comedy and music videos on YouTube each day; if you can create compelling content, someone may find your video using a simple search and enjoy it enough to post the link on Twitter or Facebook. (A note about Facebook: Facebook has its own video capability. You can upload video directly to a Facebook page, a fan site, or group or use the Embed feature to put a thumbnail of video hosted on YouTube into a status update on Facebook in the same way that you might with a blog entry.)

There was a time when videos like those produced by PharmaFriend would play only in a computer media player or perhaps in PowerPoint when projected to an audience at a single event. Their impact and effectiveness would be severely restricted by geography and logistics. Perhaps Karen might have distributed her series of videos on DVD, but even this medium would have limited the ways in which her staff could watch it, and the general public would probably never see the content. Burning and distributing a DVD is much less efficient in terms of logistics and expense than simply posting content on a site like YouTube. When hosted on a site like YouTube, the content can play back in any blog or Web page under the banner of any entity or organization that wants to redistribute the information and communicate its message, internally or externally.

CREATING POWERFUL VISUALS: POWERPOINT

Shooting a professional video is not always feasible; it may be beyond the technical or economic means of many small businesses and entrepreneurs. But the use of digital slides and computer graphics has evolved at an incredible pace. Programs like PowerPoint and Keynote on the Mac can combine the power of still images, animation "builds" and transitions, and video to create a powerful communications medium. You need look no further than Al Gore's *An Inconvenient Truth* movie to get a sense of the power of these tools to inform and persuade a mass audience and deliver a message as effectively.

SCENARIO: BUILDING A REPUTATION WITH EDUCATION

Strategic Communications was a professional graphics firm that specialized in presentations. They were hired by Premiere Pharmaceuticals in its campaign to educate psychiatrists about its latest product, NeuroPath, used for the treatment of Alzheimer's disease.

Premiere Pharmaceuticals had held educational meetings around the country, along with hosting webinars online, to inform the medical community about the efficacy of NeuroPath. Along with these programs, the company created a social network on its Web site through which leaders in the fields of neuroscience and psychiatry contributed to blogs; the site also reached out to families with Alzheimer's patients for their feedback and ideas.

Dr. Stanley Conklin, the head of Neuroscientific Studies at the state university, was engaged by Premiere as a speaker to host its seminars throughout the Midwest. The company offered Stanley a laptop and portable projector to take on his speeches to present information about NeuroPath to hospitals and clinics.

But there were a number of problems with Stanley's participation in the project. First, he refused the offer of the free projector and laptop because he wanted to remain completely independent of Premiere Pharmaceuticals. He had his own laptop and would contract for audio-visual services at the locales where he spoke. More important, he wanted to provide the seminars as part of the Conklin Neuroscience Group and not under Premiere Pharmaceuticals' banner. He had his own ideas about how to treat Alzheimer's; the administering of NeuroPath was just one aspect. Stanley was a strong believer in "talk and touch therapy" as well as the strategic involvement of the patient's family, friends, and a support network inside and outside of a hospital or care center. Finally, although Stanley was a fine speaker, he still used 35mm slides to present technical information and was just learning how to use a Windows laptop.

So Strategic Communications dispatched Julie Mayfield, one of their best consultants and trainers, to show Stanley how to effectively present technical information to his audiences using PowerPoint. The first thing Julie had to do was to earn Stanley's trust. The psychiatrist had been pressured by several managers at Premiere to present studies on NeuroPath that he did not completely accept. She explained that she was there strictly as an advisor and to help him shape his own message about his theories on the treatment of Alzheimer's. She listened carefully as Stanley explained that he was not working for Premiere Pharmaceuticals but rather would continue to represent only his own medical group. Julie asked if she could use Stanley's new laptop. She opened PhotoShop, where she brought up the Conklin Neuroscience Group logo. Using the color picker in PhotoShop (see Figure 6.4), she got the precise shade of orange in the value that the logo used.

Then Julie opened PowerPoint to a new presentation and explained how she could modify the Slide Master (see Figure 6.5), which represented the "blueprint" for the presentation, so as to truly represent the identity of Conklin's group.

Figure 6.4 To create a branded template for a presentation, first establish the color values of the logo or collateral material.

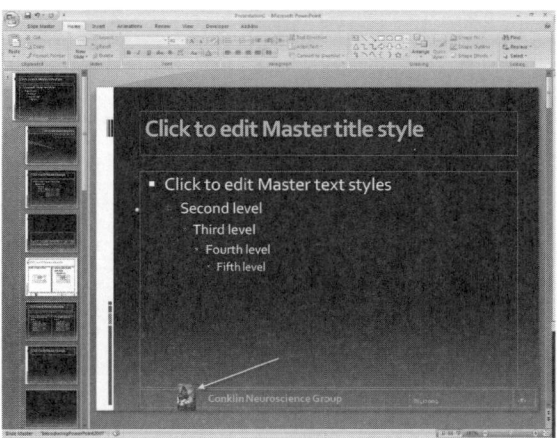

Figure 6.5 Modifying a presentation's Slide Master creates a consistent look that can represent the identity of an entity or organization.

Stanley visibly relaxed and brightened when he saw his own logo on a set of preliminary slides, and when Julie applied similar colors to create a Custom Theme that she named Conklin, he realized that he now had a presentation template under his own identity. (See Figure 6.6.)

Next, Julie put a DVD from Premiere Pharmaceuticals into the laptop's drive,

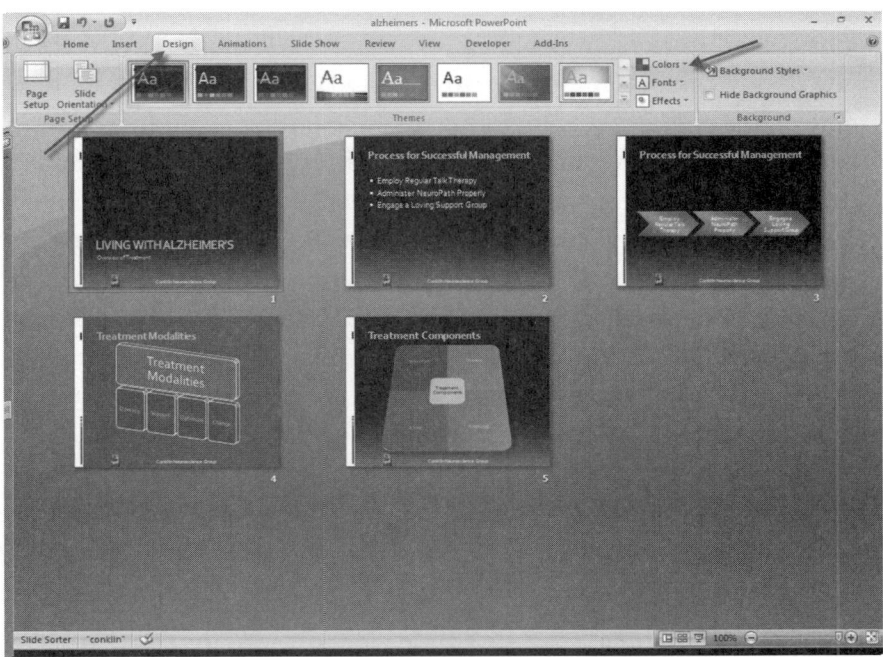

Figure 6.6 Colors chosen individually can be applied in a custom theme (in PowerPoint's Design tab) to create a consistent look throughout a slide show.

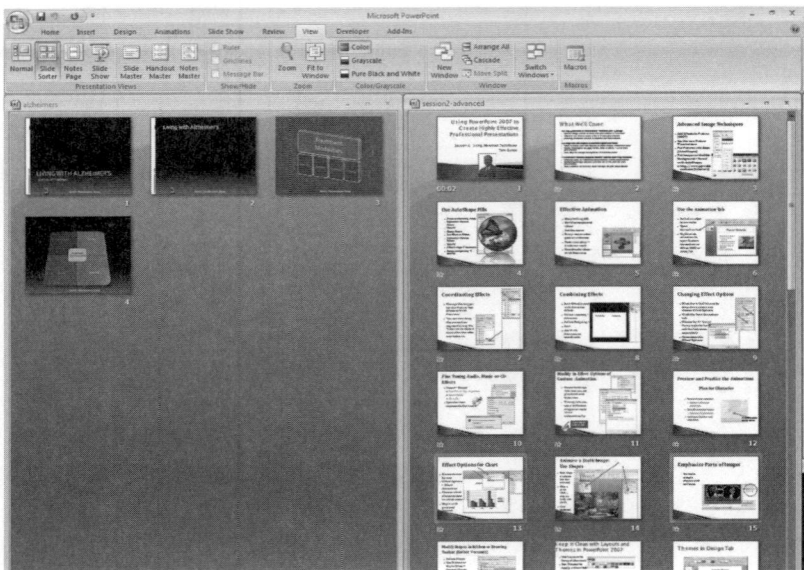

Figure 6.7 Using Arrange All from the View tab in PowerPoint allows you to move slides between one presentation and another.

right-clicked its icon, and opened it in Windows Explorer. She created a project folder on the laptop's desktop named "alzheimers" and transferred some of the company content into the folder, showing Stanley a set of MPG-format video files of patient interviews before and after treatment and another PowerPoint presentation. She opened both presentations side by side by clicking Arrange All in the View tab. (See Figure 6.7.) She selected individual slides using the Ctrl key from the Premiere Pharmaceuticals presentation and moved them into Stanley's branded slide show. (Stanley gasped when his slides suddenly took on the Theme attributes of the new Slide Master Julie had created, but Julie clicked on the small SmartTag to make the transferred slides retain their original formatting.)

Julie took a long look at some of the Conklin Group slides about their Alzheimer's regimen with NeuroPath, some of which had come from different faculty members at the university and some that Stanley had repurposed from his own textbook. Julie explained to Stanley that these slides, with up to twelve sets of bullets, each with long sentences about specific treatment concepts, would be fine for a book or document, but Stanley would be speaking to *people*.

"Dr. Conklin," she asked carefully, "if you were in the audience for this presentation, how would you react?"

He smiled and emitted a short snoring sound from his nose.

"And how much information would you retain?" He shook his head.

Julie suggested that they break up the presentation into three parts, representing Stanley's treatment philosophy, and come up with a short, active title for each:

1. Employ Regular Talk Therapy
2. Administer NeuroPath Properly
3. Engage a Loving Support Group

In this way, Julie suggested, Stanley could tell his story more naturally and engage the audience. She helped him construct individual slides with visual analogies about some treatment strategies; in one instance she found an animation of a hamster on a treadmill that Stanley could use as a representation of a patient stuck in a mental loop. When he used NeuroPath to stop the loop, the hamster (representing the patient's conscious self) could get off the treadmill. She also found some excellent stock images on iStock.com that illustrated some of Stanley's other points with visual metaphors rather than plain text.

Stanley turned to Julie and said that he needed to make sure that specific technical information was available to his audience; just having short visual messages in his slides would not be sufficient. Julie suggested moving as much of the technical information as possible into the Notes panel, reminding him that this was a visual presentation and not a textbook. To make this information available to his audience, he could print the notes as a PDF booklet and either print and distribute it or post it online on his Web site as a download. (See Figure 6.8.)

Stanley preferred the download strategy; he realized that he could write about many of the concepts on his blog and get commentary from his colleagues and students. Julie agreed and suggested that he also get a Twitter ID, but Stanley didn't think that his ideas could be accommodated in 140 characters or less. He had seen Twitter and didn't like it.

Julie saw his point and suggested Stanley check out the forums on the Premiere Pharmaceuticals Web site and perhaps open up his own

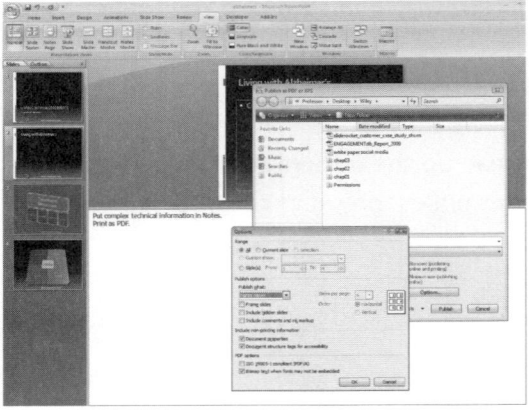

Figure 6.8 You can download an Add-In for PowerPoint that lets you save and print your notes (or handouts or slides) in PDF format.

discussion area that he could link from his blog. This would include comments from psychiatrists who were treating other conditions as well and perhaps lead to information about the combination of NeuroPath and other prescription drugs. Stanley said he'd love for Julie to show him how to do that, but first he wanted to solve one other problem.

He pointed to a photograph on one of Premiere's slides and said that he also had different images that he wanted to use in slides, and he took out his laser pointer.

"If I point to the images with this," he said, "the reference disappears when I close the presentation and turn off the laptop. How can I make it more effective and also have it shown in my handouts?"

Julie showed him how to use various AutoShapes to highlight portions of the image and then have them appear as Fade In Animations when Dr. Conklin clicked his mouse. (See Figure 6.9.)

At this point Stanley was eager to take over

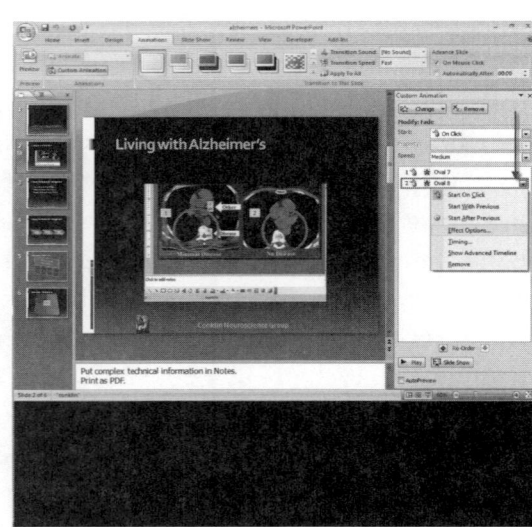

Figure 6.9 Adding a Fade In Entrance Animation to AutoShapes can highlight parts of an image to let the presenter call attention to detail.

150 Tools of Engagement

and asked Julie to stick around while he started to create his own slides. Within minutes he had reverted to an old habit and created a fairly boring three-bullet slide with his main points in sequence. He looked at her proudly.

Julie took over the mouse and selected the three bullets. She right-clicked and chose Convert to SmartArt, and in moments she had changed the bullets into a chevron diagram, depicting a fairly simple timeline. She quickly added some effects from the PowerPoint Ribbon;

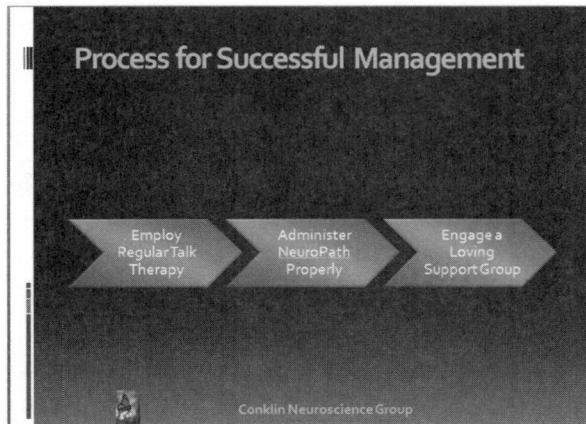

Figures 6.10–6.11 Converting a set of bullets to SmartArt can make a significant difference in how your information is presented and absorbed.

Stanley looked at the transformed slide with approval. (See Figures 6.10 and 6.11.)

"Can I animate that, one shape at a time?" he asked.

She showed him how to use the Effect Options for SmartArt in the Custom Animations panel to make the shapes appear sequentially, so that he could discuss each concept before the next one appeared in the slide. (See Figure 6.9 for the Effect Options in Custom Animation.)

Crafting a Visual Message **151**

Before she left, Julie watched Stanley rehearse the slide show with his portable mouse and showed him how to navigate to the end of the presentation if he got behind schedule instead of rushing through slides. "Just type in the slide number of the slide you want to jump to, and hit Enter," she said, so that he could wind up a presentation at any time. She suggested that he have a series of slides he could always use to wrap up and know the number where they began.

Stanley's head was spinning from all of the possibilities that the presentation software provided for explaining his ideas about NeuroPath in the context of his own treatment regimen, but he also realized he had only scratched the surface of what PowerPoint could do.

"How come this software gets such a bad rap?" he asked her. "I keep hearing about Death by PowerPoint."

"Just fill up your slides with bullets, and read them to the audience, and you'll understand," Julie said. "Any more questions before I hit the road?"

"Just one," Conklin smiled. "How would I put this presentation on the Internet?"

THE POTENTIAL OF POWERPOINT

For all of its detractors and naysayers, PowerPoint (or Keynote or some of the newer competitors) provides context for content, aids retention, and can build energy and excitement when used a good presenter who integrates effective visuals with a speech or training session. In learning how to visually convey his theories on Alzheimer's treatment, Dr. Stanley Conklin gained confidence in his upcoming speaking engagements—so much so that he asked about how the presentation itself might be distributed or viewed online.

Another advantage of using effective visuals is that it may lend *authority* to your message. But as has been noted in *Trust Agents*, by Chris Brogan and Julien Smith,[2] in the current environment, merely using PowerPoint or video, or having a position in a company or organization, is no longer enough to gain influence. Many of the examples in earlier chapters demonstrated how ordinary citizens can become communicators and agents of change by "going viral" in social media. Brogan and Smith's book provides many more examples and insights into how a reputation is earned and nurtured.

It's quite possible that even if Stanley Conklin and his colleagues use their positions to promote NeuroPath as a treatment for Alzheimer's, if its efficacy is cast in doubt on social sites like WebMD and discussions on the Web, even slides with nicely formatted charts showing test results from the manufacturer won't convince a physician to administer it or families to trust it.

But much of the groundswell of social media is about building momentum and getting attention for your ideas—and then focusing that attention on a location (Web site, blog, and so on) where more detailed information is available. That is where the true promise of PowerPoint lies. A great slide deck can't guarantee trust or credibility, but it can begin to establish trust, particularly among a core constituency like Conklin's peers.

Then it is up to the message itself and its proponent to participate in a continuing conversation that conveys the information in a manner that continues to build a following. A powerful way to distribute an important message is video, as the string of pharmacies in the scenario used to do damage control and retrain their staffs using stories to deliver an important set of messages. But some messages are complex, and budgets are tight. Using animated text and graphics (along with video) can be an effective way to deliver meaningful content with maximum impact at low cost. The issue, of course, is effectiveness. Particularly in academic disciplines (and in the military), there is a tendency to confuse a presentation with a textbook or document, leading to unreadable slides with unfocused content—and these slides are then read to an audience by a speaker or narrator. A communicator can learn an important lesson from social sites like Twitter and Facebook; even 140 characters can get people to act (click a link) if the content is compelling.

What is the secret of compelling content?

As Julie Mayfield showed Stanley Conklin, it is humanizing to *add an emotional component to your message*, something that effective Twitter users do in 140 characters but many poor presenters fail to accomplish in a lecture with hundreds of slides. The simple concept of turning bullets into visuals, whether SmartArt diagrams or analogous images and powerful metaphors, is still just catching on for many PowerPoint users. For those who seek more details, Cliff Atkinson's excellent treatment of this subject in *Beyond Bullet Points* and on his Web site, www.beyondbullets.com,[3] has positively influenced many presenters in recent years. In the book, Atkinson uses the Hollywood model to help turn any presentation into a story, generally in three acts, leaving only the emotional aspects in the slides and saving the facts and details for the slide notes and handouts.

Whether a presentation like Stanley Conklin's can work without any charts and graphs is open to debate, but certainly the use of a video of an Alzheimer's patient before and after treatment with NeuroPath would sway many more audiences than would an animated graph showing a trial study from the manufacturer. Even a series of powerful still images, accentuating the human modalities that Conklin introduced into treatment (talk therapy and loving support) would strengthen a presentation tremendously and make it effective whether delivered in a small dinner setting, an auditorium, a Web conference, or online.

If you have any doubt that effective visuals presented in a slide show can build connection and trust with an audience, you should read *Slide:ology* by Nancy Duarte,[4] of Duarte Design. Duarte is a design professional with a who's who of corporate clients; her firm worked with Al Gore on *An Inconvenient Truth* (which was created in Keynote). Duarte and her team focus entirely on the underlying story, meaning, and emotion of any project, whether for marketing and sales, training, or to change attitudes about climate. Perhaps one of the most intriguing aspects of Duarte's discipline is her belief that creating the slides in PowerPoint or Keynote should be the last parts of the process. Before anyone touches a computer, ideas are brainstormed, sketched out, walked through, and critiqued from all of their perspectives to make certain that the core values and most significant aspects of any product, service, or concept are conveyed with emotional impact.

If this sounds a great deal like the process of important ideas filtering through the matrix of social media, it's probably not a coincidence. In Duarte's case it helps that her team is comprised of polished professionals in the area of design, graphics, and storytelling. Ultimately, the connection between visuals and sound with the heart and not the head, along with a message conveyed by a polished and well-rehearsed speaker, is what lends power to any effective set of slides.

USE XCELSIUS TO DISPLAY THE TWITTER BACKCHANNEL IN POWERPOINT

In Chapter Two the backchannel was introduced as a new phenomenon that manifests as an audience commenting on a presentation, asking questions, and reacting through their PDAs or cell phones on Twitter during an event.

From a technical standpoint, it is helpful to know about a tool that lets you display the Twitter backchannel directly in PowerPoint. Created by database powerhouse SAP blogger Timo Elliot, Business Objects Xcelsius, a software program for creating effective dashboards (or interactive interfaces for data analysis) and data displays, provides a way to insert Twitter feedback and even polls of multiple choice questions directly in PowerPoint—not only encouraging the backchannel but integrating it into a presentation. More information is available at www.insidesap.com or http://bit.ly/8JD9Be.

These Twitter Tools are available for free at www.sapweb20.com/blog/powerpoint-twitter-tools.

ANYONE CAN MAKE A VIDEO OUT OF A SLIDE SHOW

The two most effective media for presenting information visually are video and graphics. YouTube and similar hosting sites work for video, but what about graphics or PowerPoint? "Real" video, like the one produced by the PharmaFriend in the previous scenario, requires complex and often expensive production and editing facilities. If you see a disaster and shoot it in poor light and quality, it may still make CNN. But if you want to make a music video to complain about how an airline broke your guitar, you will probably need more sophisticated equipment to make it effective. A low-end video producer might use a consumer camcorder (or an upscale PDA or phone), but for such a video to be effective it probably needs to rely on serendipity—being in the right place at the right time.

It is possible to save a PowerPoint file in Web (HTML) format and post it on a Web site; it will have a panel with a table of contents that show your slide titles and let the user navigate through the presentation (see Figure 6.12)—but what's missing is the vital ingredient: the presenter!

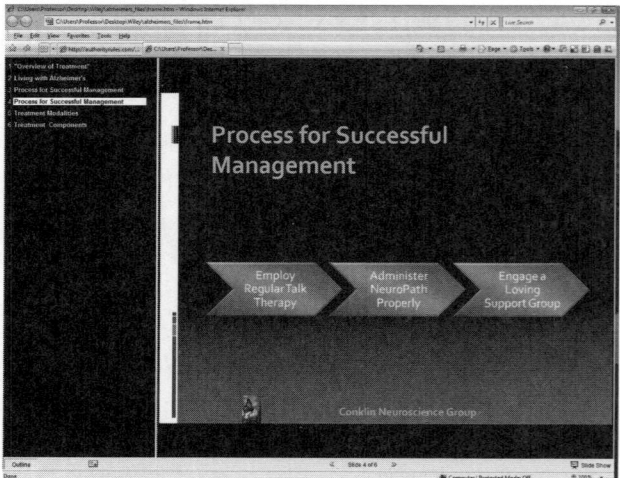

Figure 6.12 Converting a slide show to HTML format makes it available in a Web browser, but the presenter is not there to tell a story.

Another alternative is to save the PowerPoint file as a Show file so that it will open directly into a slide show full screen when viewed on a computer; such a file can be posted online for download or e-mailed as an attachment. (Older versions would be a *.PPS file rather than the standard *.PPT file; PowerPoint 2007 creates a *.PPSX file.) It is also true that such a file can have embedded audio narration, so that the presenter's voice can be heard with the slides, but embedding audio will make the file quite large (particularly if it also has images), and most important, either PowerPoint or a PowerPoint Viewer is required to watch the slide show.

But you can turn your PowerPoint into video format—all you really need is a computer and the right software. There is another significant advantage in turning a PowerPoint slide show into a video: *the presenter can be involved as a narrator (or in a window) to tell the story*. That's why turning a PowerPoint into a video is such a great way to distribute or post a presentation online.

We've already seen previously in this chapter and in Chapter Five that a YouTube video can be embedded in a blog or any Web page. The ability to create a video out of PowerPoint makes it available to a video hosting site like YouTube with the same features. These are the options for turning PowerPoint (with narration) into a video file that will be accepted on YouTube (or another hosting site):

- Use PowerPoint on the Mac and turn it into a QuickTime (MOV) file.
- Get PowerPoint 2010, which promises to have a convert to video feature.
- Use a third-party tool (see following) to create your video file.

There is also a Web hosting service that accepts PowerPoint files directly with embedded narration and will convert them into video for you for a fee and send them to YouTube. The site is www.authorstream.com—see later in this chapter for more information.

One other advantage of getting your PowerPoint into video format is that you can then burn it to a standard DVD disc that plays on a consumer video player.

THIRD-PARTY TOOLS FOR TURNING POWERPOINT INTO VIDEO

There are an increasing number of tools that will turn PowerPoint slides into a video file, and many of them also will turn PowerPoint into Flash. While Flash is a great format, it is not directly accepted by hosting sites like YouTube, and it presents other technical issues. Currently YouTube accepts four video formats: QuickTime (*.MOV), mainly on the Mac; *.AVI, a standard Windows format; *.MPG; and *.WMV, the newer Windows Media standard. Getting your PowerPoint presentation into one of these formats with an accompanying narrative audio track is the best way to post it online and make it available on any Web site without significant playback issues.

One way to do this is to download a free version of Windows Media Encoder from the Windows Media Web site. (This site keeps moving; as of this writing the URL is www.microsoft.com/windows/windowsmedia/forpros/encoder/default.mspx or http://bit.ly/4APpPO.) Windows Media Encoder will allow you to capture anything that appears on your screen (such as your PowerPoint slide show) and also record a narrator's voice and save it in the *.WMV format. The problem is that even if you use the "hotkey" to begin the capture, you will generally get extraneous material at the beginning and end of the production that will need to be edited out. Also, the program is quite complicated, although once you discover the proper set of settings they can be saved for reuse.

The most popular tool is Camtasia Studio from TechSmith, which will not only record your slide show and narrative audio, but with a webcam or camcorder the presenter can appear in the final video production in a window located on screen. (Be careful with this feature, because it will overlap your slides; you will probably need to design your slides to account for the video window or obscure some of your information.)

Windows Media Encoder

Windows Media Encoder opens with a New Session Wizard that lets you choose what you want to do. To turn a PowerPoint presentation into a movie, you will choose Screen Capture. (See Figure 6.13.)

The Wizard continues through a series of screens on which you decide how much of the screen you wish to capture (full screen), designate a filename and location, choose an output quality (high), and create

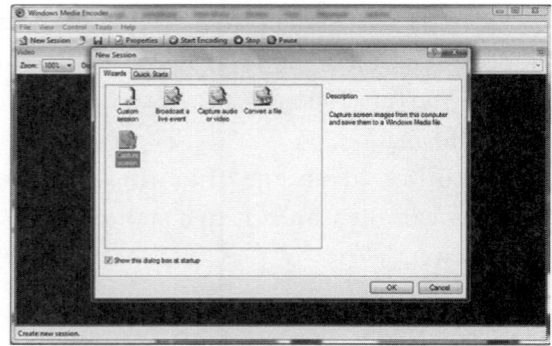

Figure 6.13 Windows Media Recorder lets you set your options through a recording wizard; to capture PowerPoint and narration, use Screen Capture and enable your microphone to record simultaneously.

a description summary. When you've set up your options, you can press the Start Recording options at the top (or a hotkey combination of Ctrl + Shift + E to start recording and Ctrl + Shift + S to stop).

With the recording started, everything you do on screen and speak into the microphone is recorded into a WMV video file. You go through your slides and speak into the microphone, giving your presentation in real time and allowing the screen capture and audio software to record what you show and say. After your last slide and close, you stop recording. It may take a few minutes for the video file of a long presentation to be saved to your hard drive.

Remember where the file has been saved (you designated a name and location in the wizard); then you can double click to open the video file and watch it in Windows Media Player.

If you're fortunate, the file will be suitable for uploading to YouTube, but chances are there will be a few seconds showing your desktop or the PowerPoint Editor unless you are really quick when you start recording. You can use the Windows MovieMaker editing program to trim the WMV clip so that it can be used on YouTube or another hosting site.

It's important to remember that the file you designate as a capture file is a WMV video file in the location chosen in the wizard. You can use the File > Save As feature in Media Encoder to save a Project Settings file (*.WME) that you can subsequently reopen, and then just start the wizard, using the settings that you put in place before saving the file. This is valuable because setting up your microphone and output options in Media Encoder can be time consuming. This process makes it unnecessary to reinvent the wheel each time.

Camtasia Studio

Camtasia has been the program of choice for creating a movie out of a PowerPoint presentation in Windows for several years. It remains to be seen whether the new "MakeMovie" utility in PowerPoint 2010 poses a threat to Camtasia. Probably the biggest advantage Camtasia affords the user is that it runs as an Add-In directly within PowerPoint, where you can set your options and trigger recording without worrying about extraneous footage being captured at the beginning of the sequence. After setting up Camtasia, you can click the Add-Ins tab of the Ribbon to see a red Record button and other features of the program. (See Figure 6.14.) If Snag-It is installed directly for PowerPoint, it will reside in this Ribbon tab.

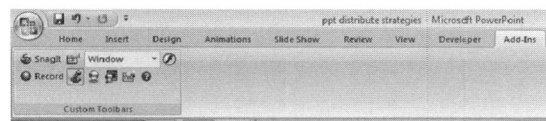

Figure 6.14 Camtasia Studio can be set up and started from within the Add-In tab directly inside PowerPoint.

Once the options are set (microphone and/or video in a window) and recording begins, you follow the same process as Windows Media Recorder: deliver your presentation, speak into the microphone, and then end recording. A pop-up screen will appear that features the other advantage of Camtasia Studio: when you conclude your presentation, you can either edit or produce your final video (see Figure 6.15). The Camtasia Editor is a full-featured interface that lets you enhance the audio, cut out extraneous material, and combine clips before

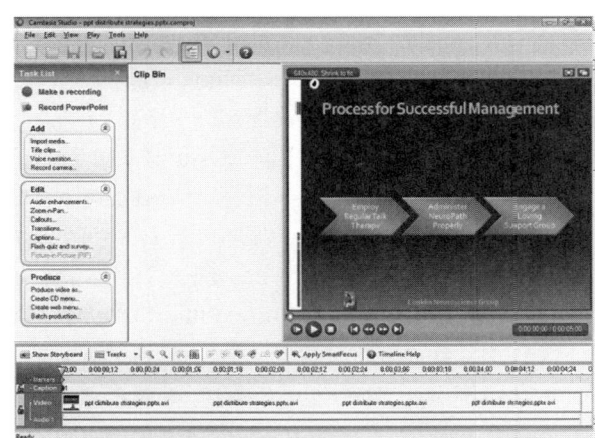

Figure 6.15 The versatile Editing program in Camtasia Studio lets you revise the final video before saving it as a new file in the production stage.

saving (producing) a final video file. There are also options to zoom into portions of a slide and then zoom out by setting key frames.

The Produce Video step is a wizard with settings that you can customize and save, but unlike Media Encoder, it is not limited to the WMV format. It allows you to save your final video in any of the three video file formats that YouTube and other video hosting sites accept. It's a good idea to experiment with various settings and then save the best one under Camtasia's custom options. Creating a Windows Media (WMV) file at a screen resolution of 640 × 480 with Best Quality and File Size is usually a good way to go, but trying different encoding options is worth the effort. (See Figure 6.16.)

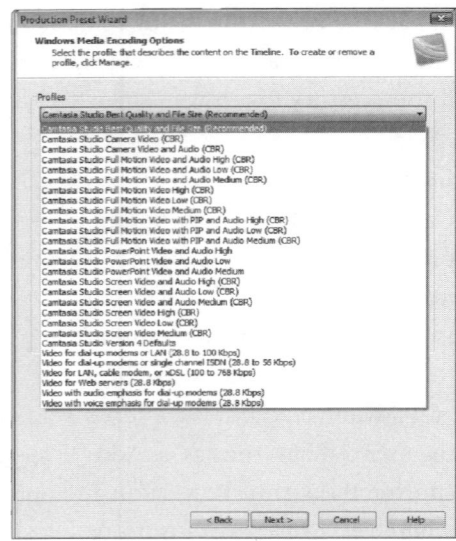

Figure 6.16 Camtasia Studio's Production Wizard lets you choose encoding options for your final output that balance quality with the size of the final file.

Remember that YouTube has a standard limit of 100 megabytes and ten minutes for uploaded files, so if your content exceeds this, you can use Camtasia to easily split up a longer presentation into shorter segments. When you do this, make sure that you save the Project file (which has the actual captured video and your editing decisions) until your project is complete. Also save the Project settings; both are under the File Menu. If you don't save the *.camrec (Project) file, you will not be able to re-edit your production, and you may lose some valuable content if you use the final video file as a source file for another project.

The Production Wizard has a YouTube option that creates an *.MP4 file that plays on the iPod, but it is limited in other playback options. Since YouTube accepts a WMV file, that is probably your best output option, since you can play that file in Windows Media Player and also reinsert it again into a PowerPoint presentation.

When you do a screen capture with Camtasia, it will pick up video that is played in PowerPoint slides and render a video within the video. This would be particularly effective, for example, when Dr. Stanley Conklin shows a video of Alzheimer's patients before and after their regimens of NeuroPath. If he records his presentation with Camtasia Studio (and with Media Encoder, in some cases), the final clip will show both video clips playing in PowerPoint as they were presented—effectively creating a video within a video. After working with Julie Mayfield, Stanley learned how to insert these files into a PowerPoint slide using the Insert > Movie from File feature and how to pause and resume playback during a presentation by simply clicking on the video clip in the slide.

Video is probably the most effective way to convey a message online. Creating a video from a slide show program like PowerPoint or Keynote can provide even more versatility when creating content for online and social media distribution.

SCENARIO: POSTSCRIPT TO CAPITAL PAYROLL SERVICES

In the social media initiative of Capital Payroll Services (introduced in a scenario in Chapter Four), Emily Porter's company began to enter a multimedia phase. Emily hired Steve Gilbert, a Web content expert, to introduce her staff to the various options the company would try out. Capital decided that YouTube would have a Capital channel devoted to PowerPoint presentations captured as they were narrated in Camtasia and conventional video of instructional sessions that were relevant to various issues as they came up.

Research was conducted online to determine out the key search terms that were used in Capital's part of the financial services industry; these could be used in the video descriptions on YouTube and added to the tags for each video that was posted. These search parameters were also distributed to the sales team as it began creating profiles on sites like Twitter and Facebook, and for their personal pages in the Capital social network where they would be blogging and participating in discussions and forums.

Capital's staff found that converting large numbers of presentations to video was time consuming and required that someone actually "give the presentation" in order to capture the audio narration as part of the video file. The company decided to take advantage of other sites on which slide presentations could be posted directly. Whenever possible, the individual who created the PowerPoint file would supply narration in one of two ways:

1. The file would be captured using Camtasia with the narration as part of the video and also as a separate MP3 file, which was an option in Camtasia's production options. Or,

2. A version of the PowerPoint file would be saved with the narration embedded in the file itself.

The Camtasia production could be re-edited and output as one or more WMV video files and posted on YouTube, with the appropriate description and tags reflecting search parameters as determined by the marketing group. Where appropriate, the MP3 file could be used in a podcast to which individuals and companies could subscribe using RSS feeds and be updated on the latest educational content from Capital Payroll Services. The same MP3 file could also be used on SlideShare.com to create a "slidecast," with the audio synchronized with the slides. (SlideShare is a hosting site for PowerPoint files with the same kind of linking and embedding features and search capabilities of YouTube. Users who found the content on SlideShare could leave comments and rate the presentations, creating a potential viral distribution pattern for any slide shows that were particularly helpful or pertinent.)

The PowerPoint files with embedded audio could be posted directly on another slide show hosting site, AuthorSTREAM.com. Steve Gilbert, the Web content specialist, pointed out that a slide show with embedded audio created on AuthorSTREAM could be converted directly to video and sent to YouTube without using Camtasia—a potential time saver—but it would cost money for this service. Steve also warned about a potential glitch with the audio files that were earmarked for podcasts or to be synchronized with SlideShare: the Camtasia audio code for MP3 files sometimes didn't work on these sites. Steve recommended a free audio utility—Audacity.com—that could be downloaded to the desktop and used to re-edit and export the MP3 audio files for reuse as podcasts and audio tracks for SlideShare.

This comprehensive solution covered all the bases for content posting and allowed the sales team to reference a number of different locations and files as they participated in the social media initiative. For example, in response to a blog about a workers' comp issue on another site, a Capital sales rep might first post a comment and suggest a solution to a problem, engaging the blog's readers in a discussion thread. Those who participated in that discussion might be invited by a link to the rep's page on Capital's social network, where a slide show or video of the solution would be embedded from one of the hosting sites.

Steve did a training session on YouTube for the Capital staff in which he went over the Video Upload form on which the full description and search parameters could be entered. (See Figure 6.17.)

Several staff members were trained in using Camtasia Studio and learned how to re-edit the videos created from PowerPoint and produce

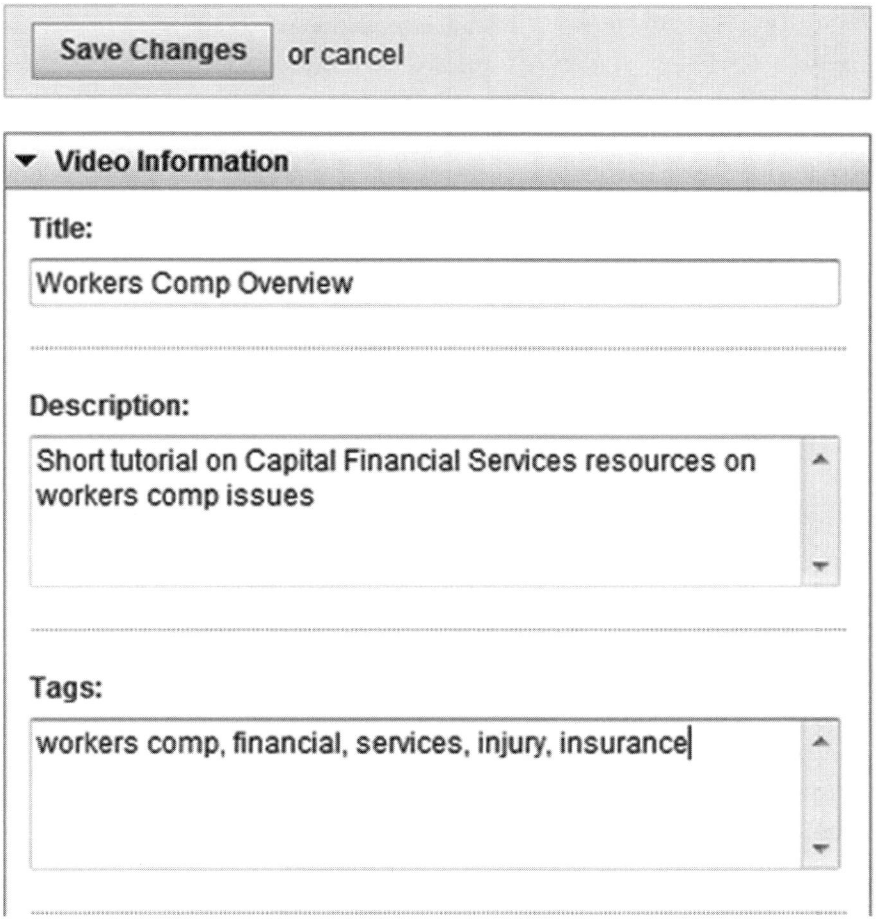

Figure 6.17 The Video Upload lets you enter a full description and searchable tags. You can revise this information or add more search tags in YouTube by clicking on Edit.

Crafting a Visual Message   **163**

them as movies and export MP3 files. Steve also showed them the audio editing capabilities of Audacity, which could create a standard WAV audio or MP3 file for playback from the Internet or use in a podcast. (See Figure 6.18.)

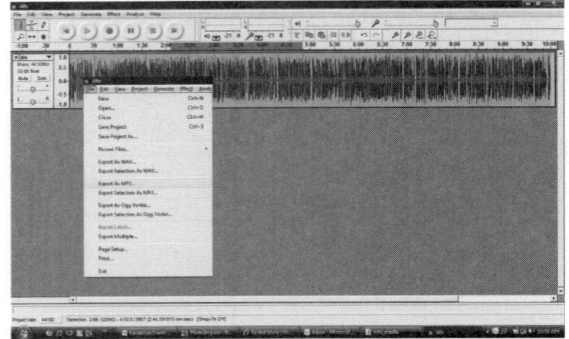

Figure 6.18 Audacity is a free full-featured audio editor that can convert, import, and export MP3 files for podcasts or to be synchronized as slidecasts on SlideShare.com.

Steve explained the pros and cons of the two main slide show hosting programs, SlideShare and AuthorSTREAM. He compared SlideShare to YouTube and showed that some posted PowerPoint files had narration included in a slidecast. He showed the staff how to attach an MP3 file to an uploaded PowerPoint show and synchronize it in the editing panel. (See Figures 6.19, 6.20, and 6.21.)

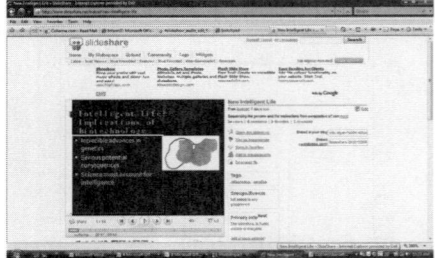

Figure 6.19 Slidecasts on SlideShare.com are PowerPoint slides with audio narration and have many of the same properties as videos on YouTube, but they are hosted in a community dedicated to presentations.

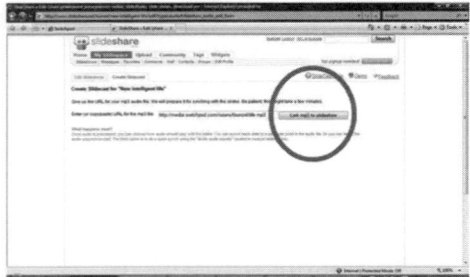

Figure 6.20 An MP3 file of the audio narration to a presentation (exported from Camtasia and converted in Audacity) can be linked to the slides in SlideShare to create a slidecast.

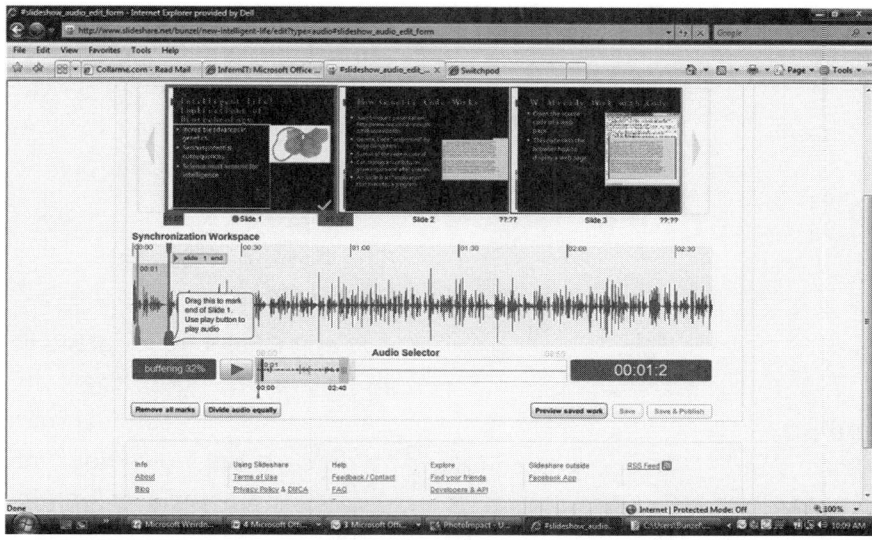

Figure 6.21 You can use the Synchronization Workspace in SlideShare to create a slidecast.

Not surprisingly, the Capital staff did not really like this complex sequence of tasks, but Steve explained that SlideShare is a mature hosting site and presentations posted as slidecasts would have a good chance of being seen by many users. Steve then pointed out that AuthorSTREAM accepted PowerPoint with embedded narration, so that anyone could simply record narration for a slide show in PowerPoint on their desktop (and not have to be videotaped or recorded while actually presenting). (See Figures 6.22, 6.23, and 6.24.)

The Capital Payroll staff loved the fact that an AuthorSTREAM post could be sent directly to YouTube, where it would be converted to a video, with

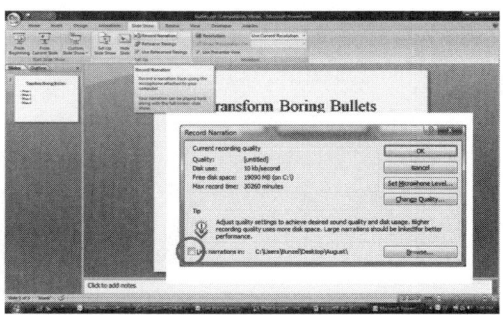

Figure 6.22 If you deselect Link narration in your PowerPoint slides, you can embed the audio to create a narrated presentation for AuthorSTREAM.

Crafting a Visual Message

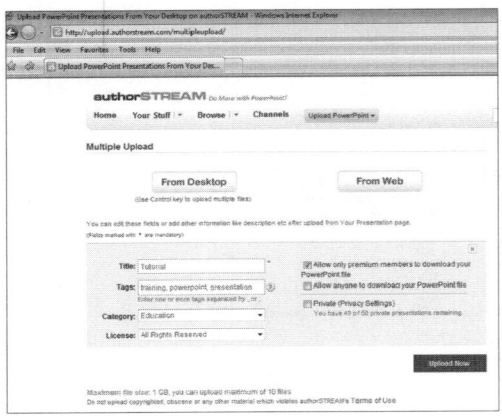

Figure 6.23 Like YouTube and SlideShare, AuthorSTREAM has a form on the upload screen to include a searchable description and keyword tags.

the same information in the description and keyword tags. It wasn't decided whether the company would pay for this service on a large scale.

The Power of Digital Storytelling

As Capital Payroll's social media initiative unfolded, the company learned a great deal from its research and interaction with clients and associates online.

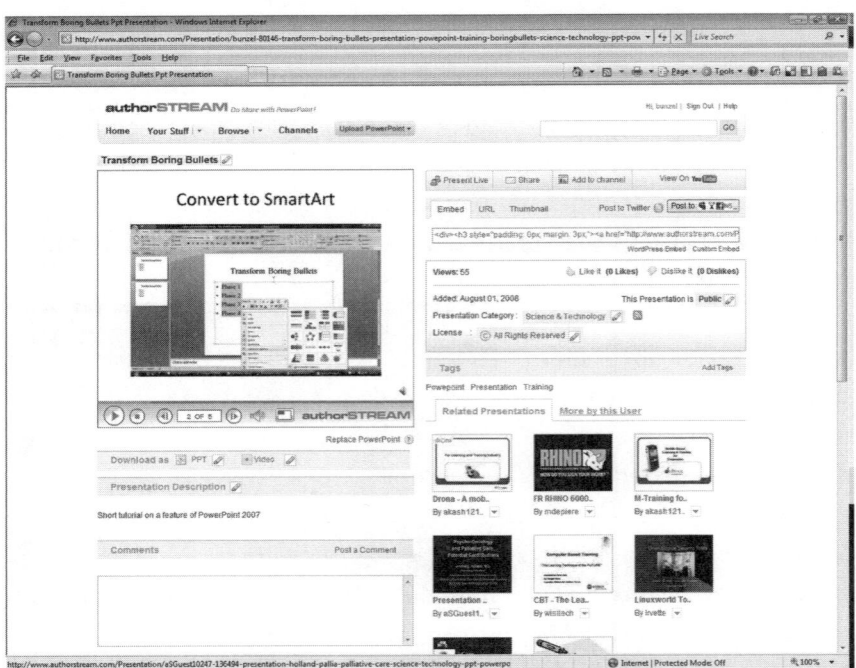

Figure 6.24 When uploaded to AuthorSTREAM, a presentation can be played with accompanying narration on the Web site or linked to or embedded just like a YouTube video. It can also be converted to video and sent to YouTube (for a small fee).

One of the great benefits was the ability to get a sense of what constitutes effective communication.

Many of the company's sales reps and trainers had become mired in old-school practices like bullet-ridden PowerPoint presentations and documents heavy with charts and graphs but without context. As they stepped into the world of social media, the departments at Capital became exposed to how customer experiences—encoded as anecdotes or stories—can help shape performance. As Emily Porter had originally found with her social training initiative, the social sites combined with images, video, podcasts and documents generated lots of energy and discussion—all of which became success (or adversity) stories.

Storytelling became such a key component of the Capital Payroll social network that Carl Taylor, the marketing and communications director, decided to shift some of his marketing efforts to harvesting case studies of how clients used the payroll services and what specific issues they dealt with. For example, instead of touting abstract terms like "401(k)" or "retirement accounts," his staff came up with a campaign that it called "The Squirrel Strategies," which simply began with some video of cute squirrels (taken by one of the sales managers) combined with questions that users of the company's services should ask when planning for retirement. (See Figure 6.25.) When the company put some of these videos on YouTube and embedded them into blogs and forum posts, they found that the images evoked an amazing array of responses and questions from participants on the social network and readers of their blogs.

Figure 6.25 Using an evocative symbol or metaphor can help communicate key concepts emotionally far more effectively than text or charts.

Suddenly issues like diversification of assets, volatility, and risk tolerance could be humanized as readers of the blog saw themselves and their wants and needs symbolized in touching and humorous short videos. Steve Gilbert suggested that they give one of the squirrels ("Stanley") a

Twitter account, in which he could share his very best saving strategies from around the Web. Stanley engaged in commentary with an increasing number of followers and got his own discussion forum on the company social network: "Don't Let Retirement Options Drive U Nuts." CNN's *Money* program picked up one of the Stanley videos on YouTube, and a large number of new members joined the forum to learn how someone as risk averse as Stanley would be able to save for retirement. Stanley sent the forum's members to the retirement calculators and tables that the company presented on its Web site and provided tips on how to use the complex tables and charts effectively.

Most important, Carl had learned his lesson and had his staff refrain from overt selling, relying instead on Stanley the Squirrel and the other strategies that the company employed. The emphasis remained on asking questions, listening to concerns, and providing value in addressing the issues that were raised not just on Capital's blogs and forums but all around the Internet. The company's training and sales teams gathered the experiences of client companies and end users as more and more fodder for Stanley, and for themselves, as they contributed to financial services blogs and tweeted regularly about what they discovered as key elements of the various payroll and financial services they offered.

IMPLEMENTING DIGITAL STORYTELLING

Without beating the cute animal symbolism to death, management consultant and facilitator Terrence Gargiulo (who features cute critters in his book, *In the Land of Difficult People*) is a serious proponent of the use of story in communicating effectively in the corporate and organizational environment. Gargiulo's use of stories echoes many of the features endemic to the rapid growth of social media, mainly that stories are a human and cultural way to encode information and to create a space for listening to others. His practice, and his book *Making Stories* (also his Web site, makingstories.net), encapsulate his theory that "not only do we communicate through stories, we also learn from them."

Gargiulo believes that "stories are efficient ways to store, retrieve, and convey information. They help us to understand business processes, create and modify corporate culture, manage change, and facilitate the management of knowledge and its transfer. They also help develop, coach, and mentor others, improve training, and help us interact with others in the organization proactively."

Gargiulo's practice concentrates on story making and storytelling as teachable skills and, as we've seen extensively, these elements are the critical aspect to effective participation and the growth of influence in the new digital frontiers.

According to Gargiulo, stories can be used to:

- Empower speakers
- Create environments
- Bind and bond individuals
- Engage our minds in active listening
- Negotiate differences
- Encode information
- Act as tools for thinking and to bring about healing[5]

This last point is particularly germane to so-called soft skills training in many organizations. As the need for diversity has been recognized and established in many corporate and academic environments, it has led to conflicts that can only be reconciled through deeper levels of understanding. Textbook approaches and direct confrontation of these issues don't often capture the subtext of on the conflicts in the same way that an anecdote or perhaps the same experience told from two or more different points of view can yield insight. Sharing such experiences and insights in the new social Web dramatically increases the capacity for feedback and understanding. And the stories that we find compelling influence the organizations we belong to both by choice and by need.

A STORY-BASED COMMUNICATION SKILLS MODEL

Gargiulo believes that "everyone is a natural born communicator. Stories are such a natural part of how we communicate. We give sense to our experiences through stories and we make sense of the world around us through stories."

He has developed a story-based communication skills model from research with Fortune 500 leaders that explore three dimensions of effective communication and nine skills that each of us possesses. (See Figure 6.26.) The related

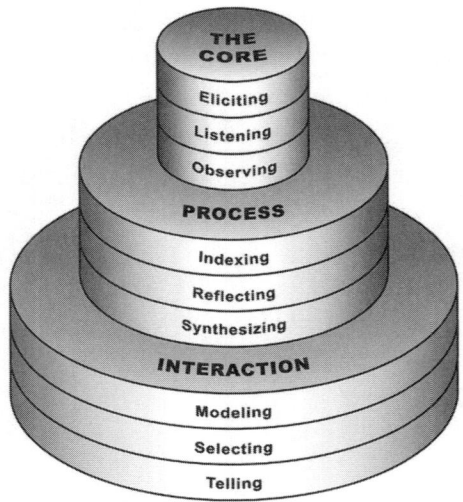

Figure 6.26 Gargiulo's story-based communication skills model can be used as an assessment tool or for coaching and facilitation.

instrument can be used as a stand-alone self-assessment tool in workshops or coaching. Three-hundred-and-sixty-degree feedback and coaching versions of the tool exist as well. Each instrument includes scoring and graphing tools, explanation of the model, and a large collection of self-development exercises.

Table 6.1 provides a brief explanation of the three dimensions and nine skills.

HOW THE LEARNING LANDSCAPE HAS CHANGED

As you followed along in this chapter, you probably realized, as Gargiulo suggests, that today's learning landscape has "a dizzying array of options." In his efforts to integrate storytelling, Gargiulo has put together a comprehensive overview of today's learning landscape, including social media, in his model along with more traditional tools. (See Figure 6.27.)

Gargiulo explains that in his snapshot

> the top and sides are essential pieces that keep all the other building blocks glued together. Inseparable from any learning intervention is the creation of business value. Learning must support the performance of individuals working to actualize organizational goals and bottom line imperatives. This is not as utilitarian as it may sound. Something interesting occurs when individual performers' energies are focused. People are more engaged because they are utilizing their talents, developing their capacities, and becoming part of something they feel a part of.
>
> The other parts of the top and side bands (Assessing Learning & Skills, Tracking/Reporting, Measurement & Evaluation, and Link to Performance) define other elements of managing learning. These

Table 6.1
Gargiulo's Three Dimensions and Nine Skills of Communication

Ring	Skill	Description
INTERACTION *Describes how we use stories to connect with others and communicate*	Modeling	Being aware of one's actions and using them to create lasting impressions in the eyes of others; employing a variety of analogical techniques to bring an idea or concept alive
	Telling	Relaying a story with authenticity that paints a vivid, engaging picture for listeners
	Selecting	Picking a story that is appropriate to the situation at hand and that clearly communicates concepts, ideas, or feelings
PROCESS *Describes how we work with experiences to transform them into meaningful and reusable stories*	Indexing	Developing a flexible, vast, mental schema for retrieval of experiences, and knowledge
	Synthesizing	Finding patterns in new experiences and creating connections between them and old ones
	Reflecting	Reviewing experiences with circumspection and extracting knowledge from them
CORE *Describes how we open ourselves to be aware and sensitive to stories*	Eliciting	Asking questions and finding ways to pull stories from others
	Listening	Absorbing stories and invoking the imagination to enter them in a fundamental and deep way
	Observing	Practicing mindfulness to become aware of the stories implicit in others' words and actions

Crafting a Visual Message

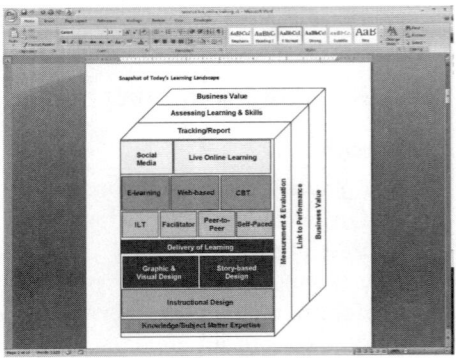

Figure 6.27 Gargiulo's diagrammatic snapshot of today's learning options.

represent the high level buckets that are a part of Learning Management System (LMS). Regardless of whether your organization uses a large scale enterprise solution or more simple systems and processes, these activities envelop learning.

The map shows how various pieces of a learning architecture build on one another. Each of the major areas (Foundation, Delivery Modes, Delivery Mechanisms) highlights the strategic choices that need to be made. There are pros and cons to any arrangement of tools and processes.[6]

The various tools and technologies covered in this chapter are integral to the successful delivery of any aspect of this model, but the foundation of meaning encoded in stories, according to Gargiulo, is a vital component that cannot be ignored if training and other organizational communication are to succeed.

Just as Gargiulo explains how the nuts and bolts of the learning landscape have changed in delivering training, along the spectrum from traditional to posting on Twitter, the core processes of eliciting, listening, and observing constitute the key human dynamics of both successful storytelling and getting grounded in social media.

STORIES DEFINE A TRIBE

One of the most powerful metaphors for how stories build understanding and belief is included in the title of the very popular business book *Tribes* by consultant Seth Godin.[7]

In many ways tribes are the essence of social communications, because they have committed and thoroughly engaged members. The very image of a tribe is highly evocative and effective, and Godin uses the concept to go deeply into the issues of leadership and loyalty that are at the heart of most organizational efforts, particularly education and training.

Godin defines a *tribe* as a group of people connected to one another, connected to a leader, and connected to an idea that inspires their passion. What truly binds a tribe, in Godin's world, is not an abstract idea ("liberty") as much as a story that supports it and the spirit of the endeavor (the Boston Tea Party). In Godin's terms, a leader is the individual who understands the essence of the stories at the heart of his or her tribe that are elicited in this way, and perhaps even "coauthors" them as he or she inspires others to face these issues in whatever environment they operate.

Godin's corporate examples of tribes are many; one of the most popular is the cult around Apple computers. The loyalty of graphic designers and media to the product is less about what it does but more about its ethos: "It's cool." Another example is the following of the Grateful Dead. He writes, "The Dead helped us understand how tribes work. They didn't succeed by selling records (they only had one Top 40 album). Instead, they succeeded by attracting and leading a tribe." (Today an influential member of that same tribe might well be someone with old video footage or reminiscences of the musical group.)

For Godin, the power of the social Web is that anyone (individual, organization, group, or company) can form and lead a tribe, as long as they come from a place of creating value and passion.

To accomplish the generation of a new tribe, one needs to come from a very deep and basic understanding of human needs and desires, which again doesn't come from slogans or mission statements but from stories and performance. How does one find and use the most effective stories in a specific environment?

Gargiulo's *Making Stories* and his Web site have many examples, but just as in social media, the key is asking questions that elicit experiences encoded in stories. Here are some of his sample questions for opening up a dialogue based on story:

- What things are difficult in your life right now?
- What are some of the hardest things you have ever had to do?
- What are some of the hardest things you have ever had to say to someone?
- Are there any hard things you are afraid to attempt?
- How have you coped with the hard things in your life?
- How have others helped you?
- What are the difficult things that you have done that have surprised you?[8]

As stories unfold, they naturally yield components that form the foundation for meaningful and effective communication: analogy and metaphor. Examples like pulling the sword from the stone in the Arthurian legend are universally encoded cultural myths.

In her book *Slide:ology*, design guru Nancy Duarte provides numerous case studies and examples of finding the analogy or metaphor to visually convey an important concept. In the chapter "Brainstorming Meaningful Metaphors," she shows how eliciting stories results in a clear vision of a solution delivered with a powerful symbol. "Collaborating with others almost always yields a stronger result," she writes. "After brainstorming at the whiteboard with an executive, we developed a fresh concept to demonstrate [the value of a product]. A combination lock serves as a metaphor; the dial spins to create the illusion of granting access."[9]

There are a number of significant elements at work here.

First, the value of the product in question was not written down in bullet points; it was elicited through brainstorming or *listening* to the concrete examples (stories) of someone intimately connected with its use (the executive). Technology was used (a whiteboard) in this case, but Duarte suggests that Post-It notes and sketch pads are equally effective at the eliciting stage; by contrast, imagine waiting for Windows to boot while you try to discuss issues of this nature and get to their core value. Finally, Duarte's metaphor was a powerful image that could be animated and turned into video using more technical expertise, but even an iStock photo could serve as an evocative means of conveying the value proposition of a product that combined multiple disparate complex components and might open up an audience's mind to a solution to a serious problem.

Once the concept is clear in a human and emotional way, the technology really doesn't matter. Duarte may well have delivered this message through PowerPoint, just as a medical practitioner could demonstrate the conflict between two states of being using a visual metaphor and animating it within a slide.

What might the metaphor be for the effective use of social media in crafting effective communication?

In the first phase, perhaps aging cheese (without the smell), since ripening takes a commitment of time and resources, and it is best served in harmony with other organic complements, like wine, bread, and fruit. Creating quality relationships takes time. For the second phase, or implementation of interactivity or delivery of content, Gargiulo uses the metaphor of the conductor of an orchestra (as opposed

Figures 6.28–6.30 Creative storytelling and PowerPoint animation can add impact to a visual metaphor.

to a speaker), who in today's world will elicit the significant meanings and contributions of a variety of sources and blend them into a harmonious message with the feedback (verbal and nonverbal) of an appreciative audience.

In both of these phases, note again the movement away from the idea of broadcast and the essential element of building relationships over time. In most cases a conductor does not take the podium in a vacuum; the audience will know something about the material and perhaps have seen him and the orchestra in the past so that a mental and emotional bond (rapport) is already in place. In the area of training and organizational communications, the presenter needs to be established before a real-time event will succeed. Particularly in the area of facilitation, the trust engendered by developing rapport between the facilitator and the audience enhances both her credibility and the results of the event.

The complementary aspect is critically important here, since as Godin argues in *Tribes*, the Internet has eliminated the barriers to leadership: those who contribute and add value gain influence. Others who cling to dying and irrelevant styles of communications are destined to be ignored. Everyone's contribution and participation, from training to marketing and every aspect of communication, matter.

Effective use of technology can help, but the essence of communication is still the message, and story, analogy, and metaphor are the most powerful means of delivery.

The conventional tools of video and graphically rich slides can be effectively used both in standard presentations and as a means for delivering content that will work across social media communities and Web sites. The effective use of stories and metaphors in concert with these tools promotes credibility, rapport, and engagement, laying the foundation for delivery of an effective message and the cohesiveness of communities and "tribes."

In many ways the technologies of social media and desktop converge in a unique new frontier—the Web conference—that eliminates other barriers (geography and time) but also poses unique challenges. The webinar or Web conference, as we'll see in Chapter Seven, combines interactivity with real-time events (which is also part of the success of Twitter), but the Web conference or webinar goes well beyond 140 characters in its ability to deliver content and value.

QUESTIONS TO PONDER

1. How comfortable do you feel using presentation graphics and/or the technology that creates and displays imagery? Do you feel you use these tools effectively? How would video increase your effectiveness and the reach of your message?

2. If you do not personally possess or seek to learn the expertise to use advanced graphics and video tools, can you conceptualize and communicate your intentions effectively to an assistant or presentation professional to create content for you?

3. How can you mine the stories that comprise your experience in your field, and also in your personal life, to best illustrate and dramatize your message? What metaphors and analogies can be used to emotionally connect with your audience beyond the technical or informational aspects of your message?

Notes

1. http://blogs.reuters.com/mediafile/2009/07/31/tweeting-hits-high-note-with-fortune-100/—http://bit.ly/3JUIo8.
2. Chris Brogan and Julien Smith, *Trust Agents: Using the Web to Build Influence, Improve Reputation, and Earn Trust.* Hoboken, NJ: Wiley, 2009.
3. Cliff Atkinson, *Beyond Bullet Points: Using Microsoft® Office PowerPoint® 2007 to Create Presentations That Inform, Motivate, and Inspire.* Redmond, WA: Microsoft Press, 2007, and www.sociablemedia.com.

4. Nancy Duarte, *Slide:ology: The Art and Science of Creating Great Presentations*. Sebastopol, CA: O'Reilly, 2008.
5. Terrence Gargiulo, *Making Stories: A Practical Guide for Organizational Leaders and Human Resource Specialists*. Westport, CT: Quorum, 2002, p. 7; MakingStories.net. See also Terrence L. Gargiulo and Gini Graham Scott, *In the Land of Difficult People: 24 Timeless Tales Reveal How to Tame Beasts at Work*. New York: AMACOM, 2008.
6. Gargiulo, MakingStories.net, and eBook *Maximizing the Value of Live Online Learning*, 2009, http://bit.ly/8YKKHj.
7. Seth Godin, *Tribes: We Need You to Lead Us*. Indianapolis: Penguin Group, 2008.
8. Gargiulo, *Making Stories*.
9. Duarte, *Slide:ology*, pp. 196–197.

chapter
SEVEN

Meeting in Real Time
Using the Power of Now

If you've ever done online dating (and even if you haven't, you can probably imagine), you know that after you've exchanged e-mails and talked on the phone to develop a connection, you arrange to meet in the real world. For a significant experience to occur between individuals or groups, there needs to be a space and time when the parties come together and directly exchange information and ideas.

In the traditional business world, this has usually been a meeting or event at which one or more people may present and an audience may watch, listen, and perhaps participate. More recently the trend on the Internet has been to create a context for an event through a continuous conversation or channels of interaction in social media that can provide research, feedback, and shape the context along with the content for an event.

A real-time event or meeting remains the basis for the majority of interactive experiences of persuasion, training, learning, entertainment, or any other similar endeavor. However, the lines between the new tools of social media and established communications programs that support real-time meetings and events are blurring.

Shel Israel, author of *Twitterville*,[1] recently held an event in which he used Twitter to answer students' questions in a classroom in New England while he stayed at home in Silicon Valley. He used Twitter to begin the communication with the students, which he aggregated with a hashtag (#[filtertopic]) so that everyone could follow (using a filter) all of the preliminary questions and commentary. The event was fun, and the students loved it because it used Twitter (and presumably not PowerPoint), but you might still wonder: Where were the visuals and the accountability?

The climax of the event was an online real-time (synchronous) class. It might seem that the best tool for this part of the project would be one that used messaging (chat or Twitter) and voice (audio conferencing) and some visuals. Suppose an important Web site came up as an answer to a question? How could it be shown or reviewed? Certainly the URL could be shared through Twitter, but in this scenario, each individual attendee would need to access the information on her own.

The alternative is to use a program or platform that supports shared visuals, audio, and other tools in real time—a Web conferencing or webinar tool. While it is true that using only Twitter, even for the real-time event, facilitated instant interaction with students using portable devices, a large screen shared between Israel and the classroom would add a very useful dimension to the conversation. A whiteboard and the ability to brainstorm, annotate, and share notes would provide even more functionality.

In Chapter Two we described the concept of using a Twitter feed on a large screen at a conference so that real-time exchanges with a panel of speakers could take place. This is an evolving trend, to be sure, but enhancing a session with projected visuals is still a staple for any online conference or webinar to enhance communication and retention.

At this point it's time to take a closer look at some of the tools that let you effectively take a conversation or social media interaction from the "online dating" phase to the real world in real time—over the Internet.

THE REALITY OF WEB CONFERENCING

The use of the Internet for holding meetings and conferences began quite a while ago in proprietary networks run by large powerhouses like Cisco. The problem was that participants had to go to a location where connections were available with sufficient bandwidth to accommodate the parties. This was the early period of the video conference, which was the preserve of Fortune 500 companies, mainly in broadcast, entertainment, and advertising, and a few large corporations and the occasional university that had the resources to implement such a system. As the Internet matured and bandwidth increased, more and more of this functionality found its way online. VOIP (voice over Internet protocol) technology also emerged for audio communication, which could eventually be merged with a video feed.

Companies like Microsoft entered the field, buying early developers like Placeware, using dedicated servers in solutions like Netmeeting, and eventually designing platforms like SharePoint and Microsoft's latest end user Web conferencing tool, LiveMeeting. Entering the field was Citrix Online, with a tool called Go to My PC that began with the ability to access a remote computer for technical support. Citrix Systems morphed Go to My PC into what is now a suite of products called GoToMeeting and GoToWebinar. More recently Citrix published a GoToTraining product with content management, interactivity, and registration features geared specifically to online training users.

Obviously there are many other companies, from small startups to Cisco and Adobe, which purchased Macromedia (which had Breeze) and more recently built conferencing into its own successful Acrobat product. Skype, which began as a pioneer in VOIP phone service, has built more and more functionality into its software; video can be shared, along with chat and file sharing, which makes it a viable alternative in some situations. Web conferencing is a solution with a wide range of features and capabilities that is widely available on the Internet. There are free services with video (and limited stability) and robust solutions built on powerful platforms that scale up to thousands of attendees.

A webinar, in fact, is simply a meeting with many more attendees than a regular Web conference (think conference room or small venue for a Web conference compared to an auditorium or stadium for a webinar). Companies that offer webinars need to have a solid platform that scales up without raising bandwidth issues.

VIDEO AND WEB CONFERENCING

Not surprisingly, the single biggest way to choke bandwidth is by including video in the equation. When Oprah Winfrey promoted a video conference or webinar with Eckhart Tolle (author of *The Power of Now*),[2] there were so many subscribers that the first few programs reached many viewers with frozen screens. That is why, for many professional or organizational programs, whether for sales, training, or education, Web conferencing typically features a module that supports a slide show, a whiteboard, chat, annotation tools, and sharing a desktop—which means that the presenter can show the audience whatever is happening on her computer screen.

While VOIP may be part of scenario, in most cases the programs that support a Web conference or webinar also provide a common conference call number that participants can dial to hear the audio portion and participate (when their lines are open; generally a moderator mutes all but the presenter's audio until Q&A).

Some applications, but not all, show video of the speakers; if there is an element that is more likely to crash a Web conference than anything else, it is using a live video feed as the speaker is shown. A great alternative is simply to use some still photos in the PowerPoint or other slide show that present the relevant content, perhaps in the opening slide, and then let your content and voice carry the program. Another solution is to use a video feed (from a webcam or live camera) in a window on the shared desktop for brief periods to minimize issues of broadcast stability.

WEB CONFERENCES AND WEBINARS VERSUS ONLINE CLASSROOM TRAINING

The key difference between a Web conference or webinar and the many different solutions for putting a classroom online is that Web conferences and webinars have a live speaker, trainer, or panel of experts present, responsive and moderating the proceedings. Online classroom solutions typically are created by such experts specifically to run in their absence—or asynchronously. As a result, a Web conference or webinar is a single real-time conference or event (a video version is usually archived so that anyone who could not be present can view it afterward). Online classrooms, however, are created to be available 24/7, so that those with access to the program can participate at their convenience.

An online classroom solution can be as simple as creating a movie with Camtasia Studio or Windows Media Encoder (introduced in Chapter Six), capturing a series of computer screens, perhaps pointing to specific screens with annotation tools, and narrating a sound track to provide the training content. Camtasia Studio makes a movie of PowerPoint (or any other series of screens) with an audio narrative and optional video track specifically so that a presenter is no longer required to be in attendance. Other more sophisticated online classroom tools may let the user interact with a series of screens using "hotspots" (or areas on the screen that are clickable as hyperlinks to other information) and offer testing at the end of a sequence or chapter. But, again, no instructor or trainer is actually present and interacting with a student. (For more comprehensive online solutions, look at the products from Articulate.com, including a new Web-based screen capture program, screenr at http://screenr.com.)

While online classroom solutions have great value, and leverage the power of social media through enhanced communication between instructor and students before and after a training session, they lack the dynamic interaction of a real-time event like a Web conference or webinar. Not surprisingly, online classrooms are seldom used for sales or marketing. And although online classroom solutions offer the benefits of students working on their own time, the absence of real-time interaction with one or more instructors or experts is a serious drawback. A discussion forum or blog, or even a microblogging tool like Twitter, can augment the situation, and social media as a support system and feedback mechanism for relatively static online tools is a great development.

THE REAL WORLD: HOW SOCIAL MEDIA PROMOTES AND COMPLEMENTS A SUCCESSFUL WEB EVENT

When Citibank wanted to promote its new Citi-Forward card, it combined a social media campaign with a webcast targeting mainly financial media and Gen Y users of financial services. The marketing team made sure that participants in the webcast were well-known bloggers in the financial industry, and a follow-up campaign to the webcast was planned on social networks like Facebook, Twitter, MySpace, and a YouTube channel. Most of the buzz about the webcast was created directly by the blogger-panelists chosen by Citi's marketing team and the moderator, a well-known financial podcaster who also worked for the Student Loan Network.

Mack Collier, a social media expert who participated in the event and wrote about it on his blog, used Twitter mainly to build critical mass; he says that he contacted only seven Twitter colleagues to help promote the webcast. Collier says in his blog that he doesn't respond to "pitches" from people who contact him for the first time with a proposal—he only pays real attention to those he knows long term. The key point here, central to social media: these were key *influencers* and those with whom Collier already had long-term trusted relationships. The result of using social media connections to promote the webinar was that media registrants (the main target audience) exceeded the hoped-for number by 100 percent, and the event was a successful launch for Citi-Forward.[3]

In the following scenario and text sections we use two Citrix tools as representative of many Web conferencing and webinar solutions. The features offered in the tools are pretty standard; where applicable, differences in features will be pointed out. Most platforms have annotation tools, shared desktop, chat, and some include a whiteboard and video of the speaker over a webcam. There are slight variations, however; Microsoft LiveMeeting has no Audience view but does feature a more robust PowerPoint playback capability with a slide preview panel of thumbnails.

SCENARIO: DR. CONKLIN GIVES HIS FIRST WEB CONFERENCE

Dr. Stanley Conklin, the expert on Alzheimer's who was introduced in a scenario in Chapter Six, did so well with his new PowerPoint skills that Julie Mayfield's client, Premiere Pharmaceuticals, wanted Strategic Communications, the graphics firm, to set up a series of webinars. Stanley loved the idea because he wouldn't have to go to an airport or rent any more cars—he would be able to deliver the content from his study. Julie set him up with Go to Meeting Corporate and Go to Webinar, two Citrix solutions, and promised to guide him through the process of planning and delivering the content.

Based on the PowerPoint presentation that Stanley had developed with Julie's coaching, the webinars would be organized under the general topic of "Managing Alzheimer's Disease: A 'Wholistic' Approach with Three Modalities." To begin raising awareness about the webinars, Stanley used his Twitter feed and Facebook page to ask a series of questions about the seminars he had already delivered to those who were now following him:

- Which of the three treatment modalities—talk therapy, pharmacology, and group support—do you find most effective?
- Are you a physician, family member, or caregiver? How does that influence your choice of modality of care or treatment?
- Which treatment modality would you like to learn more about? In what ways?

These questions garnered a wide range of responses, and although Premiere Pharmaceuticals, the sponsor of the webinars, would have preferred that the webinars not emphasize the other treatment modalities, they could not argue with the enthusiasm and energy that this preliminary research campaign on Twitter engendered.

Figure 7.1 Many Web conferencing programs let you meet instantly by inviting other participants by phone or e-mail.

When the company "suggested" a set of slides with the latest data on their product, NeuroPath, Stanley agreed to include some of them and blogged about the issue, gathering more commentary and increasing his transparency and credibility among the public and the medical community.

But, as he had been in using PowerPoint, Stanley was nervous about embracing yet another technological tool. To increase his comfort level, Julie invited him to a two-way conference. Since she had the Citrix products installed on her computer, she clicked the program icon in her system tray and chose to "Meet Now." (See Figure 7.1.)

To keep things simple the first time around, Julie called Stanley when he was ready and told him what to do to join their meeting. (See Figure 7.2.) On other occasions she sent him e-mails with links to click and instructions on how to log in.

During this first meeting, Stanley saw that they were connected

Figure 7.2 Participants can join the meeting by entering information into their Web browser or clicking a link provided through e-mail or discussed by telephone.

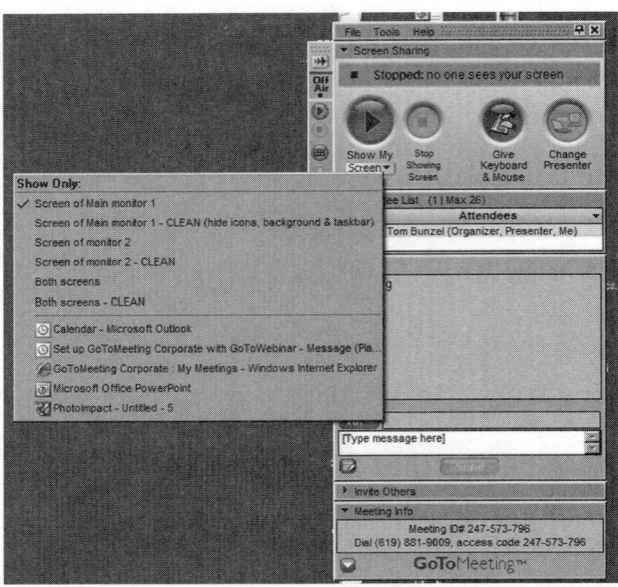

Figure 7.3 The presenter in a Web conference or webinar can share her desktop view or display any open program to the audience.

through the Internet (and simultaneously by phone), and that when Julie clicked Show My Screen, he saw the desktop of her computer through his Web browser. He also had a program window floating above the browser that let him see who else was in the meeting and he could participate in chat. (See Figure 7.3.) On her end, Julie decided not to show Stanley her cluttered desktop and clicked a drop-down menu to determine what she could share—which included any of her open programs—PowerPoint, Outlook, and an image editor called PhotoImpact. (See Figure 7.4.)

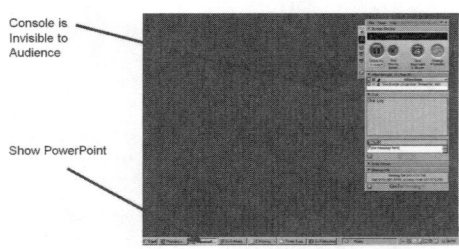

Figure 7.4 The presenter can show a clear screen to the audience (instead of a cluttered desktop) and then click a program from the Task Bar to show it on a shared desktop.

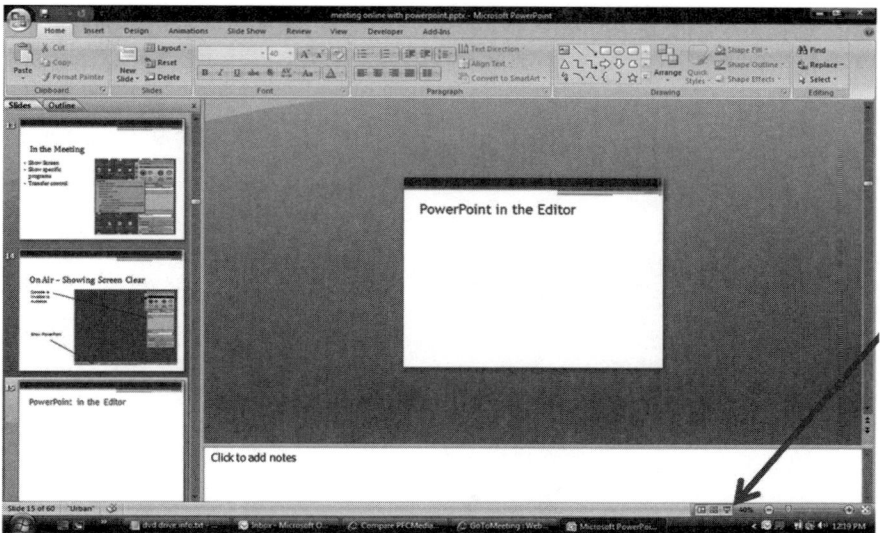

Figure 7.5 During a Web conference or webinar, opening the PowerPoint program will show the Editor to the audience. You can click the Full Screen view or press F5 to show your presentation.

Julie clicked to show PowerPoint, which opened as a program in the Editor (where new slides and graphics could be created). (See Figure 7.5.)

During their training, Julie had explained to Stanley that it's best not to display a PowerPoint slide show to the audience until it is in full-screen mode. Julie went over the distinction again, explaining that if she wanted to train Stanley in PowerPoint, she could keep the Editor open and go through various steps, which he could follow. But when Stanley was presenting, instead of showing a cluttered desktop or the PowerPoint Editor, it would be best not to share his screen until the presentation was up full screen, with his first "welcome" slide—so she clicked the icon at the bottom of the PowerPoint screen to display her slide show full screen.

With a Web conference or webinar, instead of being projected on a screen in a conference room or auditorium, the content was visible to the audience through their Web browsers (along with some interactive features like polling, annotation, and chat).

Julie went through a few slides with images and animation and then said, "Okay Dr. Conklin, now you try it!" She made Stanley the presenter, and he had more options in his console to show his screen. Julie talked him through it, and now he was "live" in a practice session. After sharing his desktop and opening his PowerPoint slide show full screen, Stanley opened a window to see what Julie (and the rest of his potential audience) would be seeing as he presented. (See Figure 7.6.)

Stanley went through a few slides, practicing his timing and animations, and also tried out some of the annotation tools, like the highlighter.

Julie explained that he now had three ways to emphasize information in a slide:

1. Animate a shape within PowerPoint, as she'd taught him before.
2. Use the PowerPoint highlighter during the slide show.
3. Use the Web conferencing tool's highlighter.

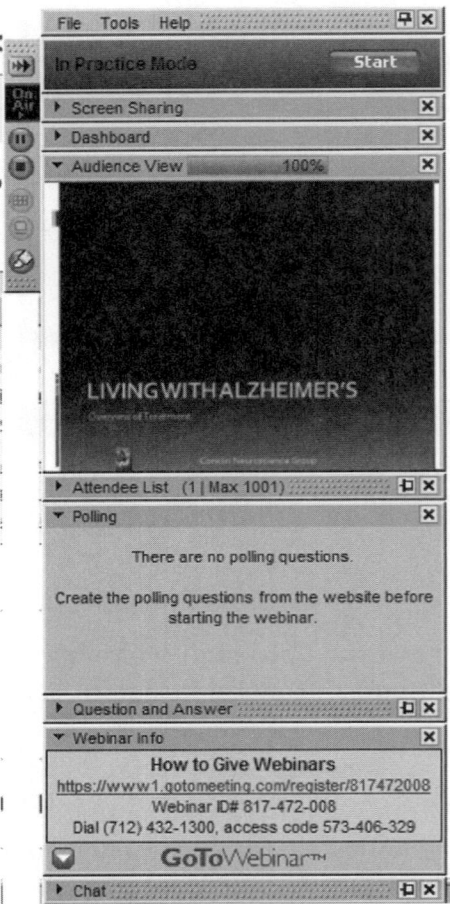

Figure 7.6 While online, the presenter can open a window to monitor the pace and see what the audience is seeing, handle Q&A, or present polling questions.

To avoid confusion, and not unwittingly save the annotations with the slide show, Stanley decided to play with the highlighter in the conference console. When they exited the practice session, Stanley was considering the possibilities of what had just happened.

"So now that I have this program loaded on my computer," he said, "I can start a meeting with anyone I know just by sending them an e-mail invitation or calling them up?"

Julie said yes, adding that the only extra step would be needed if audience members never used the particular webinar or conferencing tool. They might need to spend a few minutes loading and installing the software. Stanley realized that while he would be getting the tools from either Julie's company or the sponsor, Premiere Pharmaceuticals, he'd be able to use the Web conferencing tool in conjunction with his teaching and private practice.

"I guess what I could do," he said, "is put together a few presentations that I could use during my office hours with my psychiatric students—so that if they raised a question on Twitter or by e-mail, I could just say 'Let's meet now' and give a short presentation and talk to them during the slide show to answer their questions."

Julie suggested other alternatives. When Dr. Conklin was conferring with patients, if he wanted to provide support, he didn't need to have preset PowerPoint presentations.

"But I have to show something," the doctor said.

Sure, Julie reminded him, but you can show anything on your screen. "So if you turn on the webcam on your computer, you can move video of yourself into the shared screen area and communicate visually one on one. Or you could set up a series of Web pages or even Word documents or pictures that you could discuss with your patients' families or support groups, for example. It doesn't have to be just PowerPoint."

Stanley was considering the possibilities; with Julie's help he had grown a large online community of followers on Twitter, Facebook, and on his blog, in addition to his students and the families and support groups of the patients he treated.

"Can I show the before-and-after videos of the patients?" he asked her.

Julie explained that if he tried to show video from within PowerPoint, as she had taught him, it often did not display through the Web browser. (The playback program inside of PowerPoint—the media control interface—does not work quite right through the Internet.) As a workaround, however, she suggested that he could post the videos to run from YouTube from his Web browser. As part of his previous social media participation, he had already uploaded some of his most effective videos into his own channel on YouTube, where he had received and responded to numerous comments from colleagues and caregivers. He realized that he would just have to keep the Web browser available during a presentation with the videos ready to play (or place a hyperlink to the YouTube page into his PowerPoint slide).

Stanley said, "Okay, this is great, but we just did a Web conference—which I suppose might have included some other people?" Julie confirmed this. "So what's a webinar?"

A webinar, she explained, used a slightly more robust program that is scaled to more users; there might still be more than one presenter but essentially he'd be presenting to a larger audience that could communicate with chat, questions and answers, or through the polling questions that he would need to set up in slides before the event.

"Yes, I saw that polling feature," he said. "How do I use it?"

Julie told him that her company, Strategic Communications, would be managing the webinars so that he just had to e-mail the multiple choice questions to the main coordinator, who would add the polling element to the presentation that Stanley could access at any time—first displaying the poll, giving the audience a few minutes to vote, and then displaying the results before returning to his presentation.

It quickly became apparent to Julie that Stanley was getting excited and wanted to do some webinars on his own. Julie opened the module in GoToWebinar, where a polling question could be created for an upcoming webinar. (See Figure 7.7.)

"Okay," he said, "so how would I put together a webinar for a larger audience?"

Julie explained again that most of the details would be handled by her company, which had compiled e-mail lists and had a sophisticated strategy for promoting the event. But Stanley wanted to be able to invite attendees himself and see how that was done. Julie explained that he could start a webinar right away, just as they had started their ad hoc

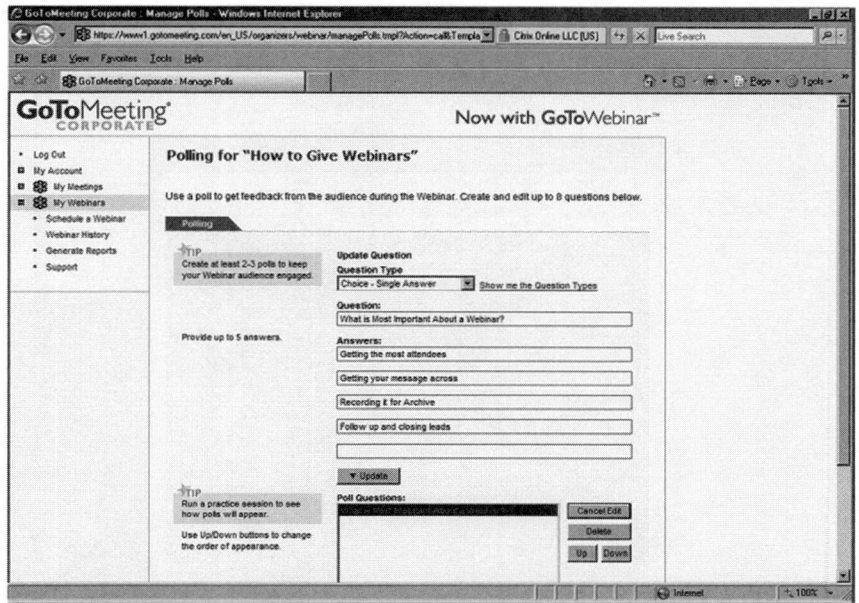

Figure 7.7 To get feedback from the audience during a conference or webinar, you can ask a polling question and show the results during the presentation.

practice meeting, or more likely schedule one down the road, using either the pop-up menu that was now installed in his system tray (see Figure 7.1) or a Web page from the main program (see Figure 7.8).

Julie showed him the Scheduling window (see Figure 7.9) where he could begin to set up and describe his own

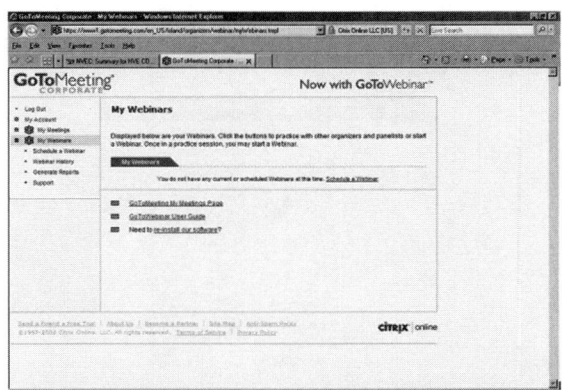

Figure 7.8 The main program for the Web conference provider will let you begin or schedule a conference or webinar (GoToMeeting Corporate shown here).

Meeting in Real Time: Using the Power of Now

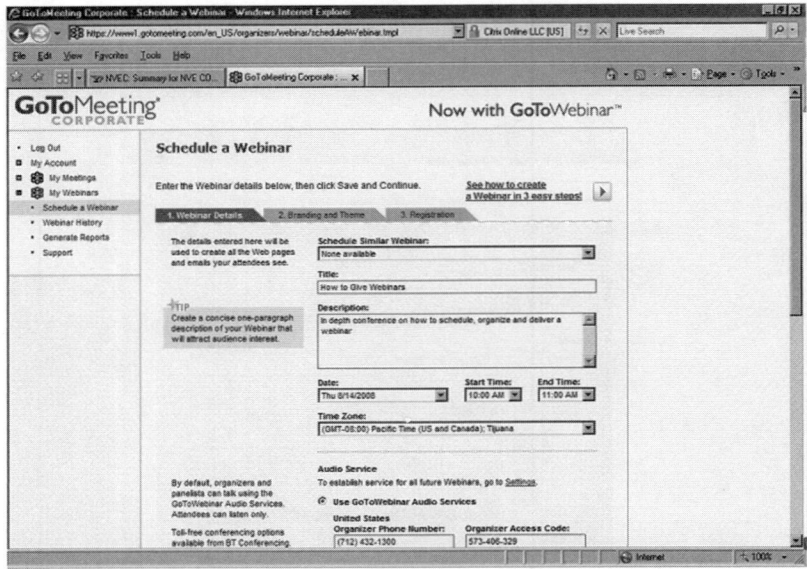

Figure 7.9 The Schedule window provides a form to describe the event, pick a date and time, and set up audio services (instead of limiting the audio to computer speakers and microphones).

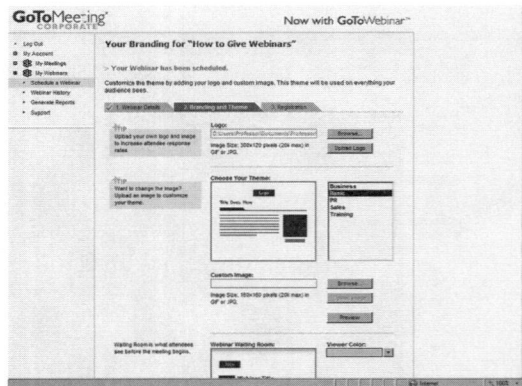

Figure 7.10 When setting up your own webinar, using your own branding in the invitation and waiting room, with a background and logo, adds consistency and professionalism.

session. Julie showed him that if he wanted, at the bottom of this screen he could also include other organizers and panelists.

Since Stanley would be giving his own seminars separately from those sponsored by the pharmaceutical company, he wanted to add his own unique look to the invitation page and waiting room, which attendees would see when they signed up and entered the event. (See Figure 7.10.)

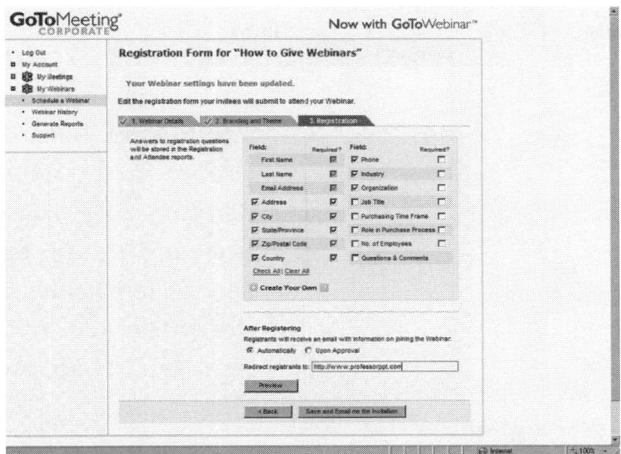

Julie also went over the options for the Registration page (see Figure 7.11), where Stanley could collect additional information about those who would be attending, and how he could manage the webinar once it was set up.

Figure 7.11 The Registration page can be set up to collect specific information in a form to add to a database for follow-up and research. You can mail a copy back to yourself for a preview or to copy and paste into other e-mail invitations.

Since Julie had Stanley e-mail the invitation to himself from the Registration page, she had him open the message in his own e-mail program (Microsoft Outlook), where he could copy and paste, forward, or otherwise send the invitation out to others. Julie pointed out that the Web link for registration could also be copied and pasted into Stanley's blog, Twitter posts, or any other areas of the Internet where he wanted to provide access to the webinar. (See Figure 7.12.)

Stanley tried out the Web link to preview the registration page the potential attendees would see if they decided to attend his own webinar. (See Figure 7.13.)

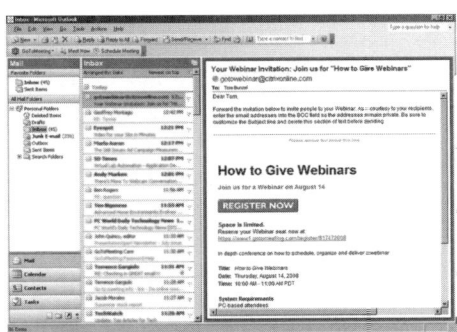

Figure 7.12 Webinar invites can be received and responded to with direct links to the Registration page from any e-mail program.

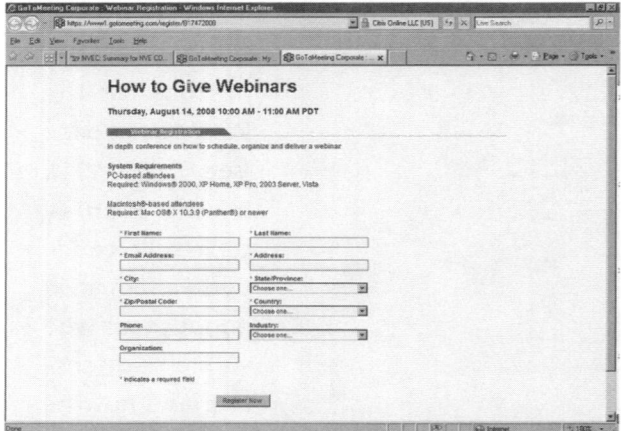

Stanley had done everything except actually give a webinar. A week before the event, Julie had him do a practice run-through to become familiar with the interface and test the software on his computer.

Figure 7.13 The Registration Web page for attendees has fields in a form with a Register Now (submit form) button. These are the fields chosen when the webinar is set up (as was shown in Figure 7.11).

> Since Stanley had both a laptop and a desktop, Julie suggested he deliver the session from the desktop and log in from his laptop *as a participant* to get a better idea of how the audience was following along with his visuals. (This is also a good idea if the conferencing program does not have an Audience View built into its presentation module.)

On the big day Stanley was nervous but prepared and excited. It wasn't until the moment when he was about to be introduced to his audience that he realized: *he couldn't see them—was anyone there?* He referred to the audience view and his secondary screen on the laptop to reassure himself and took a look at the list of attendees on his dashboard (see Figure 7.14) in his presenter module to see that, due to extensive social media and promotional efforts, there were several hundred viewers watching his screen. Stanley recognized a few of the names and welcomed them personally to the webinar, relaxing and developing rapport with the group.

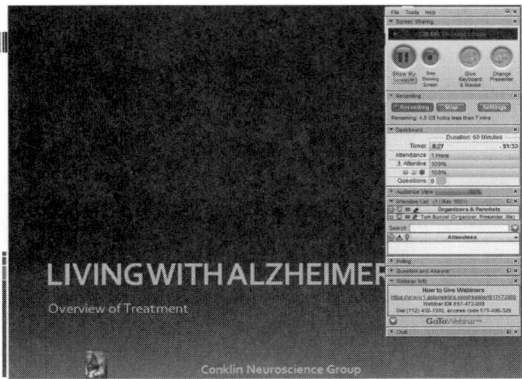

Figure 7.14 As the webinar begins, the presenter can see the attendee names as they enter, greet them, and make sure that the conference is being recorded for archived video.

Behind the scenes, Julie and her staff were ready to handle some of the logistics, including introducing Dr. Conklin and handling the Q&A as well as monitoring chat and helping any attendees who were having trouble logging in. In addition, Julie's technical expert had set up the recording options to make sure that the entire event would be saved as a video file for archiving, so that anyone who had missed the seminar could watch and listen later on. Julie's crew made sure that Recording was enabled under the Tools submenu for the webinar, along with the other functions that might be available to the presenter in his console. (See Figure 7.15.)

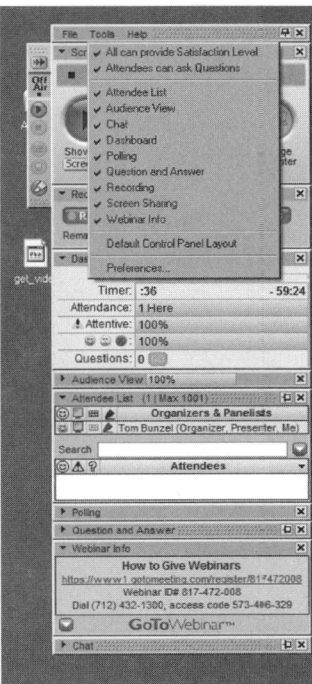

Figure 7.15 Before the webinar, the Tools submenu should be checked to make sure that all services are available and that Recording is enabled if the conference is to be archived as a video file.

TIPS FOR GETTING THE VIDEO RIGHT

Under the Recording Preferences, it is important to be sure that audio is enabled and that the microphone or default audio device is working properly. Windows Media is the default output file for this webinar, and the crew decides to save the

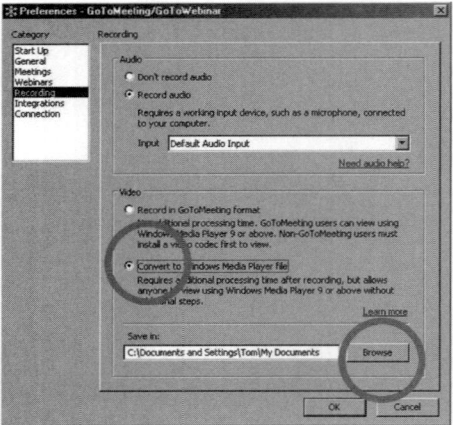

Figure 7.16 The webinar coordinator should check the Preferences window to make sure that audio is enabled and that the proper video output and folder locations are selected.

file locally in order to be able to use it in different ways: upload to YouTube, distribute on DVD, or to post on a Web page. (See Figure 7.16.)

Finally, the speaker should be prompted to put up his first slide in full screen view (not in the PowerPoint editor) so that recording can begin.

Whoever is in control of the meeting should now press the begin Recording red button (see Figure 7.17).

Depending upon what you chose in

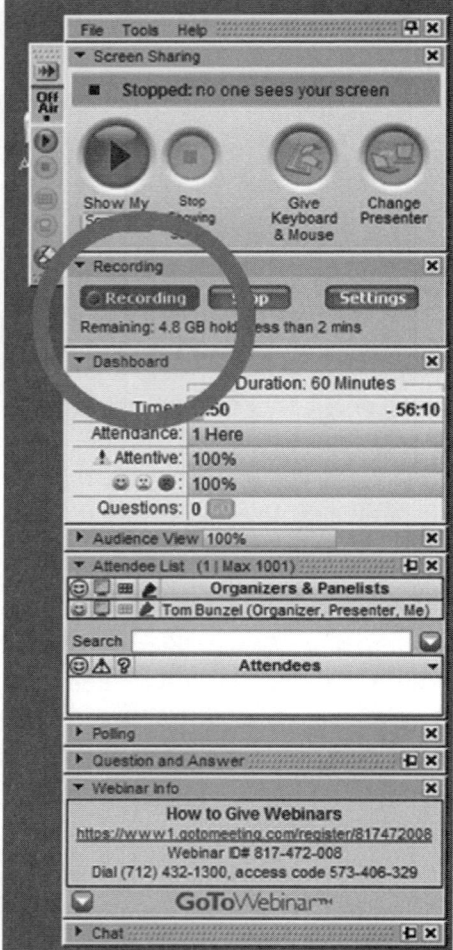

Figure 7.17 To avoid heartache or heartburn, make sure that someone is responsible to begin recording just prior to the speaker introduction.

the Recording Options (Figure 7.16), you will have the final recorded file in a local folder or you will receive a URL from the webinar software provider (in this case Citrix) to let you know the video can be accessed. In the latter case, another registration screen for viewing the archived video will collect more user information from anyone accessing the file for your follow-up database. (See Figure 7.18.)

Tools of Engagement

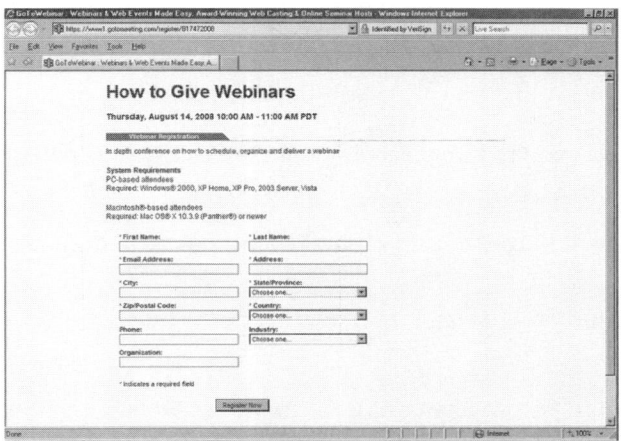

Figure 7.18 If the service provider for the webinar has archived the video online, users should fill out a form to view the archived file so that you can collect more information.

If you've chosen to have the file converted to Windows Media and stored locally, make sure you locate it in the folder where it was saved (*Back it up!*) and if necessary, edit the file in a video editor and output it in a format (Windows Media 9 or earlier) that can let others see it. Probably the best reason to store the file locally is to be able to upload it to a video hosting service like YouTube. Using YouTube to host the file will make it unnecessary to re-encode the video, since YouTube converts it to Flash format, and again, provides you with linking and embedding code to use the video in your blogs, link to it from social media posts, and send a link to the file by e-mail. Unless you have set up your YouTube video as private, posting it on your channel will allow people you have not specifically invited to watch it, who may search for it (using the keywords and metatags you used in the description when you posted the file) and will be able to view the archived webinar video. More users will watch, comment on, and rate the video, providing more potential for mass distribution of the information.

PROFESSIONAL WEB CONFERENCE OR WEBINAR TIPS

A webinar or Web conference is quite different from an in-person event for which there is an audience that the speaker can see and with whom she can interact. In a Web event, grabbing and holding the audience's attention is critical to establishing a connection that will keep attendees focused throughout the conference or seminar. Presentation and speaker expert Patricia Fripp has a series of tips for adding impact to your webinar both visually and through content and delivery. At the outset, she suggests using one or more looping slides in PowerPoint that introduce the session and deliver housekeeping information like the dial-in number and help information. For the initial slide, she says to "Think Hollywood" to grab the audience's attention. Fripp suggest that you also use a "hook" such as:

- A catchy fact: "It may interest you to know Ferraris hold their value more than polo ponies! I first learned this lesson when . . ."
- A startling statistic: "Did you know that if you had spent a million dollars a day, every day, since Jesus was born, you would not have spent a trillion dollars. Please keep that in mind as we strategize how to increase sales by only 5 percent."
- An intriguing challenge: "Ten years ago we were the market leaders. This year we are thirteenth. You are now in an exciting position to turn that around."

If you can, relate your hook directly to the essential message that may have built interest in your event through your blog, Twitter, Facebook, or other social sites. For example, in a training or educational event, you might say, "Many of you are here to learn how to grow nutritious vegetables in your own garden. Did you know that home grown organic gardening has grown 65 percent in the past three years?"

Only at this point does Fripp recommend that you introduce yourself. Like many presentation professionals, she stresses the need to focus on the audience's needs over the speaker's; use both intellectual and emotional issues to connect with an attendee's focus on "What's in it for me?"

For example, Fripp suggests that you don't say, "I'm going to talk to you about webinars." Instead say, "In the next fifty-six minutes, you will learn the six secrets of making a webinar work; the four benefits of using webinars as part of your client interaction; and the three mistakes our competitors are making when they use them." Of course, this could also be a great way to build excitement about your content in your promotional efforts and on the registration page.

Pausing for questions or handling them through chat, using polling questions, using a whiteboard or interactive diagram to build a concept with the audience are important practices for keeping your audience involved. Visuals that use analogies, metaphors, stories, and anecdotes are even more vital to maintain a connection with the audience in a conference or webinar. Remember that in most cases the audience can't see the speaker, so practice using a strong voice and avoid the use of filler words like *uh, huh, ah*, and so on. It's good to end with an action item or next step for the audience, and use vocal energy to end on a high note.[4]

Nancy Duarte, in her book *Slide:ology*, offers the reminder about slide design that when an audience member sits close to a screen, rather than in a boardroom or auditorium, slides can be formatted differently. Details are more readily visible and more text can go on the screen. However, because of the possibility of distraction and multi-tasking, Duarte recommends that you "break your content into bite-sized bursts so the viewer's interest stays piqued."[5]

It is worth reminding yourself that the audience is invisible—so keep consulting either the Audience view screen or to another monitor logged in as part of the audience. This lets you maintain proper pacing by noting whether your screen is being updated quickly enough for the audience to keep up.

Bear in mind that audience members vary and their attention may drift. Work with your voice and your visuals and use polling, chat, and Q&A to keep them connected. Whenever possible, involve the audience at regular intervals by using a question, scenario, or other technique that makes them (inter)active rather than passive.

Training expert and train-the-trainer Bob Pike gives webinars on how to give webinars. He suggests setting goals at the beginning of any online event and then testing at intervals to see how you're doing. (Some programs let you monitor the "mood of the audience" with colored graphics.) Pike suggests that an audience's highest need is to be valued and appreciated, and he expresses such sentiments throughout an event. He uses verbal reinforcement to acknowledge feedback, questions, or contributions of any kind, and he has several other tips for the end of a webinar:

- Tie things together at the close to reinforce knowledge and aid retention.
- Create a close that allows for celebration (meeting your stated goals and objectives).
- At the close, recommend that attendees take a specific action.
- Don't ask for an evaluation at the close—it's distracting.

Pike believes that attendees can listen with attention for about 90 minutes, retain subject matter for about 20 minutes, and need to be involved every 8 minutes for key points to stick in their consciousness. He also provides incentives at his events to make people pay attention and receive the appreciation that makes them attentive. Pike tells a story of an event for corporate executives at which he gave away potatoes as "prizes," and at lunch executives were wondering, "What do I have to do to get a potato?"[6] Recognition is a powerful tool.

For more ideas on how to get your audience's attention, look at *Better Beginnings* by Carmen Taran.[7]

TO VIDEO OR NOT TO VIDEO (THE SPEAKER)

Using a webcam image of the speaker can personalize a Web conference, and in some cases (such as with Skype) multiple webcam feeds can be used to create a video conference, but this can impede bandwidth and cause problems, particularly for a large-scale webinar. If the platform you're using does not have a webcam capability, you can show your image using your shared desktop simply by moving the preview window for your webcam program into the viewable area of the screen. (See Figure 7.19.)

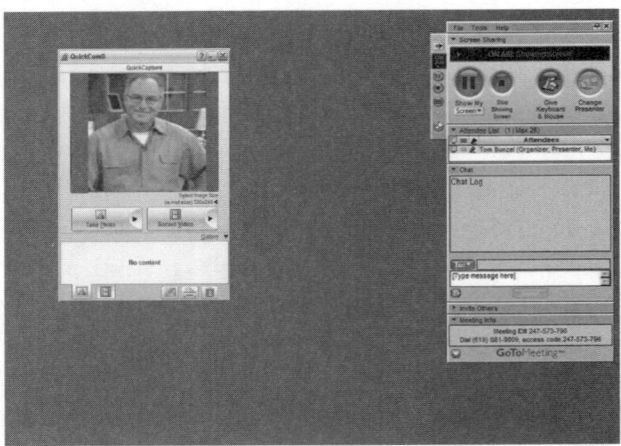

Figure 7.19 To show the speaker on screen, you can move the preview panel for a webcam program into the viewable desktop area of the Web conference or webinar.

SCENARIO: DR. CONKLIN'S WEBINAR

After some initial nervousness, when he realized there was no one to look at during his presentation, Dr. Conklin performed admirably and covered his material well. While focusing on his sponsor's pharmaceutical solution to the extent that he felt comfortable, he showed the before-and-after Alzheimer's treatment videos through his Web browser from their YouTube page and, using Adobe Acrobat Reader, he opened some testimonial letters from families whose loved ones had gained immeasurably from Dr. Conklin's family support, talk therapy, and physical exercise theories. This created a buzz at the conclusion—especially since

Dr. Conklin emphasized that the talk therapy involved a great deal of listening—and he followed up with several days of blogs and posts on Twitter and Facebook that stirred up quite a bit of commentary.

Caregivers and facilities from around the world now began to follow both Dr. Conklin and NeuroPath (the Alzheimer's drug being discussed) on Twitter, with questions and discussions flowing back and forth. Many Internet users, both individuals with Alzheimer's issues in their families and representatives from medical and psychiatric facilities, viewed the video after it was posted on YouTube, adding more commentary. In addition, Premiere Pharmaceutical used a registration page for hospitals and physicians who wanted to see the video after the webinar and built up a solid database of potential new speakers and proponents of their treatment regimen.

For his part, Dr. Conklin had learned how to give a webinar; he had managed to pace his slides fairly well, although he did run out of time and had to access the last few slides by number in order not to go over the allotted schedule. He made the mistake of using his laptop on battery power for monitoring what his audience was seeing, and it went to sleep midway through the conference. Not panicking, he opened the Audience View in his presenter module to make sure that the audience was keeping up with his visuals.

Finally, Dr. Conklin was extremely interested in the impact of his theories on the Alzheimer's community, and he carefully monitored the comments on his blog, read the Twitter and Facebook posts, and responded to questions. He saw that there was quite a bit of interest in the archived video on YouTube, the link to which he had sent out from his e-mail contact list. He asked some of his students to help him as his number of followers on Twitter and readers on his blog increased; they forwarded the most important comments that he may have missed when he was traveling or treating patients and responded to some on his behalf.

The psychiatrist's own contact database expanded dramatically, with both families of patients, psychiatric colleagues, and caregiving facilities contacting him by e-mail and phone. Julie Mayfield counseled him to add categories with color coding to his Outlook database to sort his contacts into appropriate groups. (See Figures 7.20 and 7.21.)

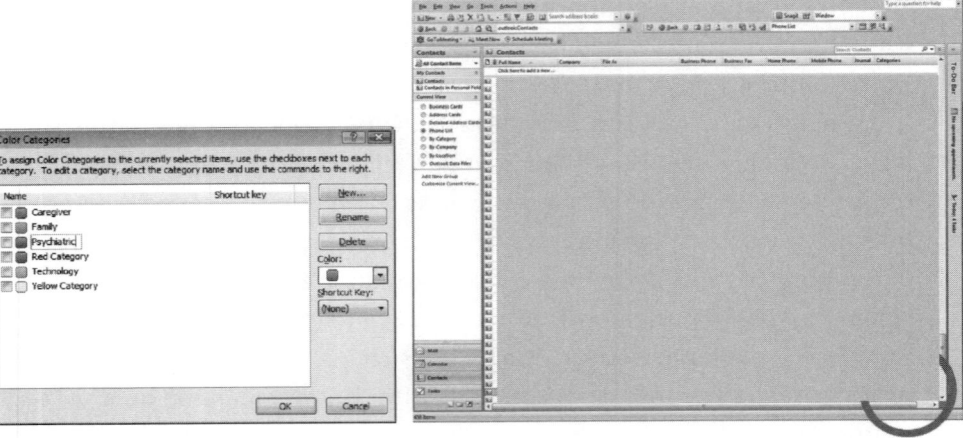

Figures 7.20 and 7.21 Outlook's Contact database lets you add color-coded categories to sort through large numbers of individuals and companies.

Copy2Contact for Capturing Database Information

Since Stanley was receiving a lot of e-mail and accessing Web pages with additional contact information, as well as data that he wanted to bring into his Outlook Calendar, Julie showed him how to use Copy2Contact (formerly known as Anagram and downloaded from copy2contact.com) to create a hotkey system through which he could copy and paste multiple fields of data directly into Outlook's Contact and Calendar areas. He just needed to select data, press a hotkey (the default is F12), and review the information in either the Contact or Appointment window of Outlook before saving the information. (See Figure 7.22.)

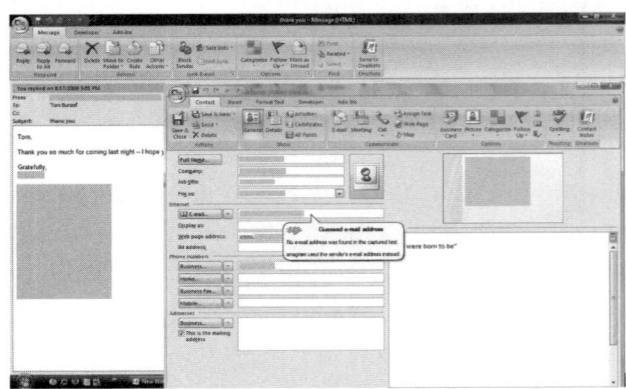

Figure 7.22 Copy2Contact is a utility that lets the user select a block of data and press a hotkey to place the information directly into the appropriate fields of the Contact database or Calendar.

Tools of Engagement

BRAINSTORMING WITH A WHITEBOARD

Although in the scenario Dr. Conklin used chat and fielded direct questions in his webinar, it was not a full-on collaboration session. In some cases, particularly in planning conferences, brainstorming and the input from multiple sources is more important than presenting information. For example, if the psychiatrist hadn't already created a PowerPoint presentation, he and Julie Mayfield (and perhaps a rep from Premiere Pharmaceutical) might have collaborated together to select a set of slides to communicate a specific concept.

Presentation specialists like Nancy Duarte (author of *Slide:ology*) frequently advise clients to sketch out ideas for the flow of a story before committing them to electronic media. The whiteboard tool of most Web conferencing solutions supports this by allowing the main presenter as well as other participants to share ideas on an electronic blank page using markers and then save the content in a graphics format.

Visual assets can be shown by various participants during the conference (graphics, charts, PowerPoint slides, even video), and then a flow of ideas to educate, sell or motivate can be worked out in real time on the whiteboard.

Leveraging the need for audience involvement, the participatory nature of a whiteboard can energize any online conference or webinar. To structure time for such a session, some presentation experts advise that the whiteboard be set up with a defined grid for each participant on which he or she can enter input, but in many cases the blank page supports a free flow of ideas that can be structured at the conclusion of or after the session.

When telling a visual story (set of anecdotes, metaphors, analogies, and so on), a whiteboard is a very effective way to elicit input from a variety of sources during an online conference. As we've seen with Twitter, even aggregating microblog posts through a Web browser can contribute to brainstorming and add content to the mix.

The combination of blog commentary, Twitter conversation, and a more structured setting in which the input can be aggregated and organized among a set of participants while still supporting multiple inputs and changes (whiteboards are easy to add to and erase) can be the focal point of a Web conference that has high energy and dramatic results.

USING DIMDIM TO PRESENT WITH PERSONAL VIDEO AND A WHITEBOARD

DimDim.com is an open source Web conferencing program that is available for free. You can use it to run a meeting at which you show a presentation, share your desktop, use a whiteboard, share PDFs or other documents, or perform most of the basic tasks involved in communicating through a Web browser. A nice additional feature is that the Flash capability of DimDim will work with most webcams, making it relatively easy to let the other participants in the conference see you.

The free version supports up to twenty users; the Pro version supports up to a hundred participants and costs less than $100 per month.

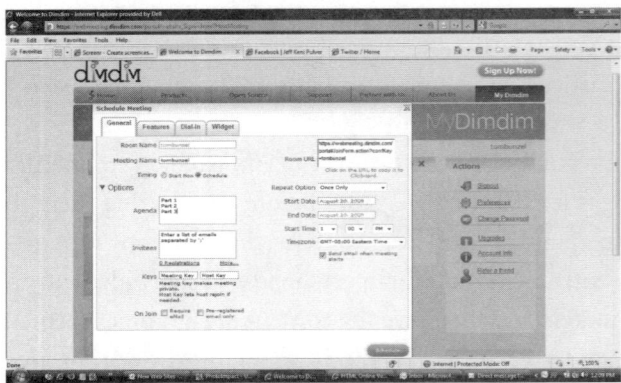

Figure 7.23 When you set up a scheduled DimDim conference, you can enter an Agenda that will be included in your e-mail invitations to others.

In a DimDim conference, you can share webcam views and hear one another through each person's microphone, send public and private messages, and record the conference. The recorded file can be downloaded, or you can use the supplied embed code to paste into the HTML (hypertext markup language) of any Web page or blog. DimDim is a great way to get started in Web conferencing and try out different scenarios. Once you've signed up for an account, you can host a meeting or join someone else's meeting (when they've sent you the log-in information). (See Figure 7.23.)

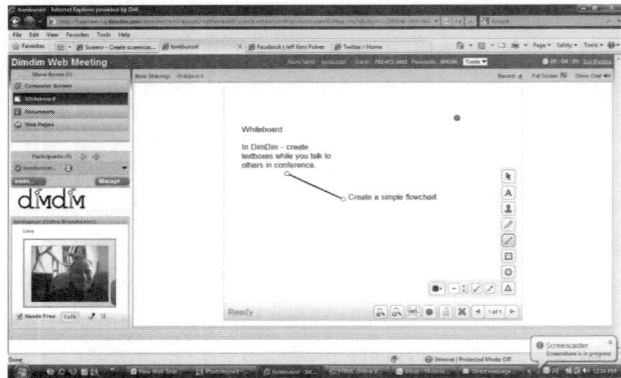

Figure 7.24 A DimDim meeting has the standard Web conference features, including a video window for webcam views of speakers and a shared Whiteboard.

Once the conference begins, you can interact through the microphone and speakers on the users' computers, over a telephone conference line, or via chat. (See Figures 7.24 and 7.25.)

Figure 7.25 You can invite additional participants from within a DimDim meeting so that you can start the meeting, set it up, and then have others join the event.

DimDim is a free, quick, and easy conferencing solution that also demonstrates the use of a whiteboard and a webcam of a speaker in a window. While DimDim captures the screens as the meeting is recorded, it does not have the capacity to save any shared files or whiteboard annotations. Files could be saved and then distributed by one of the users, and a whiteboard state can be saved as a graphic image by pressing the PrtScr key on your keyboard, which places the entire screen into memory, and then making sure that you paste the image into an image editing program (like PhotoShop) to crop and save the file to distribute after the meeting.

USING MICROSOFT WORD AS A WHITEBOARD

You can click to open the Office Clipboard with the down arrow in the Home tab and paste up to twenty-four items into your clipboard in Word, PowerPoint, or Excel. A great idea is to copy some AutoShapes

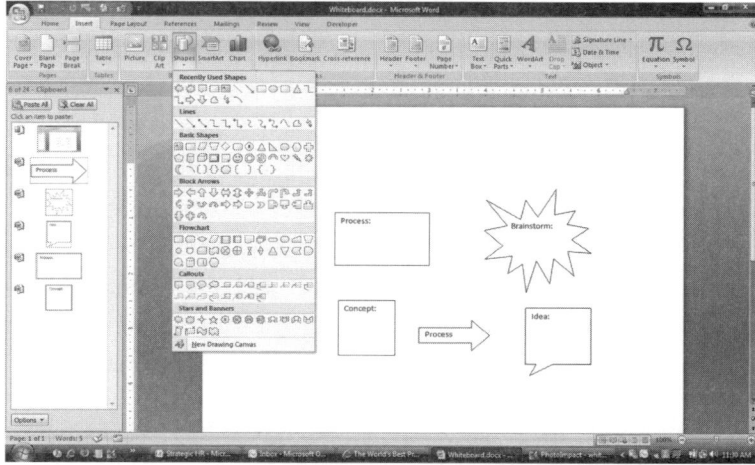

Figure 7.26 By copying AutoShapes or Text Boxes to the Office Clipboard and then pasting them into Word, you can create a whiteboard-like brainstorming diagram that you can save in Word format.

Meeting in Real Time: Using the Power of Now

that represent ideas to which you can add text and then copy them to the clipboard (see Figure 7.26). Then, as participants add their ideas, paste the appropriate AutoShape and revise its text to create a brainstorming diagram, and save it in Word format for reuse or distribution.

You could also use Word to store up to twenty-four screen captures from a program that does not permit saving a whiteboard. Click PrtScn and paste each successive image from the Whiteboard into Microsoft Word. This will give you an electronic version of the consecutive screens in your whiteboard.

SETTING UP AN EVENT ON FACEBOOK

The lead-up to a real-time event can be effectively orchestrated with a number of social media tools. You can place the URL for meeting registration in a blog post, on a social site like Twitter, or in an e-mail. Facebook is a particularly effective launch pad for a real-time event, conference, or webinar. Events is one of the available tabs under your Facebook Profile; you can add the tab by clicking the "+ Add a new tab" button (see Figure 7.27).

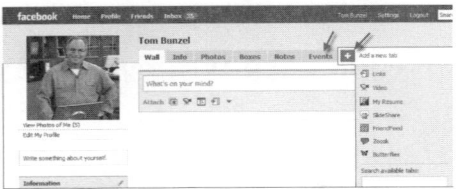

Figure 7.27 You can add an Event tab under your Profile in Facebook or click it directly if it's already been enabled.

Clicking Events will take you to an Events page that lists any events that you have added to your My Events area, but you can create an event by clicking the + Create Event button. The key step here is *naming the event*. Once created, the name cannot be changed, so it's important to choose a search-friendly and meaningful name. Then it's just a matter of filling out the relevant details including a URL that registrants can use to sign up for a conference or webinar. (See Figure 7.28.)

The Customize window Access area lets you choose the level of access: people can add themselves and invite others to the event; the event can be restricted to those you invite, but others can see the details without participating; or the event can be secret (outside Facebook search) and only specifically invited people can see the details. (See Figure 7.29.) The Publicize option lets you enable

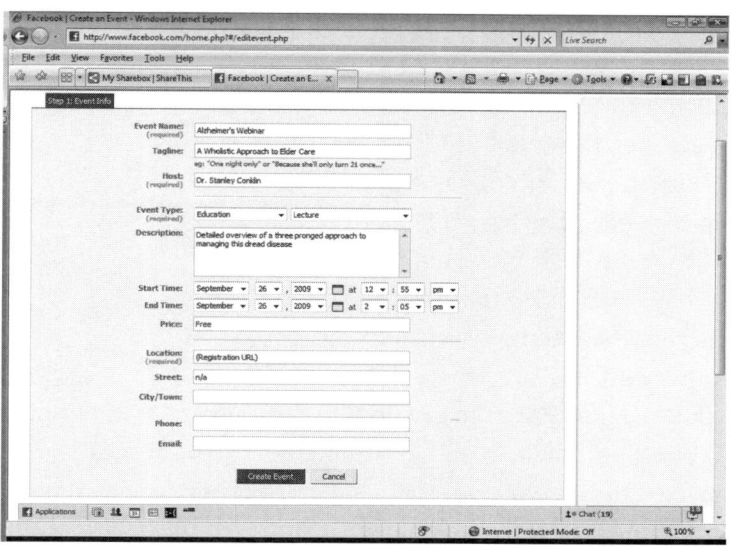

Figure 7.28 The Create Event window in Facebook is a great place to detail the particulars of a webinar or conference and then invite others within your Friends or any Groups or Networks to which you have access on Facebook.

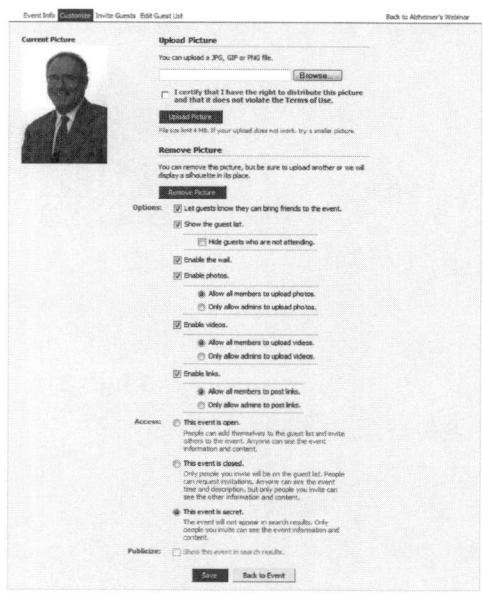

Figure 7.29 The Customize window lets you decide who can attend or be invited to the event and set it up for Facebook search.

the event for Facebook search. Click Save, and your event is set. (See Figures 7.30 and 7.31.)

Within Facebook there is an RSVP area that you should encourage attendees to click *after* they have registered online for the event. However, make sure they *don't* think that by RSVPing they have signed up.

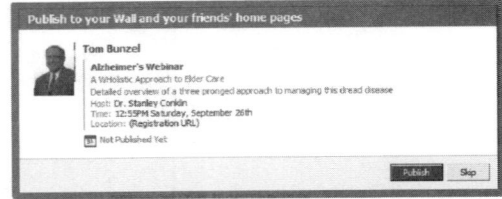

Figure 7.30 After saving your event, you have the option of publishing it to your Wall and to your Facebook Friends' home pages.

Now your event has the power of Facebook behind it. It can be distributed through any number of invitations within Facebook, and invitees and group members who receive the notification will be contacted through their e-mail with a direct link to the event page, where they can learn more and then click the link (for a Web conference) to register.

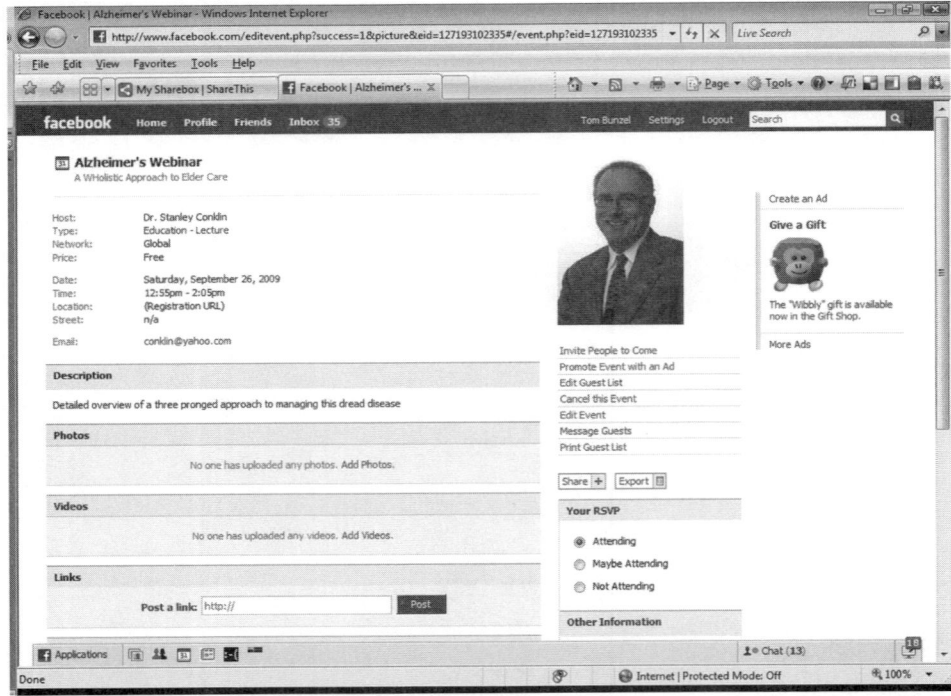

Figure 7.31 The Event page lets you see who is registered and post a direct link to the registration page for a conference or webinar in the Links panel.

PRESENTING DIRECTLY IN THE CLOUD

In Chapter Six we discussed PowerPoint as the preeminent slide presentation utility that lives online as video (through Camtasia and Windows Media Encoder), or hosted on SlideShare and AuthorSTREAM, or as the main visual component for most Web conferences and webinars. (Of course, Mac users are loyal to their Keynote.) But what if you didn't need to give a complete webinar—you just wanted to be able to show a presentation through the Web browser and, more important, be able to take advantage of many of the Web's other features (tags, embedding, linking, and so on) seamlessly? As competition has emerged for Microsoft Office from online applications like OpenOffice (see Figure 7.32) and Zoho (see Figure 7.33), the presentation components of these new applications have become fairly robust. Both online Office suites let you create, edit, and distribute documents (including spreadsheets and presentations) directly online.

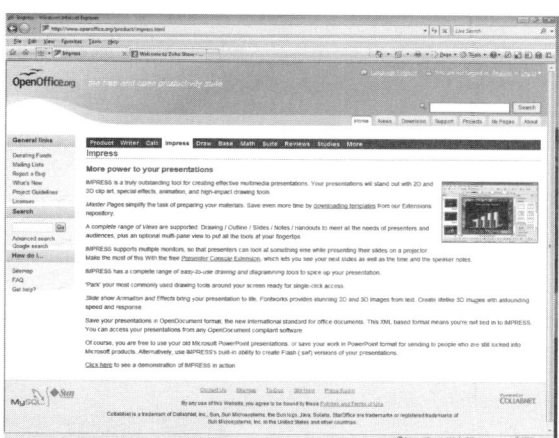

Figure 7.32 OpenOffice's Impress presentation program has many of the slide show features of PowerPoint and lives online, letting the user present directly through the browser and access other resources from within the program.

Figure 7.33 Zoho's Show online presentation tool also mimics PowerPoint, with many similar capabilities, and now works with SharePoint.

These kinds of programs can interface seamlessly with any social media or interactive forum information (each document can be accessed directly online with permission), and they invite collaboration, since multiple users can view, comment on, and even edit a given document from their respective locations. That is the essential value proposition of SharePoint, and Microsoft's new Office Web Applications (go to Windows Live to sign up: http://login.live.com and access the new Web Apps under More > Skydrive): you can create and edit online not just individually but as a team.

Of the online visual presentation tools currently available, perhaps the most mature is SlideRocket, which is not part of a suite but a stand-alone competitor for PowerPoint and Keynote that supports Flash video in its slides and lets the user access other Web documents (for example, spreadsheets and charts from another online Office suite, Google Docs).

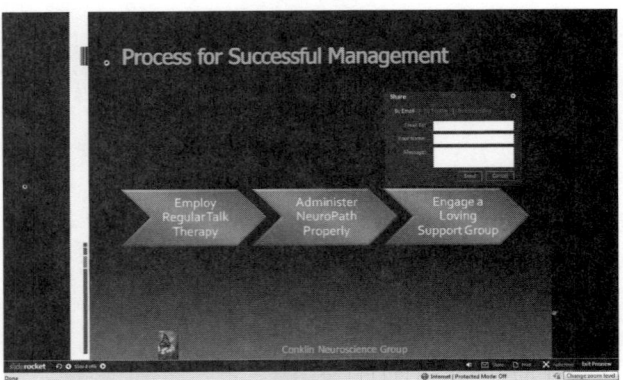

The Share capability of a tool like SlideRocket is expanding the reach of users on the Internet to communicate visually by including distribution by e-mail, directly through Twitter, or by embedding (copy and pasting code) in the same way that hosted

Figure 7.34 SlideRocket's sharing capability extends its reach; users can send links in Twitter posts or embed presentations in other Web pages, such as blogs.

applications for video and PowerPoint do. (See Figure 7.34.) This essentially makes online applications social media tools, bridging the gap between what had been limited to the desktops of end users and what lives online and is shareable among users, groups, and organizations.

As a link between the more powerful (in some respects) desktop programs, SlideRocket lets the user import and export PowerPoint files and supports some Custom Animation (mainly within individual objects, as compared to SmartArt diagrams, for example); the capabilities expand with each version of SlideRocket. (See Figures 7.35 and 7.36.)

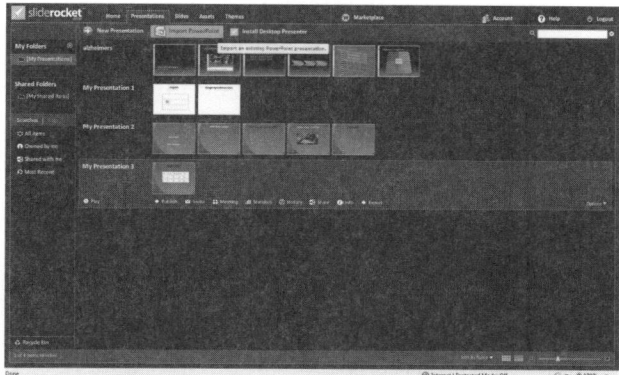

Figure 7.35 SlideRocket's ability to import and export PowerPoint expands its versatility.

All of these tools mimic PowerPoint to a greater or lesser extent to enhance usability. There are placeholders within the slides, features like transitions are supported, and there is generally a gallery of designs and backgrounds to choose from or ways of creating and uploading your own. For users who are queasy about keeping their content only on the Internet, most of these programs support the ability to download and store presentations and other documents in Office-compatible

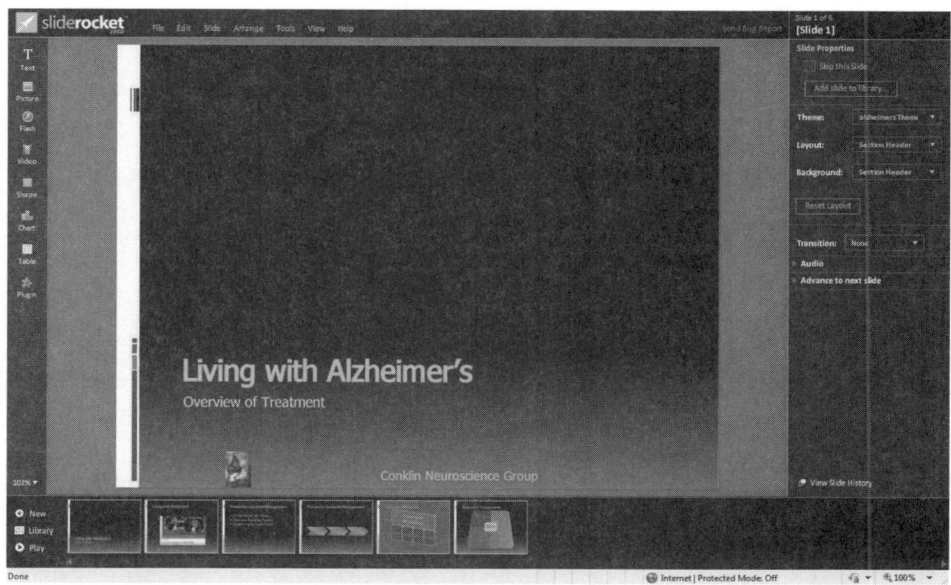

Figure 7.36 For an online application, SlideRocket provides a full array of tools to create and present slide shows with graphics, video, and animation entirely through a Web browser.

file formats. How would these applications work in a Web conference? When you share your desktop and open your Web browser, any participants in a conference can see you edit or present directly from within SlideRocket or any of the other tools mentioned.

GETTING ORGANIZED AND CONNECTING WITH ONENOTE

The organizational issue of aggregating Web content was mentioned in Chapter Four, when discussing the shared bookmark feature of Delicious.com. Another tool that combines the indexing capabilities of a database, robust search, and the ability to conference directly with others is the unsung hero of the Microsoft Office Suite: OneNote. OneNote deserves a mention for its capabilities in research and preparation for online communication as well as the collaboration needed in a real-time conference.

OneNote is a digital loose-leaf notebook on steroids. Along the top of the window are Sections, and in the right panel are Pages, each of which can be named and configured to represent projects, classes, categories, or any other areas into which related information can be placed and stored. The power of OneNote comes alive when copying and pasting information from the Internet into pages that are organized in sections according to the needs of the user. As shown in Figure 7.37, a selected section of a Web page pasted into a OneNote page takes with it its reference URL, making a return to the original source easy.

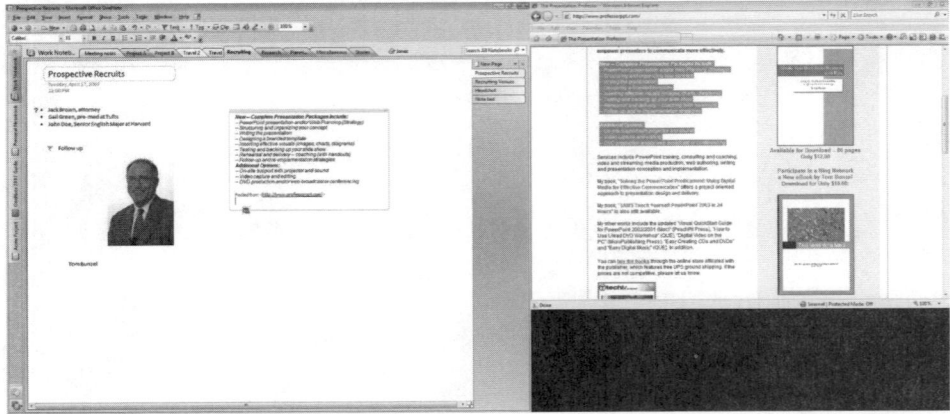

Figure 7.37 When you paste information from the Internet into a OneNote page, the URL from the original source is also included, making OneNote an excellent research tool.

In its current version, OneNote comes with lots of search capability; you can add various color-coded Tags to items and cross-reference Tasks between OneNote and Outlook. You can copy and paste video into OneNote, insert files (including entire PowerPoint presentations), and you can use the program as a voice recorder by speaking into a microphone and recording audio directly into a OneNote page. An effective way to get your PowerPoint slides into OneNote (Office 2007) is to select Print from PowerPoint and locate the Send to OneNote printer selection. The slides will go directly into a OneNote page that you can move to an appropriate section.) (See Figure 7.38.)

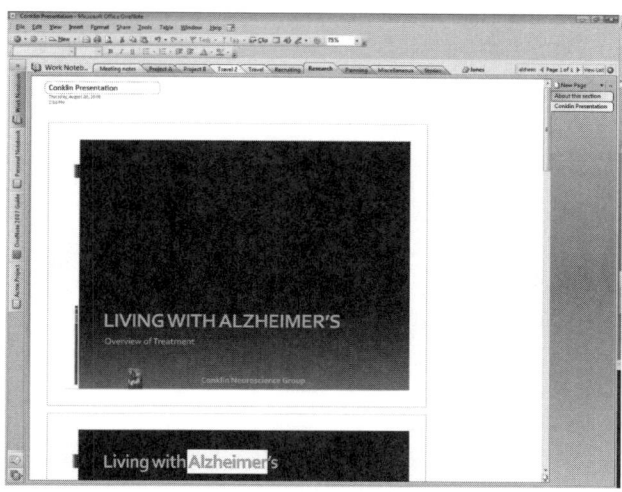

Figure 7.38 When you send a PowerPoint file to OneNote through the print feature, its slides become searchable and you can begin to add reference information in OneNote.

While OneNote is a superb tool for planning for a meeting, event, or training session, it can also be used to conference in real time to collaborate on content within its Sections and Pages. By clicking on Live Sharing Session under Share in OneNote, and selecting Start Sharing Current Section, you open a task pane that takes you through the process of sharing a section of your notebook. After designating a password, which you will need to share with any participants in the session, a window opens with Shared Address Information (an IP address) (see Figure 7.39). You can copy and paste this IP address and send it, along with the designated password, to other participants, who can then select Join Existing Session under the Share > Live Sharing Session menu, enter the IP address and password, and join the conference. At this point participants are sharing the pages in the shared section of the OneNote notebook and can suggest changes or add information. OneNote is a powerful online collaboration tool.

In OneNote 2010 the Start Live Session feature has been removed, replaced with a new Share tab on the Ribbon that allows users to share an entire notebook with other

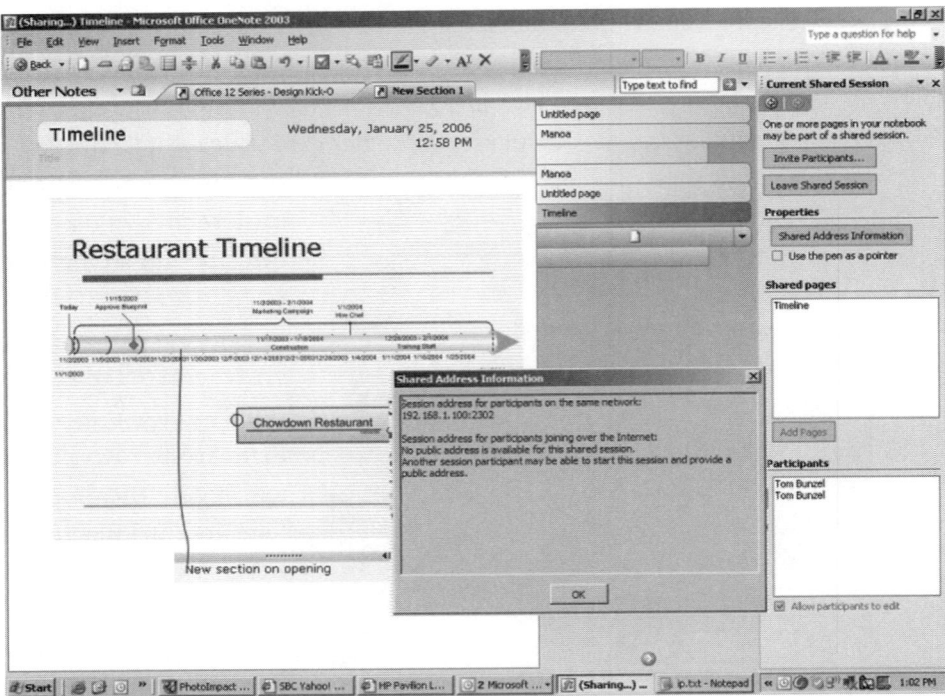

Figure 7.39 A Live Sharing Session in OneNote lets all participants collaborate on a shared page in a section of OneNote (while speaking on the phone or conference line). Shown here is the IP address information screen from a previous task pane in the process to begin the Live Sharing Session.

users using a web location. This is separate from the new OneNote Web App, which will also enable collaboration among users using an online version of OneNote.

In this way OneNote combines the best features of a powerful research and organization tool with a Web conferencing solution.

While social media is a great way to build excitement around a topic, idea, or concept, to communicate in depth and achieve tangible results there is no real substitute for a real-time event or conference. After the conclusion of the event, the process is not complete; following up a real-time event with other strategies and tools is key.

CONTINUING THE CONVERSATION

As described previously, online conferences can be archived in video format to be posted online for those who may need a review or who missed the real-time event. But that is hardly the end of the story. Communication about the event continues, in blogs, on Twitter and Facebook, via e-mail or on social networks. Follow-up initiatives can include status reports on action items, links to the content covered during the event or conference, continuing to add value and build on the subject matter of the event.

For example, in Dr. Conklin's webinar on the pharmaceutical company's NeuroPath drug treatment in the scenario, he mentioned additional treatment modalities that he believed were crucial in a comprehensive solution to issues surrounding Alzheimer's disease. After his event was archived as video, and the slides posted on SlideShare and AuthorSTREAM (with his narration), many more hospitals, caregivers, and families learned of the new modalities and became interested in them. Dr. Conklin responded to comments about the conference on his blog and began to give his own webinars on the treatment options he favored. He mentioned the NeuroPath treatment regimen in these private webinars, and he concentrated more intensely on the hows and whys of group support, physical exercise, and talk therapy, creating a ripple effect on these topics throughout his social media circle, educating others about his experiences, and stimulating further discussion on this important topic.

In this way, the content created using both desktop and Web-based tools, along with the platforms available for real-time conferencing and collaboration, complements and supports the ongoing conversations and viral distribution features of social media.

LEVERAGING YOUR DATABASE WITH A NEWSLETTER

One of the benefits of accumulating information through the registration forms and social media efforts before and after webinars is the database that is collected comprising a community of interest. Using this information strategically is an important next step in any training or marketing efforts.

WEBINAR FOLLOW-UP STRATEGIES

As more and more families, caregivers, and institutions saw the archived versions of Dr. Stanley Conklin's webinars, which emphasized a broader approach, beyond the NeuroPath drug treatment promoted by Premiere Pharmaceutical, the company finally "got it." One of the marketing managers at Premiere, who had gotten interested in social media, realized that it was Dr. Conklin's credibility—specifically because he had presented a broad-based approach to treating Alzheimer's—that was responsible for the interest in his webinars and the growth of a large database of people who had attended a webinar, subscribed to podcasts, read company blogs, or registered to watch the archived version of his conference. The company hired Strategic Communications to manage a Twitter campaign and blog that would *not* be about its drug, NeuroPath, but instead serve as a resource for all aspects of treating Alzheimer's. Dr. Conklin agreed to contribute to the Premiere Pharmaceutical blog along with his own, sometimes "mirroring" posts, as long as he felt comfortable with the company's approach.

Julie Mayfield did a series of training sessions with the company's social media team that emphasized that they were to only disseminate useful and helpful information about all aspects of Alzheimer's. Wherever possible, she recruited members of the health care community who had a personal connection with Alzheimer's patients or their care for the training effort.

The Twitter ID was not named for the drug company or NeuroPath, although the connection was disclosed on the main page. It was branded as "ElderCare," and Julie had her staff retweet (RT) any and all resources that contributed to a better knowledge and effective treatment of the disease. Wherever possible they would use Digg.com ratings, Facebook contacts, and Delicious.com bookmarks to expand this online resource well beyond what the pharmaceutical company had originally envisioned. As part of the Twitter campaign, Julie and Dr. Conklin used the hashtag "#eldercare" to filter comments from users, and also compiled User Lists in Twitter of significant contributors of feedback and information.

Premiere Pharmaceutical also realized that Dr. Conklin had aggregated a loyal group of followers through his own webinars and blog. These users were fiercely loyal and were not necessarily in Premiere Pharmaceutical's database. They asked Julie, whom Stanley trusted, to approach him about compiling a database of all of the e-mail lists—his as well as the company's—so that they would have access to these passionate and influential members of the Alzheimer's community. Stanley was not sure about this, because he felt personally connected to those who had followed him through his own blog, webinars, and Facebook and Twitter posts.

At Julie's suggestion, Stanley created his first newsletter, which carried a prominent disclosure statement in which he apologized to anyone in the mass mailing who did not want association with the drug company and promised that the newsletter would remain completely independent. Any recipients of the newsletter who did not want to continue receiving it could opt out, and they were promised that they would not be placed on Premiere Pharmaceutical's mailing list or further solicited. This transparency initiative succeeded in maintaining Stanley's credibility with his own followers and was covered in the medical and broader media, further increasing the scope of his efforts and the reach of his corporate sponsor.

To create his newsletter, Stanley had his staff use the desktop component of Microsoft Office that had an e-mail newsletter template: Publisher. After modifying the template slightly, the staff was able to use the Tools > Mailings and Catalogs option in Publisher 2007 to begin an E-mail Merge. (See Figures 7.40 and 7.41.)

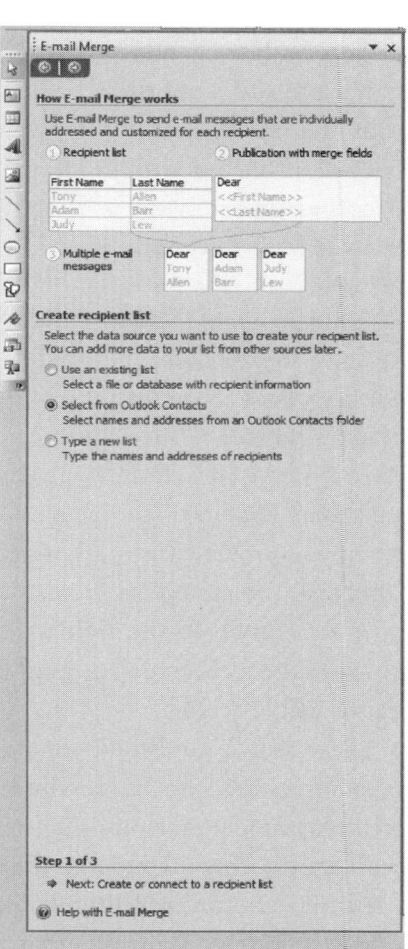

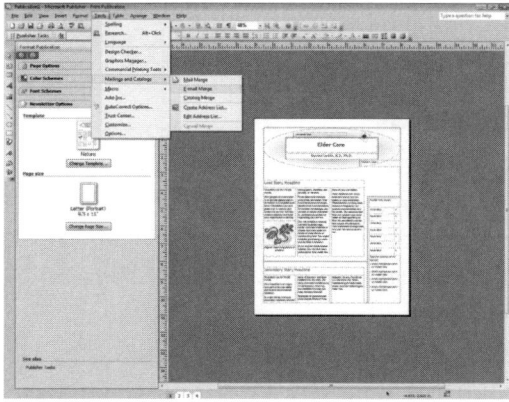

Figure 7.40 Microsoft Publisher has the ability to merge newsletter content with an e-mail list.

Figure 7.41 Microsoft Publisher's E-mail Merge File Wizard task pane takes you through the process of connecting with a database or contact list in Outlook.

Microsoft Publisher's Merge File process is nearly identical to a Mail Merge in Word, except the output will be a set of e-mail messages instead of letters. To personalize each e-mail, you add a set of fields that represent data that will be filled in with information from the database when the merge takes place and the messages are generated. The fields—for example, <Title> <First [Name]> <Last [Name]>—are placed in the newsletter where you want them to appear (see Figure 7.42). When you preview the mail merge in Publisher, the recipients in the database are shown in the fields. Then you're ready to Merge to E-mail (see Figure 7.43).

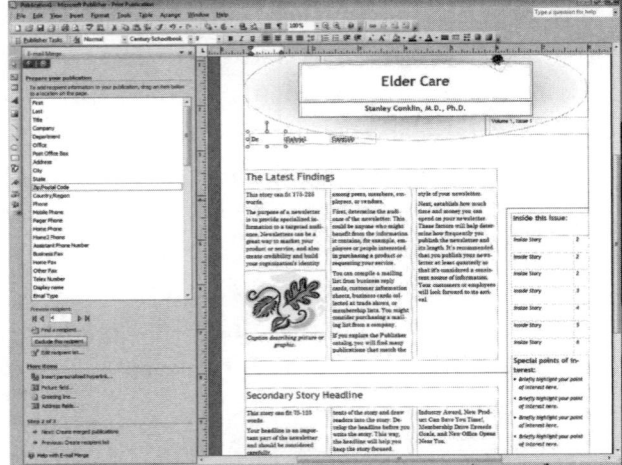

Figure 7.42 E-mail Merge in Microsoft Publisher lets you place fields or containers for data into the document and preview how it will look when merged.

The result is an e-mail generated to each recipient (or those who have been filtered in a previous step) in the Outbox of Microsoft Outlook. You can open these before sending to make a final check that they are error free and look the way you expected. (See Figure 7.44.)

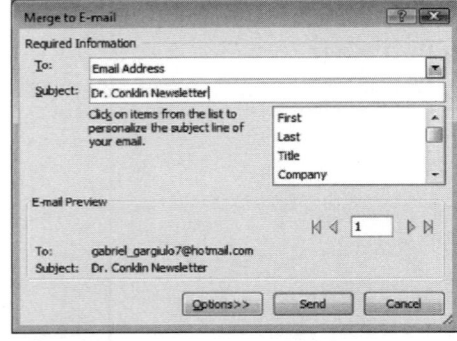

Figure 7.43 When you click Merge to E-mail in Microsoft Publisher, you can confirm the address field and add a subject line.

There is a preview feature in Publisher that generates a temporary Web page showing you the final look of the newsletter with the Mail Merge data before you generate a set of e-mails. This creates a series of e-mail messages with the newsletter in HTML format that is sent in a personalized way to each recipient. Publisher's E-mail

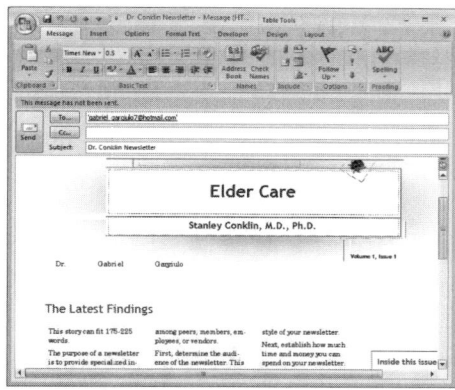

Figure 7.44 After generating an E-mail Merge in Microsoft Publisher, you can check the final results in your e-mail Outbox folder before sending.

Merge feature has filtering controls that let you localize a mailing to a particular area, or if you have the information in the database, you can target a specific age group or gender, or those contacts who have met any other searchable parameter (sales, for example).

You can combine mailing lists from a number of Microsoft Office sources, including Excel, Outlook, Business Contact Manager (a special version of Outlook), and Access. If your list is in another format (for example Palm Desktop), consider converting it to a *.CSV comma-delimited file (a basic database format). Its fields should also show up in the Publisher E-mail Merge Preview area.

There is a feature in Publisher that lets you save the information about choices you've made to one or more recipient lists as a shortcut (to your Windows Data Sources) under Step 3 of the Publisher Mail Merge Wizard (Select E-mail Merge Output). To do so, click Save a Shortcut to Recipient List, directly beneath Prepare to Follow Up on This Mailing.

Since this process is somewhat complex, if you're going to filter, sort, or combine lists, consider generating a new database with the recipients you want to target and saving that file in the database-appropriate program. But if you have one or more basic lists in Outlook, Excel, or Access, Publisher will let you quickly and efficiently filter a set of results and send a personalized e-mail newsletter.

Online Newsletter Tools

Alternatively, an entirely separate set of newsletter tools are available online. For example, the sponsoring company in the scenario, Premiere Pharmaceuticals, wanted a more sophisticated campaign. They asked Dr. Conklin to send the newsletter file to them in HTML format so that they could use an online service (MailChimp) that let them track results and integrate with Twitter, their blogging tool (WordPress), and a customer relations program (SalesForce). Besides the opportunity to subscribe to the newsletter, the e-mail linked to Dr. Conklin's blog and allowed users to subscribe to its updates, along with his podcasts, using the RSS option on those Web pages. Combined with the Twitter campaign, the result was a vibrant community that supported all aspects of Alzheimer's care through the immediacy of microblogging, events such as future webinars that distributed information and provided support, as well as the newsletter and ElderCare blog that kept people connected and updated.

KEEP THE CONNECTION FLOWING

In her book, *The Truth About Profiting from Social Networking*, Patrice-Anne Rutledge[8] coins the phrase "the virtual water cooler" to image the new Internet model for information sharing, transmission, and communication, or the modern equivalent of the watering hole in the desert. With the dynamic changes that are taking place, both in technology and content creation, one can expand this analogy to an underground spring, or a flowing tributary, because modern communication is no longer a one-time, static event or broadcast.

Whether the task at hand is communicating to convince, teach or train, or to gather information and expand the focus of one's activities, the process is continuous from the birth of a core identity, to transmitting and receiving complex ideas effectively, to taking advantage of real-time dynamic events like webinars, training conferences, and festivals, the process flows on and needs to be kept vibrant through a continuous dialogue between what was once perhaps a single presenter and her audience but is now an online community.

The process involves providing continuous care, monitoring one's profile or brand, and continuing to distribute content and commentary throughout the Internet in an organized and systematic way.

In other words, "Rinse and repeat."

QUESTIONS TO PONDER

1. How would you feel about speaking to an audience you can't see? How might visuals help your confidence and the effectiveness of your message? What is your level of confidence in handling the technical issues of conferencing online? Do you have resources or staff that might help in this effort?
2. Do you have an organizational strategy for your research and preparation? Could a tool like OneNote, or online bookmarks, or some other cataloging tool make you more efficient?

3. Do you view a conference, whether actual or virtual (online), as a one-time unique event? How much effort do you put into preparation, research, rehearsal and contact with an audience prior to delivery? Do you have a goal for your event? What kind of follow-up strategy might solidify the achievement of your goal and continued contact with your audience?

Notes

1. Shel Israel, *Twitterville: How Businesses Can Thrive in the New Global Neighborhoods*. Woodlands, TX: Portfolio, 2009. See also Israel's blog: http://redcouch.typepad.com/weblog/twitterville.
2. Eckhart Tolle, *The Power of Now*. Novato, CA: New World Library, 2004.
3. Mack Collier: http://moblogsmoproblems.blogspot.com.
4. Patricia Fripp (www.fripp.com). Published in Presentation Xpert (http://bit.ly/1xsgBC) and excerpted with permission from eLearn Magazine, July 7, 2009 (http://bit.ly/ALfwn), © 2009 Association for Computing Machinery, Inc.
5. Nancy Duarte, *Slide:ology: The Art and Science of Creating Great Presentations*. Sebastopol, CA: O'Reilly, 2008.
6. www.bobpikegroup.com.
7. Carmen Taran, *Better Beginnings: How to Capture Your Audience in 30 Seconds*. Danville, CA: Rexi Media, 2009.
8. Patrice-Anne Rutledge, *The Truth About Profiting from Social Networking*. Upper Saddle River, NJ: FT Press, 2008.

What Lies Ahead in Global Communication

chapter
EIGHT

It's always challenging to try to look ahead and even remotely predict where the world of technology and the trends in communication might be going. Even by the time this book is published, platforms, software, and, most important, how people use technology will have undergone change. That's how fast technology evolves.

Sometimes it is hard to remember that blogs are only a few years old, and that many of the other programs and trends we have covered in previous chapters are still in their infancy.

In this chapter we begin by pointing out some significant directions that communications in a socially connected world are headed: ubiquity through miniaturization in mobile devices and nanotechnology, expanded horizons through evolutionary technologies like virtual worlds and new platforms like Google Wave, and finally the meaning of communication itself, with a look at what is called the "semantic web"—and its implications beyond technology—with some far-reaching speculation about the direction of the evolution of not just technology, but of ourselves.

Certainly the trend toward adoption of social technologies is undeniable. In their white paper "Social Media: Embracing the Opportunities, Averting the Risks,"[1] analysts Carol Russell and David Baer confirm what has been suggested throughout the previous chapters—that "despite these apprehensions [security and related issues], social networking is being accepted as a key communications strategy. According to survey results, eight in 10 believe social media can enhance

Figure 8.1 Enhancing the connection between the organization and its customers and thereby strengthening a brand or identity are the key perceived values of social technologies.

relationships with customers/clients (81%) and build brand reputation (81%). Almost 70 percent feel such networking can be valuable in recruitment (69%), as a customer service tool (64%) and can be used to enhance employee morale (46%). The most popular vehicles being used include Facebook (80%), Twitter (66%), YouTube (55%), LinkedIn (49%) and blogs (43%)." (See Figure 8.1.)

Organizations today must demonstrate value and build credibility among customers and other stakeholders in a worldwide community, where consumers of information rely more on influencers and "trust agents" than on authority figures. However as this movement (or "groundswell") continues, it will transform onto different platforms, enlist new tools, and assume different cultural roles.

PRESENTING FROM MOBILE DEVICES

One area that always seems to grow is the miniaturization of technology, and communications is no different. While smart phones and mobile devices have been around for several years, the iPhone, with its myriad of applications, many of them business related, has become a leader in bringing the power of the Web to the end user in a device that fits in the palm of the hand. We've seen how Twitter feeds instead of PowerPoint slides can appear on an overhead screen during a conference, bringing the entire world and the audience into the program; this is achieved because many participants can text their input on mobile devices. Twitter and Facebook work on the iPhone, as do many other social applications that allow users to share information and opinions on travel, restaurants, traffic, shopping, child care, events, and much more without the need for a computer.

By making the web completely mobile, these new devices are also introducing the element of geo-location into applications; the latest trend, begun by FourSquare.com, is to have individuals identify how often they physically visit and frequent specific locales by "checking in." This element has become part of the Whrrl slideshow application, discussed in Chapter Five.

Computers themselves have been downsized. Inexpensive laptops called netbooks or MIDs—mobile Internet devices—are threatening the hegemony of full-scale, expensive portable PCs and Macs. With so much software available directly online (in the "cloud"), and wireless access becoming ubiquitous and reliable with high bandwidth, more and more end users are opting for the lighter netbooks with less bloated operating systems and software.

In some cases the technology simply gets smaller and more mobile. The large projectors that showed 35mm slides are giving way to units that work with ultralight handheld devices. There are several projectors that work with the iPhone under the umbrella description "pico," or small and mobile. Many of these started with the capability of projecting from iPods, which were limited mainly to videos stored on the devices, but with the iPhone, one could easily project a SlideRocket presentation or a hosted PowerPoint presentation from a Web site like SlideShare or AuthorSTREAM. In most cases these projectors won't expand the viewing area from a mobile presentation into an auditorium; rather they confine it to a small venue like a boardroom or an intimate audience that may have gathered spontaneously and watches the image projected on a wall.

Regardless of the size of the image, the principles of effective communication still apply. One company that has specialized in helping clients craft an effective message is Reximedia (www.reximedia.com), founded by Danielle Daley and Dr. Carmen Taran. Dr. Taran, the author of *Better Beginnings*,[2] provides in-depth tips on grabbing an audience's attention, maintaining it, delivering value, and getting results. She and Danielle Daley offer an online course in Visual Thinking, making them kindred spirits with Nancy Duarte, author of *Slide:ology*,[3] and Julie Terberg (www.TerbergDesign.com), another presentation graphics specialist renowned for her work with PowerPoint.

Particularly interesting about Reximedia are its two iPhone applications: Presenter Pro and Razz. Neither of these is a competitor to PowerPoint or Keynote. Rather, they are skill-building tools that profit from their portability because they can be accessed just before one steps into a boardroom or classroom to provide education, stimulation, and inspiration.

Presenter Pro (see Figure 8.2) features:

- Advanced presentation skills techniques with eye-catching supporting graphics, audio, and video clips
- A "tip shaker" for accessing hundreds of quick presentation tips; shake the device while viewing any of the sections for a quick tip
- A checklist feature, which enables you to store and e-mail any topic paragraph(s) you want to refer to later

- A Notes feature for writing (and e-mailing) comments and notes
- Exercises for practicing your skills and knowledge check quizzes to help you remember the information

Razz is a last-minute tip feature that presenters can consult if they need ideas that will grab an audience's attention.

The key point here is not the feature set or viability of these specific applications but that mobility has brought the social Web to the here and now, everywhere. One can argue as to what this does to people's attention spans and independence, but applications like these can interface with social media tools to continue online conversations and answer questions posed on Twitter, Facebook, and the like, projecting the visuals onto a nearby wall; for example, in the lobby of a hotel after meeting three strangers in the lobby bar. One could consult one of these or other mobile applications during a conference break, convene a mini-conference, and inspire, educate, or sell a concept.

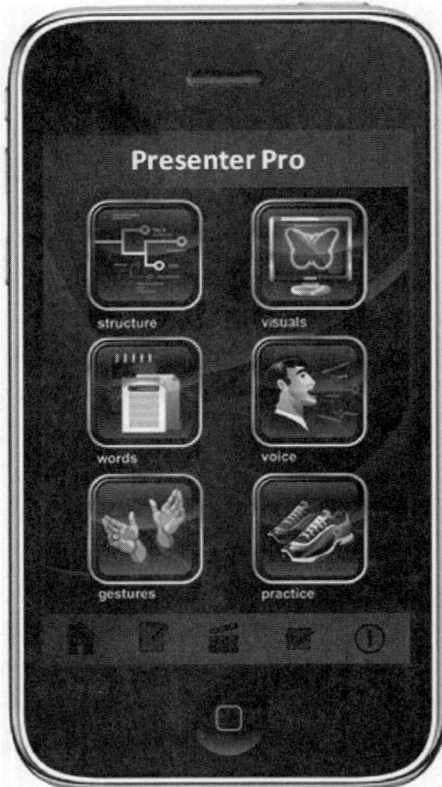

Figure 8.2 Presenter Pro is a portable application for the iPhone that provides tips, techniques, and planning features that can be accessed anywhere and any time.

A few years ago such an interaction would have required hours, if not days, of preparation. Miniature projectors and mobile devices expand the reach of the social Web in ways that we are just beginning to witness.

AUGMENTED REALITY

Augmented reality is a technology that is fast emerging on portable devices, although sports fans have seen examples for some time. For instance, when down and yardage information, or advertising, is superimposed on a live picture of a football game or other sports event, the reality is being supplemented (or augmented) by computer graphics.

In some ways this merges virtual and real worlds by integrating information from databases or other sources with what the user experiences in reality. Another example on PDAs is integration of GPS (global positioning satellite) information with maps or real-world images, incorporating information about distance, services, and transportation onto the screen on the monitor.

At this time this technology has found its way mainly on the iPhone and other PDAs for marketing and consumer-based applications, and it is working its way into military and game technology as well.

One can speculate that this technology will become prevalent in training as well. At the higher end, medical simulations could incorporate graphical information in visual imagery from body scans to colonoscopies and use such combinations for diagnosis and the education of medical professionals. In the organizational space, human resource training may eventually use integrated information in role-playing and facilitation modalities to increase realism, accountability, and interactivity. For example, a financial training class could incorporate organizational data in its visualizations, with teachers or presenters projecting potential outcomes for scenarios over video or real-time activities to educate and involve audiences.

TWINE: IS WEB 3.0 THE SEMANTIC WEB?

If life is a series of presentations, as Tony Jeary[4] wrote, then what is happening online is a dizzying transformation of the ways information is accumulated, organized, and distributed. Just the indexing and organization of Web information can be accomplished in many ways, from social bookmarks on Delicious.com (Chapter Four) to a powerful desktop tool like OneNote (Chapter Seven).

But what happens when the organizational principle is part of the message itself? In other words, what about *meaning*? This brings up the philosophical issue of whether meaning is a purely human quality . . . or . . .

Will we reach the point that the Web and its applications can discern the content of language such that items can be searched for and organized by software, but according to human needs and values?

The premise of those who are proponents of the new concept of Web 3.0 that refers to the semantic web believe that a new kind of database structure called RDF—resource description framework—can provide contextual structure to content that not only informs and expands search capability but also allows for artificial intelligence-like presentation of potentially connected and supportive content from both other humans (the essence of social media) and the system itself.

Tim Berners-Lee, sometimes considered the father of the World Wide Web, describes it as follows: "If HTML and the Web made all the online documents look like one huge book, RDF, schema, and inference languages will make all the data in the world look like one huge database."[5]

One obvious example of the power of search by meaning or intention is that if one searches for "male rooster," one is not likely to get pages of porn based on the slang equivalent. Many users have already experienced similar algorithmic attempts to understand meaning on Amazon.com (with its suggestions of titles), or the more maddening aspects of Internet Explorer (when the history tries to anticipate the sites you want to revisit), when a software program anticipates what you might want based on its interpretation of your choices to that point.

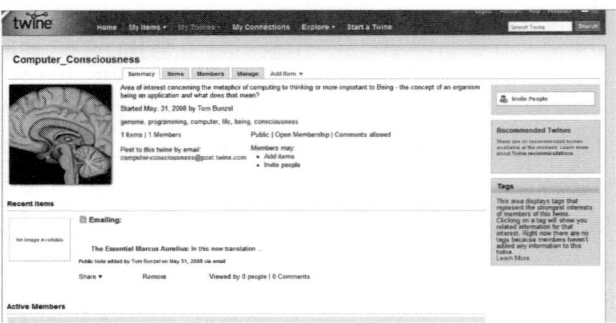

Figure 8.3 A twine is similar to a group on a social network, but soon content begins to accumulate through the connections to kindred twines.

"Twines" combine the social aspect of social media with the functionality of blogs (see Figure 8.3) into an entirely new kind of web application based on semantics—you use the Twine.com Web site to create and access "twines."

One participates in a twine by constructing a network of meaning that connects to other related networks symbiotically; the networks grow organically through collaboration—they literally evolve (see Figure 8.4). A twine begins with a concept from a single user or group, who defines the concept's scope and begins to add content using bookmarklets or a linking application that takes a specific page directly to the twine. Some Web browsers like Internet Explorer have default security settings that may need to be adjusted to allow for this.

Bookmarklets (which are not unique to Twine but are becoming popular in many applications) let the user add meta-data for search before adding a link to the host program (like Twine), increasing the likelihood that other users in related

Figure 8.4 A twine evolves as other members contribute content that is related in meaning to your concept and content you have uploaded or linked to and the comments of members.

networks will find and connect to the content. One can get a pretty good idea of the interconnectedness of twines through Twine's Explore features, with Top Twines and Top Members framing News and Announcements (see Figure 8.5). Topics of general interest generate more specific subtopics, each populated by the combination of member input and a natural proliferation of interaction based on users' direct interest in the subject matter.

Twine becomes almost a "living" network of text, images, and presentations (many of the links are to video) constructed on a foundational layer of meaning in its original concept or description. Related material is added on the basis of interaction with people who are attracted to the subject matter and a robust search mechanism built on a new database structure.

One immediate objection to the semantic web model is that it is wholly linguistic and intellectual in nature and does not embrace areas of visual or auditory meaning. Perhaps future iterations of Twine-like models will include the elements of visual search (now part of face recognition software and search engines from Google and Microsoft: Bing.com)—and perhaps there may soon be a similar pattern-tracking facility for audio search to create a new sensory web. As semantic applications like Twine evolve (Twine has now been replaced by Evri.com), it is

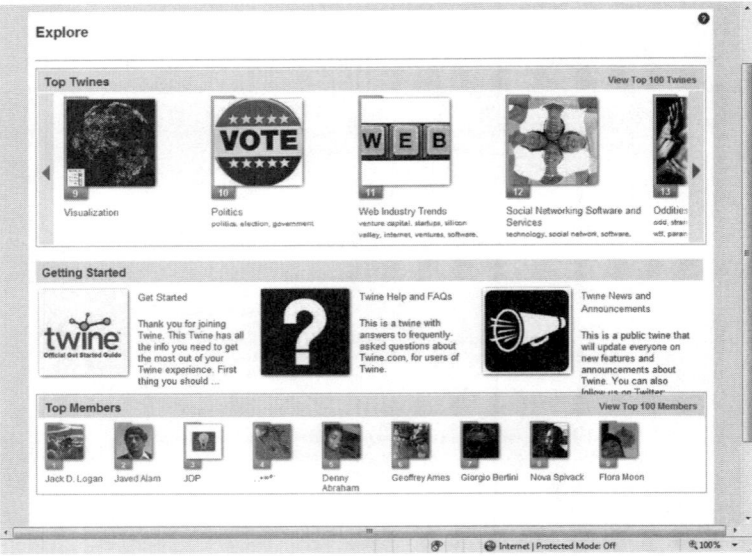

Figure 8.5 The Explore area of Twine provides an overview of the most popular topics and members; drilling down locates more specific entries with member comments and interactivity.

possible that search and meaning will not just reside in metatags or words, but be extracted directly from visual or auditory elements using a level of artificial intelligence not yet known.

GOOGLE WAVE: THE WEB AS A SINGLE APPLICATION?

Not surprisingly, one of the most ambitious new communications efforts on the Web, with the brash undercurrent of expectation suggesting that it might actually replace e-mail, is from Google: the highly anticipated new Google Wave application (see Figure 8.6). Those creating the hype around Wave (which is in beta as of this writing) suggest that with the use of Wave as a platform there will be no need for other applications; the Web will be a single unified application through the use of Wave. (Cynics suggest that this may just be a strategy for Google to promote adoption of its Chrome Web browser.) However, such a unified application is already feasible. As we've seen, due to the interoperability of APIs (application program interfaces) and the concept of "mashability," features and content from one application online can be aggregated and used in another already on the Web.

Figure 8.6 Google Wave promises a new real-time communications platform for instant communication and collaboration among participants.

Wave promises to roll everything together into one superprogram that might also be considered an operating system.

One site that followed the early buzz about Wave is Mashable.com. According to Benn Parr, "Communication within Google Wave is more like an IM conversation than email"[6]—with threads or "Waves" based on content (e-mail with search) or people (contacts with search). The IM (instant message) aspect speaks to the Twitter-like element of what Wave may be: a real-time communications platform with all elements included (and not linked)—text, voice, graphics, video, music, and more. The Mashable site suggests that in its interconnectivity all content can be edited by anyone (presumably with permission for "riding" the same Wave). The functionality of Wave is expanded through Extensions; these are Gadgets and Robots that bring the feature sets of other applications as well as content into Wave in objects referred to as "boxes" (otherwise known as windows). At this time, during the test phase of the product, the boxes available seem to be game oriented, but speculation is that a Twitter or Facebook box might well be available when the application goes public (although there is also speculation that Wave might replace both of these applications as a default social media supertool).

According to Google, a Wave is "equal parts conversation and document." Any participant can respond at any time point of a message (thread), and playback lets participants rewind a wave to see what was said, by whom, and when. And a wave is real time or live, so that participants can see what is happening *now*.

Key technologies expected in Wave are real-time collaboration, natural language (perhaps similar to the semantic web) and extensions through Google Wave APIs.[7]

VIRTUAL WORLDS: SECOND LIFE

Second Life is an online virtual world created by Linden Lab. Residents of this realm can take on any name and persona they choose, then wander about in the form of cartoon-like avatars. There are virtual companies courting their business, and some of them are listed on virtual stock exchanges where their shares are bought and sold by avatars with "Linden Dollars" and other virtual currencies.

Although Second Life, probably the best known of the virtual online worlds, was launched in 2003, the impact of these kinds of entities on the world of communication is still in the future. As of 2010, they are still viewed mainly as games or diversions. (Second Life was ranked at only 1 percent penetration by the Russell and Baer study cited at the beginning of this chapter.) But make no mistake; the participants in Second Life take their reality seriously. Citizens meet, fall in love, marry, and get divorced in the virtual world, sometimes with repercussions in the "real" world.

For example, in June 2007, a robbery took place; it seemed like an ordinary hacker had gotten into a stock exchange and made off with $10,000. Though the stolen amount translates to only roughly US$40 in real money at recent exchange rates, the heist has spurred many Second Lifers to debate whether these exchanges are just a game or serious business.[8] While the sum taken in this incident was relatively small, another exchange of virtual currency, the International Stock Exchange, got more investors after the World Stock Exchange, the victimized party, suffered the loss.

Unfortunately the same security concerns plague the virtual world as the one we inhabit.

Human affairs also take their toll. A British couple who had a Second Life "fairy-tale" wedding to augment their real ceremony divorced after the husband was caught cheating on Second Life. "I went mad—I was so hurt. I just couldn't believe what he'd done," the wife said. "It may have started online, but it existed entirely in the real world and it hurts just as much now it is over."[9] What is fascinating about Second Life is that it has become a proving ground and a staging area for live events and even business presentations. In addition to participating in weddings, denizens of Second Life interact with institutions and each other just as in the real world, and enhanced communication techniques with graphics, animation, and video, along with the nuance of digital storytelling, can be tested and implemented in venues within the virtual world.

Because jobs and businesses exist in Second Life, commerce goes on, including the sale of "real" property, and it is hardly surprising that training is also part of the community. MIT already has virtual classrooms in Second Life that provide online collaboration, and Notre Dame uses the virtual world as a cost-effective platform for distance learning. Dell and IBM are among dozens of multinational corporations doing presentations and commerce on Second Life. Smaller businesses like Reximedia (the presentation specialists described earlier) also have staked out a presence in Second Life to do real business in the virtual world and train its users on how to use the tools on the site to their advantage.

Not surprisingly, Second Life has more than 16,000 "fans" on Facebook, and the World Stock Exchange is implementing a Facebook application to restore its appeal to investors in the virtual world. On Twitter, the #SecondLife hashtag allows members to communicate in real time and discuss activities in the virtual world.

As technology in the community and the Internet at large evolves, the line between the real and the virtual may well blur even further. It is conceivable that what we now consider simulations in an online world—where organizations test and play out scenarios, some of them with disastrous consequences—may have impact in the real world. Besides interpersonal relationships, livelihoods and other aspects of the real world will be threatened. It is entirely possible that residents of Second Life, if they haven't already, will adopt the same principles of social media as we've seen throughout the Internet to form alliances of trust to protect their well-being and have the same needs as real-world residents to communicate among themselves.

The most obvious means by which Second Life can affect the outside Internet on a large scale is visual. YouTube is host to more than 240,000 videos pertaining to using the site, about its residents and organizations, and taking advantage of it as a platform for training, education, and distance learning.

For example, Twofour Communications, one of the largest training facilities in the United Kingdom devoted to organization communications, has teamed up with the Beyond Distance Research Alliance based at the University of Leicester to create an immersive teaching and research environment in Second Life called the Second Life Media Zoo, for exploration and collaboration in the virtual 3D environment. "Second Life presents us with an amazing opportunity to think in entirely new ways about teaching and learning," says Richard Wallis, Head of Twofour Learning. "Whether it's extending the classroom experience, learning through simulation, or exploring new forms of collaborative working, the possibilities are endless, and present a major challenge to educators."[10]

Second Life is not unique. In her blog, Leading Virtually, Rebecca Jestice describes various scenarios focusing on the potential of using virtual worlds for cross-cultural training. She describes how 3D immersive spaces can replicate or simulate another culture with avatars dressing and behaving appropriately, serving as successful models for students of other cultures. She cites the elements of Black and Mendenhall's social learning theory (cross-cultural relations can lead to cultural shock) with implication on training in terms of creating trust and rapport and shows how they would translate particularly well to scenarios played out in virtual worlds.[11]

NANOTECHNOLOGY: COMMUNICATING ON A MOLECULAR LEVEL

Nanotechnology is the study of the control of matter on an atomic or molecular level. For example, camera miniaturization can facilitate the placing of optical devices into human blood vessels. So far much of nanotech is in the future, but there has already been substantial progress in the field of communications. As early as 2000, according to *Science Daily*, "IBM scientists have discovered a way to transport information on the atomic scale that uses the wave nature of electrons instead of conventional wiring. The new phenomenon, called the 'quantum mirage' effect, may enable data transfer within future nanoscale electronic circuits too small to use wires."[12] The process uses an elliptical ring of 36 cobalt atoms 5,000 times smaller than the human hair, which constitutes a "quantum mirage" (see Figure 8.7). "The size and shape of the

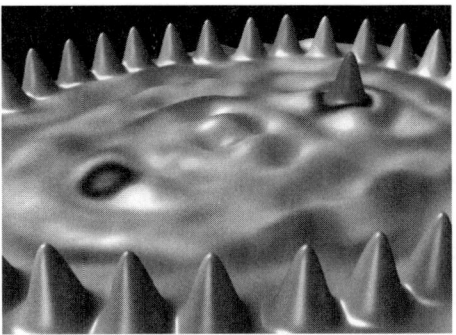

Figure 8.7 IBM's Quantum Mirage uses the wave nature of electrons instead of wire to move information on a molecular scale.

ellipse determines where information moves within the ring. The scientists at IBM's Almaden Research Center in San Jose, Calif., used a scanning tunneling microscope to position the atoms. This news was announced in the cover article of the February 3, 2000, issue of *Nature*, a prestigious scientific journal."[13] The potential for the quantum mirage is miniaturization of circuitry beyond any level currently known or employed.

Motorola has also been working in this field in the area of electronics, materials, energy, structures, manufacturing, and more. Its i870 phone featured AgION™ antimicrobial coating for its first market application in 2005. In the same year, the company announced a prototype for a Nano Emissive Display using carbon nanotubes (CNTs), which are conductors of carbon atoms less than one nanometer in size (one millionth of a millimeter) that conduct electrons 100 times as fast as copper. The prototype was created by growing carbon nanotubes directly on glass for superior electron emissions in the five-inch display prototype.[14]

Besides miniaturization and speed, nanotechnology's inroads in medicine take us firmly into the worlds of biophysics and neuroscience, where studies of the electrical impulses in the brain are already touching on issues scientists don't always like to discuss, such as meaning.

ARE HUMANS WIRED FOR STORIES?

Storytelling has always been a major theme in effective communication; in training and education in particular, narrative encodes meaning several levels beyond more mundane communications methods.

In his blog on Fast Company, Kaihan Krippendorff describes how Dr. Marco Iacoboni at the Brain Research Center at UCLA has connected the power of stories to humans' evolutionary makeup, specifically the presence of mirror neurons in the brain. Mirror neurons are information transmitters in the brain that fire equally whether they are reacting to a physical or an observed stimulus.

Observation can relate to other senses, such as a story told and absorbed through the auditory channel. It is this specific "brain technology" that has led to the power of narrative through the ages to transmit ideas and information, according to Dr. Iacoboni. In his research he was able to measure mirror neuron activity when subjects merely viewed images of others; brain activity occurred based on their feelings of empathy or identification ("This person is like me") with the image.

This is apparently why highly influential people tell stories that spark mirror neurons in others by opening their stories with images, people, sounds, smells, and feelings that others recognize and can relate to. As Iacoboni says, "Innovators create stories that others want to be part of."[15] This suggests that the nature of today's social Internet, with its emphasis on sharing information rather than imposing corporate or organizational concepts in a broadcast mode, is uniquely, well, human.

Our very nature is changing and evolving through the synergies created in these new communication modalities.

In the opening sequence of Stanley Kubrick's epic film, *2001: A Space Odyssey*, a lower primate is shown first using a bone as a tool, then as a weapon, and finally he tosses it up into space, where it transforms into a space station. This scene profoundly suggests that, for better or worse, tools are an integral part of human evolution. Our current communications technologies (our evolving tools) will either support what we consider human qualities, like storytelling and empathy, or more limiting concepts such as profit and the lust for power.

NEW TECHNOLOGIES INFLUENCE WORLD EVENTS

It's not surprising that the current regime in Iran has banned Second Life. While the specter of technological mind control and domination from George Orwell's classic novel *1984*[16] still haunts us, and rightfully so, the reality has been that social technologies have spelled the doom of some of the world's most repressive regimes. In the 1980s, there was no question that the rise of the Internet was a major factor in bringing down the Soviet Union and beginning the process of democratization. More recently it was Twitter that informed the uprising in Iran after the 2009 election was considered to have been rigged; while the results of that movement are still in doubt, there can be no issue with the fact that social media and specifically Twitter allowed those who sought personal and religious freedom to communicate freely within a repressive climate.

At least so far, the advances in technology have been mastered by those who champion progressive causes and the spirit of freedom—the government of Iran could not keep up with the features of Twitter (like hashtags), and its only response was brutal repression. While Nazi Germany nearly achieved world domination through the use of technology, and in fact a precursor of the IBM databases of today—the Hollerith machine—was used in its mass murder campaigns, it was the West that finally used technology to defeat global fascism with its own code-breaking machines and of course the atomic bomb.[17] While communications technology and the Internet have been the cause of major problems—the economic collapse of 2009 would not have happened without instant financial transfers and supercomputer calculations—it is a hopeful sign that the proponents of social media today stress that the way to succeed is to focus on the human dimension of sharing of information and community in the social Internet.

KEEPING IT HUMAN: BEYOND THE TOOLS

In their book, *Trust Agents*, Chris Brogan and Julien Smith[18] accentuate the primacy of human interaction according to principles of fair dealing as the key to effective use of social media. With a few exceptions, *Trust Agents* doesn't go into the technology itself; the authors write that "it's not about the tools," and emphasize core concepts of authenticity and altruism as the basis for accumulating social capital and reputation. Only then will a user with credibility succeed in the world of social media, according to Brogan and Smith, and achieve a following, a "tribe," or an expanding personal or organizational network.

In *Tools of Engagement* we have provided an overview of the tools that can be used to achieve this goal with the intention of showing their practical use through examples and describing the ways they work with each other to shape the evolving Internet. But it is vitally important that effective communicators keep in mind both the concepts of Brogan and Smith as well as some of the key elements of Chapter Six, in which the essentials of communication included not just tools like PowerPoint but the use of metaphor, analogy, humor, and digital storytelling—all elements that presumably would not affect the response system of a robot. But the jury is out on that.

In Chapter Six we mentioned the powerful presentations at the heart of TED, a worldwide conference of great thinkers in all fields, who share their knowledge at live venues and also online at TED.com and its social network and blog. One of the great presenters at TED is Juan Enriquez, a renowned geneticist, whose first presentation compared the genome to a computer program, citing the example of an apple as an application that "executed" when the sun's rays struck its surface, and it dropped to the earth. He showed several examples of how genetic code can be reprogrammed to alter the very nature of an organism.

In a recent presentation on TED Enriquez reviewed many of the economic issues facing us—massive debt and financial malfeasance—and suggested that the technology has emerged at this point specifically to help our species, *homo sapiens*, evolve into what he called *homo evolutus*—a new species that controls its evolution and that of all life (presumably on Earth) through technology.[19]

What this notion fails to take into account is precisely what lies at the heart of social media—namely that what makes us human—is not just our physical "technology" but something that may be called our "software"—our consciousness, mind, spirit, perhaps a quality that's nameless, but many of the humans who participate in the new Internet communication know exists. Biologist Bruce Lipton, in his book *Biology in Brief*, has offered proof that Life itself (with a capital *L*—the evolution of organic life on Earth) does not evolve randomly, by chance or accident, but that even the tiniest organisms evolve in ways that will help ensure their survival—consciously.[20]

Perhaps that is why the evolution of social media on the Internet—a humanistic movement that has exploded because it is based on trust and influence that are earned through human and not organizational or authoritarian means—has occurred in precisely this moment in human development.

In his recent book, *Life Inc.*, Douglas Rushkoff[21] provides a compelling overview of the historical and societal factors that have contributed to the measurement of worth by wealth and its many consequences. Chris Brogan and Julien Smith, among others, have made the case that the movement toward social media as the foundation for a new ethos of communication and cooperation is a necessary reaction to this branch of our evolution and a movement back toward an emphasis on human rather than corporate or externally measured values.

THE INTERNET AS A PLANETARY NERVOUS SYSTEM

As a young man, at around the time I was loading slide carousels, a close friend said something to me that I never forgot. At that time the beginnings of amazing scientific technologies were at hand—miniature radios and televisions, electronic microscopes and telescopes, and more amazing inventions on the near horizon—and my friend said, "All of these technologies are mere reproductions of sensory capabilities that we once possessed but have lost."

Perhaps this sort of esoteric musing is beyond the scope of this book, but it is fascinating to consider that all of the breakthroughs in the area of communication are essentially expansions or enhancements of sensory capacities we already possess—our human technology. Only those technologies we cannot see or touch, such as electronic or light waves or even electricity, are difficult to compare to what is human because science has not yet widely acknowledged the reality of consciousness or mind. The fields of biology and physics are rapidly converging into biophysics, and neuroscience is rapidly expanding in its understanding of the brain as more than a repository of electric impulses.

Part of Bruce Lipton's thesis in *Biology of Belief* is that just as individual cells of our bodies connect and communicate intelligently (and have grown more intelligent through evolution and the addition of a powerful brain to the entire organism to help regulate performance), the human organism is also evolving through social structures into a higher life form (higher intelligence), with individual human cells sharing and contributing to a greater entity that is still evolving. Smaller versions of such entities have evolved during previous centuries—first kingdoms, then republics, more recently corporations, all of which have their own lives, goals, and eventually their demise, in ways that are parallel to ordinary living organisms. One might ask precisely what would be the nervous system or communications pathway for such an organism, comprised of connected, intelligent humans?

It would be the Internet.

And as we've begun to see, this evolving Internet has changed into something greater than just a pipeline for data with increasing bandwidth. It is imbued today and continues to grow in response to precisely those aspects of our nature that make us human: cooperation, sharing, and compassion. Without question there are negative forces that operate in opposition to these impulses, but if the new social media shows us anything it is that technology disconnected from our humanity cannot exist.

Would the Internet exist without humans? Everything online, from a server farm hosting applications in the cloud to a single tweet, was created, after all, in our image.

QUESTIONS TO PONDER

1. Do you fear or are you excited about the advent of ever-evolving new technology in the communications field? Reconsider the question in the Introduction: Can you now appreciate or accept the presence of intrusions by PDAs and cell phones into the relationships you have with an audience or at a meeting?

2. How could participation in a virtual world expand the reach of your message in a positive way? Might anonymous role-play be of value in your field? What about exploration of diverse cultures and viewpoints?

3. Do you think about the meaning of what you are doing and its contribution on a larger scale? Do you see yourself as an isolated unit in your field, building your own niche, or are you considering your place in a greater whole when you work, teach, or communicate?

4. Is there a higher purpose to your message? What might it be?

Notes

1. Russell Herder and Ethos Business Law, *Social Media-Embracing the Opportunities, Averting the Risks*, 2009; http://bit.ly/L2X09.
2. Carmen Taran, *Better Beginnings: How to Capture Your Audience in 30 Seconds*. Danville, CA: Rexi Media, 2009.
3. Nancy Duarte, *Slide:ology: The Art and Science of Creating Great Presentations*. Sebastopol, CA: O'Reilly, 2008.
4. Tony Jeary, *Life Is a Series of Presentations: Eight Ways to Inspire, Inform, and Influence Anyone, Anywhere, Anytime*. New York: Fireside, 2005.
5. http://thinkexist.com/quotation/if-html-and-the-web-made-all-the-online-documents/1558820.html.
6. http://mashable.com/2009/05/31/google-wave-test.
7. http://wave.google.com/help/wave/about.html.
8. ZDNet-Asia: http://bit.ly/qY3Vz.
9. CNN:http://bit.ly/vin9j.
10. Second Life Media Zoo on YouTube: http://bit.ly/vin9j.
11. Rebecca Jestice, *Virtual Worlds: A Potential Tool for Cross-Cultural Training*: www.leadingvirtually.com/?p=224; J. S. Black and M. Mendenhall, "Cross-cultural Training Effectiveness: A Review of Theoretical Framework for Future Research." *Academy of Management Review* 15:1 (1990), 113–136.
12. *Science Daily Online*: http://bit.ly/xKxhe.
13. IBM Research: http://bit.ly/15TIMb.

14. www.motorola.com/mot/doc/6/6445_MotDoc.pdf.
15. Kaihan Krippendorff, Fast Company blog: http://bit.ly/j7SSI.
16. George Orwell, *1984*. Indianapolis: Plume/Pearson, 2003. Originally published 1949.
17. Edwin Black, *IBM and the Holocaust: The Strategic Alliance Between Nazi Germany and America's Most Powerful Corporation.* New York: Crown, 2001.
18. Chris Brogan and Julien Smith, *Trust Agents: Using the Web to Build Influence, Improve Reputation, and Earn Trust.* Hoboken, NJ: Wiley, 2009.
19. www.ted.com/search?q=enriquez.
20. Bruce Lipton, *The Biology of Belief: Unleashing the Power of Consciousness, Matter, and Miracles.* Carlsbad, CA: Hay House, 2008.
21. Douglas Rushkoff, *Life Inc.: How the World Became a Corporation and How to Take It Back.* New York: Random House, 2009.

GLOSSARY

Augmented Reality   Superimposing visual graphics and/or audio of computer information onto an audience or viewer's field of vision, using a screen, monitor, or headgear to combine what is "real," or viewed, with data that enhances meaning or comprehension.

Backchannel   The interconnected communication of those on mobile devices during a presentation, commenting on its content and participating and even interrupting.

Channel   Groups of videos and commentary comprising a community built on movies on YouTube.

Cloud   The presence of all applications and data on the Internet and resident on servers rather than on client desktops, able to reference and share information among them.

Crowdsourcing   The strategy of soliciting and then taking advantage of the know-how of your customers, colleagues, associates, employees, or other online community members.

Dashboard   The graphic display of data, frequently with interactive capabilities like sliders, buttons, or dials. SAP Xcelsius creates such dashboards in Flash from Excel for display in PowerPoint or on a Web page.

Followers   Those users who are interested enough to follow you on Twitter.

Hashtag   The # symbol used in Twitter to help users filter out messages or tweets on specific topics.

HTML (Hypertext Markup Language)   The programming code of the Internet that describes for a Web browser what to display on a screen as a Web page.

List (on Twitter)   A feature that lets you add specific users you follow to a filtered list to see just their tweets; can be based on a special interest, client, topic, or group.

Mashable, Mash-up, or Mashing   The cross-referencing or repurposing of content hosted on one site by using a link or embed code on another site, making duplication unnecessary.

Mirror Neurons   Cells in the brain that respond or fire as a result of a visual or narrative stimulus in the same way as if they were responding to an actual physical event.

Podcasts   Audio updates of content that can be aggregated in a program like iTunes to be listened to offline, and usually subscribed to using RSS.

Retweet   Repeating a useful update or tweet on Twitter, usually with a helpful or insightful comment, to be shared by one's own followers.

RSS (Really Simple Syndication)   A means by which Web users can subscribe to feeds to get automatic updates in an RSS Reader or other application like Outlook of regularly published content as text or audio (Podcasts).

SMS (Short Message Service)   A communication service standardized in the mobile communication system, using standardized communications protocols allowing the interchange of short text messages between mobile telephone devices.

Tweet   A status update or post on Twitter.

Twine   A kind of Web application based on semantics and artificial intelligence.

ABOUT THE AUTHOR

Tom Bunzel specializes in knowing what presenters need and how to make technology work. He has appeared on Tech TV's *Call for Help* and has been a featured speaker at InfoComm and PowerPoint LIVE as well as working as a technology coach for corporations including Iomega, MTA Films, Nurses in Partnership, and the Neuroscience Education Institute. He has taught regularly at Learning Tree International, West LA College Extension, and privately in southern California and does presentation and video consulting in southern California.

He has authored a number of books; among his latest was *Master Visually Microsoft Office 2007*. Published in 2006, *Solving the PowerPoint Predicament: Using Digital Media for Effective Communication* is a detailed, project-oriented approach to creating effective multimedia presentations. His new eBook, *Do Your Own Ning Thing: A Step-By-Step Guide to Launching an Effective Social Network*, is available at www.professorppt.com/ning_how.htm. Among Bunzel's other books are *Teach Yourself PowerPoint 2003 in 24 Hrs*, *Easy Digital Music*, *Easy Creating CDs and DVDs*, *How to Use Ulead DVD Workshop*, *Digital Video on the PC*, and the update to PeachPit Press's *Visual QuickStart Guide to PowerPoint 2002/2001*.

Tom can be reached through his Web site, www.professorppt.com, or his blog, tbunzel.blogspot.com.

INDEX

\# (hashtag), 16, 125, 243
@ (on Twitter), 16, 65, 112, 113

A

Alpha Moms, 46–47
AlterPoint, 26
Armano, David, 26
Arrington, Michael, 20
Atkinson, Cliff, 15, 16, 154
Audacity, 96, 162, 164
Augmented reality, 226–227, 243
AuthorSTREAM, 157, 162, 164, 165–166, 225

B

Backchannel: defined, 15, 243; displaying, in PowerPoint, 155; taking advantage of, in presentation, 16
Baer, David, 223–224
Baker, Glen, 43–45
Beal, Andy, 58
Bendt, Steve, 27, 28
Berners-Lee, Tim, 228
Bernoff, Josh, 15, 40, 46, 48–49, 57, 68, 74
Best Buy. *See* Blue Shirt Nation (Best Buy)
Better Beginnings (Taran), 200
Beyond Bullet Points (Atkinson), 154
Bio, 34, 53. *See also* Profile
Biology in Brief (Lipton), 238, 239
Blog Marketing (Wright), 67
Bloggers, types of, 67
Blogs: attracting traffic to, 63–67; comments feature of, 61–62; creating, 62–64, 67–68; Fortune 100 companies using, 137; tools for monitoring, 57; tools for sharing content of, 101–104; Web sites vs., 61–62. *See also* Google Blogger
Blue Shirt Nation (Best Buy): crowdsourcing by, 45; overview of, 6, 27–29; reason for success of, 40, 41
Bookmarking, social, 73–77
Bookmarklets, 228–229
Braiker, Zach, 126, 127
Brainstorming, with whiteboard, 174, 203, 205–206
Brandjacking, 40
Brogan, Chris, 8, 35–37, 50, 65, 152–153, 237, 238
Brookes, Dave, 122
Bullet lists, transformed into visuals in PowerPoint, 151, 153–154
Business networks, 68–73

247

C

Camtasia Studio, 157, 159–162, 182
Capital Payroll Services: online training program, 81–88; relationship-building using social media, 88–98; social media video initiative, 161–168
Carroll, Dave, 24
CelluLink, 25–26
Cisco, 180
"Cisco Fatty" incident, 109–110
Citibank, 183
Citrix Online, 181, 183–184, 185
Cloud: accessing information in, 23; defined, 62, 243; tools for presentations in, 209–212
Collier, Mack, 20–21, 101, 183
Comments: on blogs, 42, 57, 61–62, 65; on Facebook, 80–81; Twine and, 229, 230
Communication: by audience members during presentations, 13–14, 15–16; before implementing new strategy or product, 34, 37–39; story-based model of skills for, 169–172; strategies for successful, 36–37; using multiple social media for, 8–9. *See also* Storytelling, digital
Communications identity, 34–35
Compete.com, 49
Conklin, Stanley: gave series of webinars, 184–195, 200–202, 215; upgraded presentation with visuals, 145–152, 153, 154, 160–161
Content ownership, 14–15
Conversation: continuing, after Web conferences, 214–215; Internet as, 15; presentations as, 12, 20, 30; Twitter as real-time, 124–125
Conversation Prism, 17
Cooper, Anderson, 111
Copy2Contact, 202
Cornwell, Malcolm, 37
Corrie, Anda, 123
Crowdsourcing, 45–46, 243
Current Media, 122
Customer service: ROI on using social media for, 26–27; social media's impact on, 24–25

D

Daley, Danielle, 225
Dashboard, 155, 243
Davis, Eleanor, 75–76
Delicious.com: examples of using, 75–77; overview of, 73–75
Dell Computers: crowdsourcing by, 45; Dell Outlet Twitter initiative, 7, 120–121; social media use by, 120
Democratization, of information distribution, 23–24
Digg.com, 19–20
DimDim, 203–206
DIRECTV, 26
Duarte, Nancy, 154, 174, 199, 203, 225

E

Education, impact of social media on, 6
Elliot, Timo, 155
Endicott, Jim, 13
Engle, Karen, 139–142
Enriquez, Juan, 238
Etsy, 123
Events: on Facebook, 206–208; real-time, social media as component of, 21–23; world, social media's influence on, 236–237
ExxonMobil, brandjacking incident, 40

F

Facebook: Fortune 100 companies using, 137; overview of, 78–81; producing events on, 206–208; video capability of, 144; webinar support from, 184, 189, 201
Facilitators, presenters as, 20
Falls, Jason, 41
Followers (on Twitter), 111–114, 243
Fortune 100 companies, social media use by, 137
Fripp, Patricia, 197–198

G

Gardner, Heather, 110
Gargiulo, Terrence, 168–172, 173, 174
Gilbert, Steve, 96, 161–168
Godin, Seth, 37, 50, 172–173, 175
Goeghegan, Michael, 49
Google Alerts, 55–56
Google Analytics, 49
Google Blogger, 61, 63, 64, 142–143
Google Reader, 56
Google Wave, 111, 230–232
Gore, Al, 145, 154
Graphics. *See* Visuals
Groundswell (Li and Bernoff), 15, 40, 46, 48, 68, 74

H

Hashtag (#), 16, 125, 243
Heath, Chip, 13
Heath, Dan, 13
Hilton, Perez, 37
Hiring process: social bookmarking in, 75–76; Twitter in, 109–110
Holtz, Shel, 39–43
Homeless people, social media used to help, 50–52, 98–101, 126–127
How to Present with Twitter (and Other Backchannels) (Mitchell), 16
HTML (Hypertext Markup Language): defined, 244; familiarity with, for blogging, 62–63, 64, 101–103, 142–143; newsletter in, 218, 219; saving PowerPoint file in, 155, 156; widgets in, 105
Hyperlinks, truncated, 115

I

Iacoboni, Marco, 235–236
ID. *See* Profile
Identity: communications, 34; tools for managing, 58. *See also* Profile
In the Land of Difficult People (Gargiulo), 168
An Inconvenient Truth (Gore), 145, 154
Intel, 26
Internet: barriers to leadership eliminated by, 175; as ongoing conversation, 15; as planetary nervous system, 238–239
Iran, 236–237
Israel, Shel, 179–180

J

Jantsch, John, 53
Jeary, Tony, 13, 227
Jestice, Rebecca, 234
JetBlue Airlines, 121
Johnston, Morgan, 121
Jones, J. A., 104–105
Judge, Barry, 28

K

Kanter, Beth, 101
Karter, Trish, 126
Keynote, 144, 152, 154, 161, 209, 210. *See also* PowerPoint

Koelling, Gary, 27, 28
Krippendorff, Kaihan, 235
Kubrick, Stanley, 236
Kutcher, Ashton, 111

L

Li, Charlene, 15, 40, 46, 48–49, 57, 68, 74
Life Inc. (Rushkoff), 238
Life Is a Series of Presentations (Jeary), 13
LinkedIn, 68–73
Lipton, Bruce, 238, 239
Lists: bullet, transformed into visuals, 151, 153–154; on Twitter, 116, 117, 244
LiveMeeting, 181, 184

M

Made to Stick (Heath and Heath), 13
Madonna, 37
Making Stories (Gargiulo), 168, 173
Marketing: convergence between training and, 7–8, 49; social media used to build relationship for, 88–98
Marriott, Bill, 7
Mashable.com, 81, 231
Mashing: defined, 244; overview of, 98–101; services for, 101–104
Masters, Rita, 43–44, 65
Mayfield, Julie: hired Web content expert, 161; oversaw publication of newsletter, 216–220; produced series of webinars, 184–195, 200–202; taught presenter to use visuals in presentation, 146–152
Media, social media vs. traditional, 19–21
Meetings. *See* Events; Online meetings
Mel's Grocers, 139–142

Microblogging, 110
Microsoft: crowdsourcing by, 45; Office Web Applications, 210; Publisher, 217–219; Web conferencing tools, 181, 184
Mirror neurons, 235–236, 244
Mitchell, Olivia, 15–16
Mobile devices, presentations from, 224–226
Monroe, Jane, 25
Monroe, Keith, 81–82, 92
MySpace, 78

N

Nanotechnology, 234–235
New strategy/product: communication before implementing, 34; traditional vs. modern scenario for implementing, 37–39
NewHope, 50–52, 98–101
Newsletter, post–Web conference, 215–220
1984 (Orwell), 236
Ning, 127–134; communicating with members, 133–134; example of online training program network, 81–82, 87–88; number of users of, 109; overview of, 127–129; planning and creating network, 129–133; purposes of networks, 128

O

OneNote, 212–214
Online classroom training, web conferences/webinars vs., 182–183
Online meetings, 179–220; Facebook events, 206–208; online presentation tools for, 209–212; overview of, 179–180. *See also* Web conferencing

Open Office, Impress presentation program, 209
Orwell, George, 236

P

Parr, Benn, 231
Participatory information exchange (PIE), 30
Petouhoff, Natalie L., 26–27
PharmaFriend, 139–142, 144
Photobucket, 84, 86, 87
Picnik, 99–100
Pike, Bob, 199
Plaxo, 68
Podbean, 96
Podcasts, 96, 162, 164, 244
Polling questions, 190, 191
Pomona PetroChemical, 37–39
Porter, Emily: set up online training program, 81–88; used social media to build relationships, 88–95
Posterous.com, 104
Powell, Allie, 50–52, 98–101
PowerPoint: creating video from slide show in, 155–161; creating visuals using, 144–152; displaying Twitter backchannel in, 155; popularity of, 4, 13; realizing potential of, 152–154; TED presentations created with, 138; transforming bullet points into visuals in, 151, 153–154; webinar using, 187–190
Premiere Pharmaceuticals, 145–148, 184, 215–216, 219
Presentations: capturing audience attention for, 13; changed paradigm for, 11–12, 33–34; communication by audience members during, 13–14, 15–16; as conversation, 20; defined, 12; from mobile devices, 224–226; people interested in using social media for, 4–5; tools for, in cloud, 209–212; traditional vs. modern preparation for, 37–39
Presenter Pro, 225–226
Presenters, as facilitators, 20
Procter & Gamble, 45, 49
Profile: building, 66; as online identity, 34; planning, 53–54; tools for managing, 55, 59; on Twitter, 111, 113–115
Public relations (PR), social media as responsibility of, 41
Pulver, Jeff, 124, 125

R

Razz, 226
Relationships, building: social media initiative for, 88–98; of trust, 35–36, 38–39, 93
Reputation, tools for monitoring, 57–59
Return on influence (ROI), 50
Return on investment (ROI), 26
Retweet (on Twitter), 112, 244
Reximedia, 225–226
Richards, Michael, 50
RSS (Really Simple Syndication): defined, 244; Google Alerts and, 55–56; for podcasts, 96, 97; on YouTube, 144
Rushkoff, Douglas, 238
Russell, Carol, 223–224
Rutledge, Patrice-Anne, 220

S

Sawyer, Karen, 76–77
Scribd.com, 96–97, 98
Search engine optimization (SEO), 53, 69

Second Life, 232–234, 236
Seesmic Desktop, 115–116
Semantic web, 227, 229
SharePoint, 181, 209, 210
ShareThis, 101–104
Skype, 181
Slide:ology (Duarte), 154, 174, 199
SlideRocket, 210–212, 225
SlideShare, 162, 164–165, 225
Small businesses, social bookmarking used by, 76–77
Smith, Julien, 8, 35–37, 49, 152–153, 237, 238
SMS (Short Message Service), 123–124, 244
Snag-It, 83–84, 85
Social bookmarking: examples of using, 75–77; overview of process of, 73–75
Social capital, 35, 37
Social media: categories and examples of, 18; as component of real-time events, 21–23; Conversation Prism formed by, 17; Fortune 100 companies using, 137; human evolution and, 237–238; impact on training and development, 6–7; marketing using, 7; people using, for business purposes, 4–5; perceived value of networking on, 223–224; power of individual with, 24; tips on getting most out of using, 126–127; traditional media vs., 19–21; using, to build trust before implementing new strategy/product, 38–39; using multiple, for successful communication, 8–9; women's participation in, 46–48; world events influenced by, 236–237. *See also* Social media strategy
Social Media Answers, 57
Social Media Club (Los Angeles), 21–22
"Social Media: Embracing the Opportunities, Averting the Risks" (Russell and Baer), 223
Social media strategy: to build relationships, 88–98; for customer service, 24–25, 26–27; monitoring component of, 54–59; for online training program, 81–88; people in organization responsible for, 39–41; responsibility for implementing, 43–45; steps in implementing, 26; tasks necessary for, 41–43; tips on profiles for, 53–54. *See also* Blue Shirt Nation
Social networks, custom, 127–128. *See also* Ning
Southwest Airlines, 7
Stories: brain anatomy and, 235–236; communication skills model based on, 169–172; tribes as defined by, 172–176
Storytelling, digital: power of, 166–168; reasons for implementing, 168–169
Strategic Communications: hired to improve presentation, 145–146; hired to manage Twitter campaign, 216; produced series of webinars, 184–195, 200–201
Sturgess, Denise, 38

T

Tagging, impact on brand or profile, 74–75
Taran, Carmen, 200, 225
Taylor, Carl, 89–95, 167, 168

Taylor Guitars, 24
TechCrunch, 20, 81
Technographics Profiling Ladder, 40, 46, 48–49
TED, 138, 237–238
Terberg, Julie, 225
Teusner (Australian winery), 122
35mm slides, 11, 145, 225
Tolle, Eckhart, 181
Training: convergence between marketing and, 7–8, 49; impact of social media on, 6–7, 25; online program for, 81–88; in use of social media, 41
Tribes: defined, 37, 173; stories as defining, 172–176
Tribes (Godin), 50, 172, 175
Trust, relationship of, 35–36, 38–39, 93
Trust Agents (Brogan and Smith), 8, 35, 37, 50, 57, 152, 237
The Truth About Profiting from Social Networking (Rutledge), 220
Tweet (on Twitter), 2, 16, 87, 109–110, 244
TweetDeck, 56, 117
Twine, 227–230, 244
Twitter, 109–127; @ on, 16, 65, 112, 113; backchannel on, 16, 155; brandjacking incident on, 40; case studies of business use of, 120–123; creating online pictorial stories for, 117–120; current status of, 110–111; following and getting followers on, 111–114; Fortune 100 companies using, 137; hashtag (#), 16, 125, 243; hiring process using, 109–110; Iranian election and, 236–237; maximizing impact of using, 126–127; monitoring feeds on, 56–57; online training program using, 87, 88; organizing desktop for, 115–117; posting to, with SMS, 123–124; Profile on, 111, 113–115; as real-time ongoing conversation, 124–125; relationship between Facebook and, 81; setting up account with, 111; truncated hyperlinks on, 115; webinar support from, 184, 189, 201
Twitterville (Israel), 179
2001: A Space Odyssey, 236

U
United Airlines, damaged guitar incident, 24, 54

V
Verizon, 26
Videos: Camtasia Studio for producing, 157, 159–161, 182; as component of Web conferencing, 181–182, 195–197, 200; example of company using, 161–168; transforming PowerPoint slide show into, 155–161; Windows Media Encoder for producing, 157, 158–159, 182; YouTube hosting, 141–144, 157, 163
Virtual water cooler, 220
Virtual worlds, 232–234
Visuals, 137–176; to ease problems with new software introduction, 139–142; transforming bullets into, 151, 153–154; using PowerPoint to create, 144–152; value of, 138; Whrrl tool for creating, 117–120. *See also* Videos
VOIP (Voice over Internet protocol), 181

W

Wallis, Richard, 234

Web 2.0, defined, 2

Web conferencing: audience invisible when, 194–195, 199; brainstorming with whiteboard during, 203, 205–206; follow-up after, 214–215; history of, 180–181; OneNote for planning and producing, 212–214; online classroom training vs., 182–183; publishing newsletter after, 215–220; social media's role to support, 22–23, 183–184; tips on, 197–200; using DimDim for, 203–206; video component of, 181–182, 195–197, 200. *See also* Webinars

Web sites: blogs vs., 61–62; supplementing book, 3; tools for evaluating impact of, 49

Webinars: to boost online shopping, 47–48; defined, 181, 190; online classroom training vs., 182–183; series of, supported by social media, 184–195, 200–202; tips on giving, 197–200; video in, 181–182, 195–197, 200. *See also* Web conferencing

Whiteboard, brainstorming with, 174, 203, 205–206

Whrrl, 118–120

Widgetbox.com, 105, 106

Widgets: custom, 104–106; ShareThis, 101–104

Wiggly Wigglers blog, 7

Wikis, 68

Williams, Gary, 88–94

Windows Media Encoder, 157, 158–159, 182

Women: as driving force behind social media, 66; social media participation by, 46–48

WordPress, 67, 98–99

Wright, Jeremy, 67

X

Xcelsius, 155

Y

YouTube: content ownership and, 14–15; as video host, 141–144, 157, 163

Z

Zoho Show presentation program, 209

What will you find on pfeiffer.com?

- The best in workplace performance solutions for training and HR professionals
- Downloadable training tools, exercises, and content
- Web-exclusive offers
- Training tips, articles, and news
- Seamless on-line ordering
- Author guidelines, information on becoming a Pfeiffer Partner, and much more

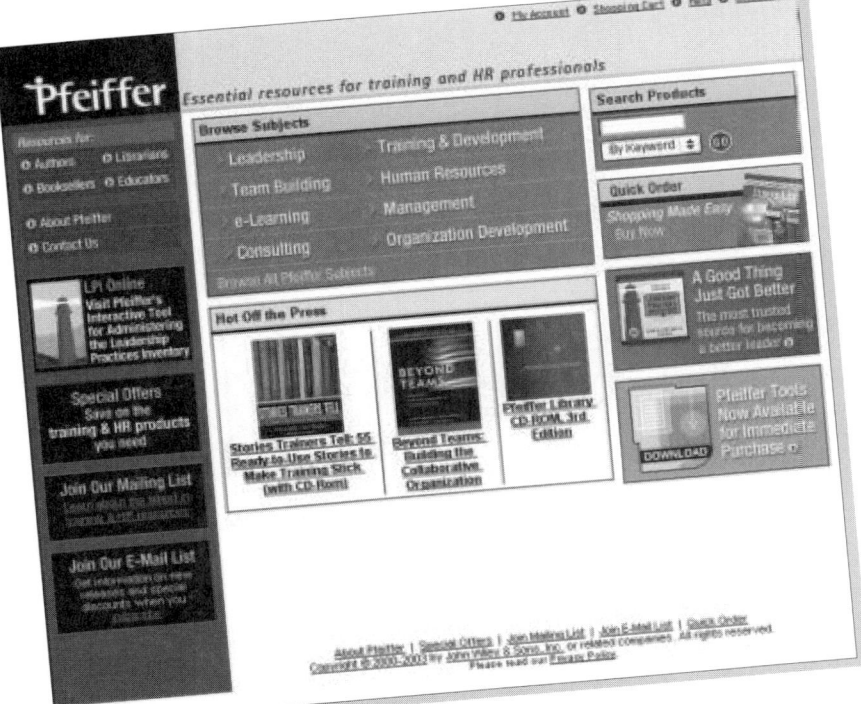

Discover more at www.pfeiffer.com

CENTENNIAL COLLEGE
LIBRARIES